The

foreclosureS.com

Guide to

Advanced Investing Techniques

You Won't Learn Anywhere Else

The foreclosures.com

Guide to

Advanced Investing Techniques

You Won't Learn Anywhere Else

Alexis McGee

WILEY

John Wiley & Sons, Inc.

Published by John Wiley & Sons, Inc., Hoboken, New Jersey.
Published simultaneously in Canada.

For general information on our other products and services or for technical support, please contact our Customer Care Department within the United States at (800) 762-2974, outside the United States at (317) 572-3993 or fax (317) 572-4002.

Wiley also publishes its books in a variety of electronic formats. Some content that appears in print may not be available in electronic books. For more information about Wiley products, visit our web site at www.wiley.com.

Library of Congress Cataloging-in-Publication Data:
McGee, Alexis, 1960–
    The foreclosures.com guide to advanced investing techniques you won't learn anywhere else / Alexis McGee with Susan J. Marks.
       p.   cm.
    ISBN 978-0-470-17104-2 (pbk.)
    1. Real estate investment—United States.   2. Foreclosure—United States.
I. Marks, Susan J.   II. Title.
HD255.M37248 2007
332.63'240973—dc22

                                                          2007045586

Printed in the United States of America.

10   9   8   7   6   5   4   3   2   1

To Tim,
who loved me and encouraged me to be true to my beliefs.

To Cooke and Kaliope,
who waited patiently for Mom to finish two books in one year,
so life can be normal again.

CONTENTS

ACKNOWLEDGMENTS   ix

INTRODUCTION   xi

PART I   Get Ready to Advance: The Next Step in Foreclosure Investing

CHAPTER 1   Why Bother with Advanced Foreclosure Investing?   3

CHAPTER 2   Essentials That Seal the Deal   17

PART II   Deeds of Trust

CHAPTER 3   A Primer on Buying Deeds of Trust   39

CHAPTER 4   Finding the Deal That Adds Up   57

PART III   Trustee and Courthouse Auctions

CHAPTER 5   The Reality behind the Hype   79

CHAPTER 6   The Dollars and Sense of Finding and Figuring the Deals   95

PART IV   REOs and Short Sales

CHAPTER 7   Another Option, Another Opportunity   115

CHAPTER 8   The Deal: Find It, Figure It, and Win   127

CHAPTER 9   Short Sales   143

CONTENTS

PART V   REO Auctions

CHAPTER 10	The Phenomenon Is on a Roll	161
CHAPTER 11	Time to Deal	179

PART VI   Selling in a Soft Market

CHAPTER 12	Winning in Today's Market	193
EPILOGUE		203
APPENDIX A	Sample Documents	205
APPENDIX B	State Foreclosure Laws in Brief	235
GLOSSARY		247
INDEX		263
ABOUT FORECLOSURES.COM		269
ABOUT OUR EDUCATION PROGRAMS		270
FREE TELE-CONFERENCE!		271

ACKNOWLEDGMENTS

This second in my series of ForeclosureS.com guides to foreclosure investing is the culmination of more than 20 years working in the real estate business with all kinds of people in all types of situations.

When I started with Grubb & Ellis Commercial in the mid-1980s and then into the early 1990s, it was a tough time to be in the real estate business. The Tax Reform Act of 1986 had laid the foundation for a soft real estate market, and, as a result, many great agents left the business. Undaunted, I searched for another way to be successful. That's when I first began to realize the potential in foreclosures and foreclosure investing.

Back then, no books, tapes, or seminars were available to help aspiring foreclosure investors. I learned on the job by trial (and error) and experience. I also learned—and continue to learn—from those around me. To each and every person who has touched my professional life and helped me and the education program at ForeclosureS.com grow into what we are today, thank you. It's a pleasure to share with new investors the right way to speed up their learning curve. Their successes are my successes, too.

I owe special thanks to my loving and supportive husband, Tim, the behind-the-scenes hero at ForeclosureS.com, and to my patient and wonderful children Cooke and Kaliope for their unwavering support.

My gratitude goes to many other people who helped with this book, including:

- Susan J. Marks, the word wizard who so aptly translates my thoughts.

- Cynthia Zigmund, my agent from Literary Services Inc., who had the vision for my foreclosure investing series and the tenacity to make it work.

- Shannon Vargo, senior editor at Wiley, whose patience and direction have guided the ForeclosureS.com books to reality.

- Sarah Garlick, Tim Rhode, Daryl White, and Mary Kay, ForeclosureS.com coaches, successful investors, and dear friends who shared their ideas and experiences.

- Liz Orio, our ForeclosureS.com research director, who helped assemble many of the details that make this book complete, along with my entire loyal ForeclosureS.com team for all their help.

- Jim Rohn of Jim Rohn International (www.jimrohn.com) and Brian Tracy of Brian Tracy International (www.briantracy.com), professional speakers, authors, consultants, and business philosophers, for their continued words of wisdom.

- Tom Daves (Keller-Williams Realty, Roseville, California), Ian Maker (REO Deal Makers Inc., Sacramento, California), Christian Rooney, and Doug Pereyda, all former students and successful foreclosure investors; and Marsha Townsend (ForeclosureLink.com), for their willingness to share their experiences and expertise with others.

- Other former Alexis McGee students and successful investors who also contributed to the book include Marcel Ford (Property Partners, Palm Desert, California); Michael Ballard (Edmonds, Washington); Leslie Bach, (Austin, Texas); Lisa Carlsen (Madison, Wisconsin); Trish Spurlock (Denver, Colorado); Brenda Coté (American Home Buyers Network, Anaheim, California); David Mack (Sacramento, California); LJ Nielsen (Sacramento, California); and Jan Caldwell, Esq. (Pleasant Hill, California).

- The Mortgage Bankers Association, American Land Title Association, First American Core Logic, The Tower Group, and Challenger, Gray & Christmas, for graciously allowing us to use their statistics to paint the economic reality of foreclosures.

- The following journalists who graciously shared their thoughts: Jessica Swesey, vice president of content, Inman News (www.inman.com); Kathy Fettke, CEO of RealWealthNetwork.com, host of the *Real Wealth* Radio Show; Hubble Smith, Business Writer, *Review-Journal*, Las Vegas, Nevada; George Warren, reporter, KXTV News10 (ABC), and Jeff Poor, Business & Media Institute (http://www.businessandmedia.org), Alexandria, Virginia.

- Last, but certainly not least, special thanks to Barbara Corcoran, Bill Bronchick, Wendy Patton, Diane Kennedy, and Steve Bergsman, who took time out of their hectic schedules to review this book.

The waves of foreclosures sweeping the nation have dramatically altered the landscape for foreclosure investing.

Not since the housing downturn of the 1990s have so many pre-foreclosure and foreclosed properties offered so much opportunity for savvy investors. You don't have to be a seasoned professional, but you do have to be knowledgeable and able to draw on the necessary information, approach, and guidance to become an advanced, senior-class foreclosure investor. *The ForeclosureS.com Guide to Advanced Investing Techniques* will show you how to take your foreclosure-investing skills to the next level honestly and ethically. We share our secrets on how to maximize this opportunity to fulfill your personal and financial dreams and achieve tremendous success.

How much opportunity lies in foreclosure investing? In the first nine months of 2007 alone, 5 of every 1,000 homeowners in the United States lost their homes to foreclosure. That's up almost 40 percent from a year prior, according to numbers from ForeclosureS.com, a California-based real estate investment advisory firm that tracks and analyzes foreclosure and property information for investors, media, and the public (www.ForeclosureS.com).

Those same numbers also tell the tale of almost 400,000 residential properties that reverted to banks and lenders—became *real estate owned* (REO) or bank/lender-owned real estate—because homeowners couldn't work out their financial problems. That staggering figure doesn't even include the more than 800,000 additional property owners who defaulted on their mortgages and were in pre-foreclosure in the same nine months of 2007!

Looking at the numbers in different ways, outstanding mortgage debt in the United States totals approximately $10 trillion. Subprime mortgages—those loans made to people with little or no credit—account for $1.3 trillion, or about 13 percent of that.[1] As of the second quarter 2007, 3.2 percent of conventional subprime

---

[1]John M. Reich, director of the U.S. Office of Thrift Supervision, in testimony before the U.S. House Subcommittee on Financial Institutions and Consumer Credit of the Committee on Financial Services, March 27, 2007.

mortgages were 60 days or more past due.[2] For all loans outstanding in third quarter 2007, the delinquency rate for mortgage loans on one- to four-unit residential properties was 5.59 percent, according to the Mortgage Bankers Association's (MBA) venerable National Delinquency Survey.[3] A total 16.31 percent of subprime loans, and 3.12 percent of prime loans were delinquent during that same time period, according to seasonally adjusted numbers from MBA.

All these numbers translate into millions of dollars in opportunity if you know how to tap it. Successful pre-foreclosure investing often involves working closely with individual homeowners in default—when their properties are pre-foreclosure and they still, for the moment, own their homes—to help them find the best solution to their financial woes. But potential deals in this business aren't always clear-cut. What if you can't find the owner who has defaulted on a mortgage? Or what if a property is vacant? What if a homeowner in default has no equity in his property and no option but foreclosure? Or perhaps a bank or lender has already foreclosed and holds the property as REO (bank-owned real estate). Do you ignore these properties and move on?

Absolutely not! You don't have to walk away from these potential deals. You can, instead, learn how to capitalize on such situations and turn them into extremely profitable deals that are win-win for all parties involved. Your options can range from purchasing deeds of trusts—buying the mortgage note instead of the property—to buying foreclosed properties at trustee or courthouse auctions; buying REO properties that didn't sell at the courthouse auction from banks or lenders; short sales, in which banks forgive a portion of the debt; or buying properties at REO auctions when banks and lenders pool their REO properties for sale.

Beware, though. These approaches are not for novices in real estate or foreclosure investing, and, like successful pre-foreclosure equity investing, are not for people looking to turn a fast buck the easy way. Deals like these require a thorough understanding and analysis of the numbers involved in foreclosures, REOs, auctions, your local and national housing markets, and more. You also need to know the ins and outs of working with large banks and lending institutions; the required legal processes and procedures in your state; where and how to get the information you need; and how to navigate the minefields that threaten your success.

Thanks to the Internet, today's approach to this business is very different from that of 15 years ago. This book addresses all these issues and more with

---

[2]Mark S. Sniderman, "The Economy in Perspective," *Economic Trends*, covering September 13, 2007, to October 14, 2007, published by the Research Department of the Federal Reserve Bank of Cleveland; see http://www.clevelandfed.org/research/trends/2007/1007/oct.html.
[3]December 6, 2007; see http://www.mortgagebankers.org/NewsandMedia/PressCenter/58758.htm.

the help of Alexis McGee, *the* nationally recognized foreclosure industry expert who sets the gold standard for honesty and ethics in the business. With more than 20 years experience in commercial and residential real estate, foreclosure and pre-foreclosure investing, as well as 15 years of teaching others how to do it right, she knows what works and what doesn't. Her first book, *The ForeclosureS.com Guide to Making Huge Profits Investing in Pre-Foreclosures* (John Wiley & Sons, September 2007), was an instant hit even before its release in September 2007. Californian McGee is also president and co-founder with her husband, Tim, of ForeclosureS.com (www.foreclosures.com), one of the most popular and reliable foreclosure information web sites in the country—and the longest-running.

Here's what some people are saying about Alexis and her expertise:

"As the host of radio's *Real Wealth* Show, it is my job to sift through these so-called experts to find the real deal. Alexis McGee is one of those rare gems. She is not only the real deal when it comes to solid information on foreclosures, but her unique services and resources are used by experienced foreclosure professionals around the world. She is a true player in the industry, yet remains quite genuine—a rare combination."

> —Kathy Fettke, CEO of RealWealthNetwork.com,
> host of the *Real Wealth* Radio Show

"Alexis is beyond a doubt the guru's guru on how to successfully invest in foreclosures—ethically. Alexis not only brings to the table a proven and ethical process to buying foreclosures, but also a supporting infrastructure that both novices and seasoned pros rely on. Hands down, Alexis is not only a wonderful person but also provides her students, novices to professionals, the tools required to truly excel in the foreclosure market."

> —Marcel Ford, Property Partners, Palm Desert,
> California; former Alexis McGee student,
> successful investor

"Whatever road led to you having a book by Alexis McGee in your hands, *stay on it*! Undoubtedly, in this book, you will find all of the technical knowledge that you are seeking pertaining to real estate transactions, but you will get a lot more. You will learn a proven way of doing business about which you can feel proud and for which you can have passion. . . . There are multitudes of people out there, including myself, who are a daily testimony to Alexis' skills in real estate, education, and motivation."

> —Michael Ballard, Edmonds, Washington;
> former Alexis McGee student, successful
> foreclosure investor

"Alexis is my foreclosure guru. She's not only the most knowledgeable source I have in the industry, she's ethical as well. Her "white knight" approach to foreclosure investing is refreshing."

—George Warren, Reporter, KXTV News10 (ABC)

"There is no other authority better at helping prospective and active foreclosure investors than Alexis McGee. Her approach to teaching is not only comprehensive, she shows you specifically how she has done it, and how you are to do it. What master would tell their students everything they know about being a success in their respective business? Alexis *is* the genuine article!"

—David Mack, Sacramento, California; investor

"Alexis has always been a reliable source on foreclosure issues. Her advice centers on hard work, rather than the get-rich-quick schemes that permeate much of the foreclosure coaching landscape. She has a well-grounded approach with the background to prove it."

—Jessica Swesey, vice president of content,
Inman News (www.inman.com)

"Alexis is a smart and reliable resource when it comes to navigating your way through the massive amount of misinformation out there about real estate foreclosures. At a time when there is such volatility in the market, having the teachings of Alexis is essential."

—Jeff Poor, Business & Media Institute
(http://www.businessandmedia.org/),
Alexandria, Virginia

"Having listened to various real estate gurus, and having reviewed their programs—and having experienced some, too—it occurs to me that Alexis is the gold standard. Her formal education and her experience all through the years have been in real estate. She absolutely knows both theoretically and practically what she is talking about, and she combines that with personal warmth, approachability, clarity, and a commitment to ethics. If you are interested in real estate investing, pay attention carefully to what Alexis says. She is right."

—Jan Caldwell, Esq., Pleasant Hill, California;
investor, former Alexis McGee student

"Alexis has the most humane approach to foreclosure investing in this business. She teaches the foreclosure investor to always put the needs of the homeowners first, which often results in the homeowner keeping their home. This refreshing, ethical approach allows the investor to help homeowners, to buy houses, to make good money, and it allows everyone involved in the process to sleep easy!"

—Leslie Bach, Austin, Texas; former Alexis
McGee student, successful investor

"Alexis McGee has been providing me with updated, accurate statistics on fore-closure filings in Las Vegas and Nevada for a number of years now, long before monthly foreclosure stories proliferated in the national media. She's been an in-telligent source for quotes about the housing market not only in Vegas, but throughout the nation."

—Hubble Smith, Las Vegas, Nevada, Business Writer, *Review-Journal*

"Alexis's ethical approach to foreclosure investing helps me to fulfill my goal of making a positive difference in people's lives while making a comfortable living for myself."

—Lisa Carlsen, Madison, Wisconsin; former Alexis McGee student, successful investor

"Alexis McGee's program really works! I had a deal under contract two weeks after [taking her] class and netted $27,100 in four weeks after leaving the ForeclosureS.com lab. Not bad from a $500 earnest money down payment."

—Trish Spurlock, Denver, Colorado; former Alexis McGee student, successful investor

"Alexis' approach to the foreclosure business has always been honest and ethical investing. . . . Alexis *is* the real deal. She is a very enthusiastic person who truly cares about the success of her students. She is boldly honest, straightforward, and compassionate—a rare combination for any businessperson these days—and has developed her own business built on these rock-solid values. This master teaches by example. So if you want to succeed, do exactly as Alexis does *to the letter*."

—LJ Nielsen, Sacramento, California, investor, graduate of Alexis McGee's training program

"Alexis McGee is a champion! I was already investing in real estate before going to Alexis, but with the help of her teachings, approach, generosity, and conviction, my business has reached new levels. Alexis and her team at ForeclosureS.com have been there for me every time I needed help. Thank you, Alexis!"

—Brenda Coté, American Home Buyers Network, Anaheim, California; broker, investor, former student, coaching client of Alexis McGee

This book hopefully will help you, too, learn how to experience this kind of success as an advanced foreclosure investor.

The book is divided into six parts:

Part I—Get Ready to Advance: The Next Step in Foreclosure Investing

Part II—Buying Deeds of Trust

Part III—Trustee and Courthouse Auctions

Part IV—REOs and Short Sales

Part V—REO Auctions

Part VI—Selling in a Soft Market

Throughout the book, real-life examples spell out step-by-step what it takes to succeed at each type of foreclosure investing—from the components of the deal to the financing and figuring. Each chapter includes checklists and sources for more detailed information as well as stories from Alexis McGee's students, coaches, and others in the form of "Tales from Foreclosure Experts" and more. In most cases, except for the experts, the names have been changed to protect individual privacy. In other cases the stories are compilations of real experiences, and any similarities to real people are coincidental. The back of the book features a Glossary and various Appendixes that provide valuable information, documentation, and insight for would-be senior-class foreclosure investors.

While the first ForeclosureS.com guide focused on working closely with homeowners in default and the importance of connecting with them on an emotional level, this book instead emphasizes the numbers. It examines more advanced techniques in foreclosure investing and how to successfully work with large organizations, corporations, and more. If you don't like working with individual homeowners, this alternative approach to making money at foreclosure investing while sleeping well at night could be just right for you. If you do enjoy working with homeowners on an individual basis, this book will expand your knowledge of the business and provide you the necessary flexibility to turn the best deals for all parties while fulfilling your own dreams.

So don't wait any longer. Get ready to get better at what you do, and turn the page.

PART I

GET READY TO ADVANCE: THE NEXT STEP IN FORECLOSURE INVESTING

Today's market is tailor-made for win-win foreclosure investing if you have the right knowledge and understanding of how to make it all happen.

—Alexis McGee

CHAPTER 1

Why Bother with Advanced Foreclosure Investing?

No matter the state of real estate markets or the economy, great deals are made every day. The question is, will one of them be yours?

—Alexis McGee

oreclosure-investing is H-O-T with profits if you know where to look, what to do, and how to do it effectively. Too many false steps, though, and you can slide into a treacherous money pit!

Today's foreclosure investing world is much different from even a few months ago when, as a pre-foreclosure equity investor, you could easily work with thousands of homeowners in default who hadn't yet lost their homes to foreclosure and likely had plenty of equity in their property—a combination tailor-made for a win-win pre-foreclosure deal.

In the third quarter of 2007, 2.74 percent of all U.S. residential real estate loans were delinquent, up from 2.32 percent in the second quarter, and up from only 1.74 percent the same time a year ago. That figure includes loans secured by one- to four-family properties and home equity lines of credit, according to statistics from the Federal Reserve Board.[1] Delinquent loans are those 30 days or more past due.

---

[1]See "Charge-Off and Delinquency Rates on Loans and Leases at Commercial Banks," at http://www.federalreserve.gov/releases/chargeoff/delallsa.htm.

The Foreclosure Tidal Wave

As defaults have skyrocketed, so have foreclosures—the final stage in the process by which people who have defaulted on their mortgages actually lose their homes. Record numbers of properties have been lost and continue to be lost at a staggering pace. In the first nine months of 2007, 5 of every 1,000 homeowners in the United States lost their homes to foreclosure. That's up almost 39 percent from a year ago, according to numbers from ForeclosureS.com, a California-based real estate investment advisory firm that tracks and analyzes foreclosure and property information for investors, media, and the public (www.ForeclosureS.com).

Many homeowners—especially those classified as subprime borrowers because they have little or no credit—find themselves tapped out financially. Thanks to creative financing and adjustable rate mortgages (ARMs), many were able to buy their homes with little or no money down. As a result, they have no equity in their properties. As their initial, low monthly payments adjust upward, their once affordable homes become a nightmare, their credit dries up, and their alternatives to foreclosure shrink rapidly.

The subprime lender shakeout and its repucussions on general credit markets further limits financially strapped homeowners' options. Scores of subprime lenders, including some of the nation's largest, have shut down, declared bankruptcy, been sold, or pulled out of the market entirely. In early 2007 Freddie Mac, the congressionally chartered private mortgage-market investor, toughened its subprime lending standards to lessen the risk of future defaults. It no longer buys subprime ARMs unless a borrower qualifies at the fully indexed, fully amortizing rate. In other words, it's no longer enough that a buyer simply qualify for a loan at a low teaser rate. Even with Congress, public and private institutions, and organizations offering bailout options for certain overextended borrowers that meet specific qualifications, many others still find themselves with nowhere to turn for help.

Banks and lenders are swamped physically and financially by the waves of foreclosures. Their portfolios of REO or lender-owned real estate are bulging. Thousands of properties end up available at courthouse auctions every month, and REO auctions in which banks/lenders bundle their properties for sale are a hot ticket.

As an investor, you can capitalize on this surge of foreclosure deals and opportunity *if* you have the knowledge to recognize what's happening and the flexibility to work the deal required for each unique situation. We're talking about buying deeds of trust, buying REO properties from banks or lenders or at foreclosure and courthouse auctions, and buying at REO auctions. These opportunities tend to be more cyclical in nature than pre-foreclosure investing, but they present a lucrative way to grow your foreclosure-investing business as the market changes and people have less equity. With the proper background and know-how, the opportunity to achieve your financial dreams is limitless.

> *As a 20-year veteran investor, I have never had trouble finding motivated sellers. That's because I first assess the current real estate market—hot (a seller's market) or cold (a buyer's market)—so I know where the deals are. Then I take the right foreclosure-investing approach to purchase a property at a discount.*
>
> —Alexis McGee

By the Numbers

It's no secret that the nation's foreclosures are on the rise. But to better understand exactly what's happening in the foreclosure-investing arena and why, you need to know the numbers. Here are a few key ones from John M. Reich, director of the U.S. Office of Thrift Supervision (in testimony before the U.S. House Committee on Financial Services' Subcommittee on Financial Institutions and Consumer Credit, March 27, 2007):

- U.S. mortgage debt totals $10 trillion.
- Subprime mortgages account for $1.3 trillion, or about 13 percent of that.
- Approximately $567 billion of those subprime ARMs were set to readjust in 2007.
- Subprime hybrid ARM holders are in trouble:
  - 8.6 percent of loans originating in 2005 were seriously delinquent after only 11 months.
  - 6.2 percent of 2004 originations were seriously delinquent at the 11-month mark.
  - 5.6 percent of 2003 originations were seriously delinquent at the 11-month mark.

Delinquency rates increased for all categories of loans in the third quarter of 2007 versus the second quarter of the year, and compared with the same time period a year earlier for all but VA loans (which were unchanged), according to the

Mortgage Bankers Association's (MBA) venerable National Delinquency Survey. The delinquency rate does not include loans in the process of foreclosure. A few third-quarter 2007 numbers (seasonally adjusted) from the MBA include:

- 5.59 percent of all mortgage loans on one- to four-unit residential properties were past due, the highest delinquency rate since 1986.

- 1.69 percent of all loans outstanding were in foreclosure at the end of the third quarter, the highest level ever (not seasonally adjusted).

- 43 percent of all foreclosures begun during the third quarter were subprime ARMs (subprime ARMs represent 6.8 percent of all outstanding loans); 18.7 were prime ARMs; 12 percent subprime fixed loans; 17.6 percent prime fixed loans, and 8.7 percent FHA and VA loans.

- 3.12 percent of all prime loans were delinquent, and 16.31 percent of all subprime loans.

- 1.31 percent of prime loans were seriously delinquent (90 days or more past due or in the process of foreclosure), and 11.38 percent of subprime loans.

A March 2007 study from First American CoreLogic, part of First American Corporation (NYSE: FAF), predicts 1.1 million foreclosures in the next six to seven years. The study[2] focused on 8.37 million ARMs that originated from 2004 to 2006 and specifically examined the impact of mortgage payment reset on the lending industry and national economy. That study also found that in the absence of homeowner equity:

- 32 percent of teaser loans will default.

- 7 percent of market-rate adjustable loans will default.

- 12 percent of subprime loans will default over the next six to seven years.

All is not doom and gloom, however. In the same report, First American CoreLogic points out that, although some homeowners may lose their properties to foreclosure, "on a national basis, the losses will translate to less than 1 percent of total U.S. mortgage-lending projected . . . and will not significantly impact the economy or the mortgage-lending industry."

That 1 percent of the market, though, certainly can translate to very fertile ground for your investment skills.

---

[2]See *Report Projects Patterns by Year for Adjustable Rate Mortgages*, http://www.firstam.com/pressrelease.cfm?pr_id=1526.

Advanced Foreclosure Investing

Those skills are based on advanced foreclosure-investing strategies, an area of study that's a step up from pre-foreclosure investing, which we categorize as *Foreclosures 101*. The advanced approaches to foreclosure investing that aren't for the neophyte investor include:

- Deed of trust or note buying: buying the note instead of the physical property, gaining ownership through foreclosure, then flipping, or rehabbing and re-selling, the cleaned-up property.

- Trustee sale auctions: purchasing property at courthouse foreclosure auctions.

- REO properties: buying a foreclosed property from a bank or lender.

- Short sale: also known as a short payoff, when a lender agrees to take a *short*, or less than full balance due on a property loan, in order to help the owner in default close a sale pre-foreclosure.

- REO auctions: when banks or lenders pool their REO properties and hire an auctioneer to try to sell them.

Why Learn Something New?

About now you may be thinking, "Why take the time and make the effort to learn something new and more complicated? After all, pre-foreclosure equity investing works just fine." Consider this: If you limit yourself to simple pre-foreclosures, you're closing the door on some very big and—once you've learned the ropes—simple opportunities to make solid, sizable profits from buying deeds of trust, trustee sale auctions, REO properties, REO auctions, and more.

Gain Flexibility

Also, without learning the techniques of advanced foreclosure investing, you rob yourself of the investment flexibility gained from understanding how to move on any deal in any situation. Perhaps one of your advanced foreclosure-investing techniques will give you a second chance to get that great property you missed out on the first time around.

Alf J. devoted a lot of effort to helping Sondra work out her default problems, but he just couldn't help her. This was the single mom's second default on her home's $95,000 first mortgage. She also had a second mortgage for $55,000, so she owed a total $150,000 on a house worth only $160,000. The first default, 15 years earlier, culminated with Sondra declaring bankruptcy. With her lack of equity in the home, her lenders refused to work with her on her current mortgage or offer her a new one. Without the minimum 30 to 40 percent equity in her house to make it appealing to a pre-foreclosure investor, the numbers didn't add up for Alf to buy it, either. (In slower or colder markets, it generally takes an investor longer and costs more to flip a property, so more equity is required for a deal to make financial sense.) Even though Sondra liked and trusted Alf, he also couldn't get her to understand that her home was the noose strangling her ability to get ahead. She simply didn't want to give up the home. In the end, she lost it to foreclosure.

Alf was an advanced foreclosure investor who understood how to buy properties at foreclosure auction. Because he couldn't help Sondra and was aware of what was happening with her property, he was able to take the next step. When the $95,000 first mortgage went to auction, he bought it for just over the amount of the loan—$99,000—which was well below the home's market value of $160,000 even after figuring the costs of rehab and repair. Because the first mortgage lender's foreclosure extinguished the second loan for $55,000, Alf now owned the home free and clear.

No Equity, No Owner

Roger had tapped out the equity in his popular, starter-size bungalow to pay off his charge cards. He was a gadget fanatic and always had to have the latest, hottest gizmo—from massage chairs to iPhones. He viewed his home only as a place to store his stuff, and he let the mortgage slide. The day after he received the notice of default, he packed up his gadgets and simply skipped town, never to be heard from again.

As a potential investor, you're faced with a great property, no equity, and no owner. Now what? What if your market is full of Rogers or, at the very least, homeowners with little or no equity so that pre-foreclosure deals don't make sense? Does that mean you stay out of work until conditions change—you're unemployed for two, three, five, or seven years? Of course not. Instead, you look for other ways to get the deal done. That's the basis for advanced foreclosure investing.

This kind of investing is about dollars and cents, not about the roof over someone's head!

—Sarah Garlick, ForeclosureS.com coach
and successful foreclosure investor

If Pre-Foreclosure Intimacy Makes You Squeamish . . .

What if you're not a people person and find the one-on-one nature of pre-foreclosure investing excruciating? Advanced foreclosure investing may be the ticket for you. These approaches to the business focus on numbers, not people. You generally deal only with private-party lenders, finance companies, large lenders, asset management departments, real estate agents, impartial trustees and auctioneers, and dollars and cents. If you figure the numbers correctly and present your case properly, you will make the sale. You won't have to coax the truth out of a homeowner or persuade him to sell the family home or urge him to kick his drug habit before it's too late.

That doesn't mean, of course, that you don't deal with people at all. You deal with them on a different level, though, and without the personal intensity and intimacy of the pre-foreclosure process. "It's not about the roof over their heads," says Sarah Garlick, ForeclosureS.com coach and veteran successful foreclosure investor.

Inherent in the nature of these advanced deals, too, is that many properties already may be vacant, hence no homeowner issues at all. This kind of investing rarely involves turning an unsuspecting homeowner out in the cold.

Of course, occasionally you may end up taking the steps to eviction, but cash-for-keys often is all it takes. We talk more about that in Chapter 2.

Forget the Excuse That the Downturn Is Over

In case you think the current housing downturn is almost over and it's not worth your time to brush up on advanced foreclosure investing, think again. We're not at the bottom yet, and the recovery is expected to be geographically sporadic and to take a long time. That's the word from the experts:

> *Subprime mortgage losses that triggered uncertainty . . . have reverberated in broader financial markets. . . [T]he turbulence originated in concerns about subprime mortgages, but the resulting global financial losses have far exceeded even the most pessimistic estimates of the credit losses on these loans.*
>
> —Federal Reserve Chairman Ben S. Bernanke, testimony September 20, 2007 before on the House Committee on Financial Services (see http://www.federalreserve.gov/newsevents/ testimony/bernanke20070920a.htm)

It will take time to stabilize housing prices and the mortgage market . . . [but] Even if the liquidity crisis that began last month [August 2007] were alleviated today, there would still be rough waters ahead for some borrowers, lenders, and investors.

—John M. Robbins, chairman of the Mortgage Bankers Association, speaking to the U.S. House Committee on Financial Services at a September 20, 2007, hearing on "Legislative and Regulatory Options for Minimizing and Mitigating Mortgage Foreclosures" (see http://www.house.gov/apps/list/hearing/financial svcs_dem/testimony_-_robbins.pdf)

It's expected that it will take years for the housing market to recover to "normal," a situation likely to be exacerbated in the short run by changes in the legislation affecting the mortgage industry.

—UCLA Anderson Forecast, and David Shulman, its senior economist, September 12, 2007 (see http://www.uclaforecast.com/contents/ archive/media_9_07_1.asp)

Tighter credit for home mortgages will measurably dampen home sales in the short term and postpone an expected recovery for existing-home sales until 2008. The forecast calls for slow steady gains throughout 2008.

—National Association of Realtors, September 11, 2007 (see http://www.realtor.org/press_room/news_releases/ 2007/sept_forecast07_dampen_home_sales.html)

The e-Connection

Thanks to the Internet—which means e-mail and instant messaging to converse and communicate, electronic access to a wealth of information, sophisticated web marketing tools, and software management solutions—the foreclosure investment game and its playing field are vastly different today from even a decade ago.

Culling through stacks of papers in search of a document or a signature, keeping track of dozens of tiny notes and scribbles as your contact list, and driving around the state to various bureaus, agencies, and institutions to acquire information simply doesn't add up to efficient use of your time or real success in this business.

Sophisticated, computerized operating systems add greater efficiency both to buyers and sellers. Banks and lenders have greater capacity to do more with what they have, and so do you. As different institutions capitalize on e-efficiencies, you must, too, if you hope to succeed.

The Changing Face of Foreclosure Investing

Forget the lone loan officer who's responsible for a bank's entire portfolio of REO properties and is willing to unload them at huge discounts simply to get rid of them. Banks and lenders today have sophisticated management teams and departments to handle their REO properties, which are considered viable moneymakers, not deadwood. Banks are in the business of making money with REO properties, too!

Although not yet extinct, handwritten legal documents are an endangered species. Many government and other document offices are paperless or heading that way. If you need the document, you must know how to access it electronically as well as manually. You may be able to get away with door-knocking and handwritten scribbles to win at pre-foreclosures, but that doesn't cut it in advanced foreclosure-investing class. Now you're playing with the big boys—established corporations and others. You must become more sophisticated in your approach. Get wired. Turn on that computer, get proficient at it, and watch your efforts yield big returns.

Foreclosure Listing Services

Your success in the business today starts with finding a solid source for foreclosure listings. For many of us, that means subscribing to a good foreclosure-listing service. Of course, I'm partial to ForeclosureS.com for obvious reasons. (See sample listing in Figure 1.1.) Other ways to find reputable listing services include:

- Ask your county recorder's office or courthouse for the names of any local company that collects and sells foreclosure data.
- Check the classified section of newspapers and local media online and off for default and foreclosure notice postings.
- Check your county recorder's office online or off to collect data as it's recorded.

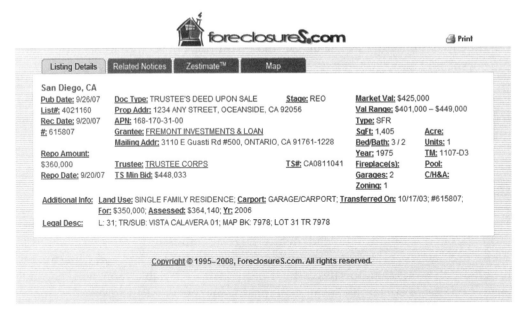

FIGURE 1.1   Sample REO Property Listing on ForeclosureS.com

More Information Sources

To check out REO auction schedules as well as pick up on some of the basics and view samples of documents such as contracts, pre-sale forms, and more, visit the web sites of reputable auctioneers and auction-related organizations. Several major auctioneers include Texas-based Hudson and Marshall Inc. (www.hudsonand marshall.com); Irvine, California-based Real Estate Disposition Corporation (www.ushomeauction.com); and Tulsa, Oklahoma-based Williams and Williams (www.williamsauction.com). The web site for the almost 6,000-member National Association of Auctioneers (www.auctioneers.org), especially its free auction finder tool (http://auctioncalendar.auctioneers.org/), is another good source.

If you're looking to buy deeds of trust from private lenders or REO properties from banks and corporations, be prepared to search them out. To find private lenders, Google (www.google.com) or DogPile (www.dogpile.com) are good starting points. Other sources include information directories, online court and county records (www.netronline.com), reverse directories that enable you to locate someone by an address, and more.

For telephone numbers, try Skipease.com (www.skipease.com), Yahoo's People Search (http://people.yahoo.com/), InfoSpace (www.infospace.com), and other

Internet white pages' directories such as AnyWho (www.anywho.com). WhitePages (www.whitepages.com) and Searchbug (www.searchbug.com/peoplefinder/) are solid free sources. 411.com (www.411.com) can work for you, too.

Another option is ZabaSearch (www.zabasearch.com). That site links to tons of free state, national, and even international databases loaded with information that includes bankruptcy records and tax liens.

It doesn't hurt to network with friends, acquaintances, and business associates, either. Often they can help turn up solid leads to small, private lenders.

To find REO lender contacts, start with your foreclosure-listing service. It should provide you a web link to the lender's site as well as its main telephone number. If the site isn't available, the listing service should at least direct you to search engine results for that lender. Once on the bank's web site, search by the terms *REO*, *foreclosures*, or *real estate available* and locate its REO department with asset managers' names and contact information, including phone numbers and e-mail. The lender also may redirect you to its outside asset management firm and provide a main contact, or to the Realtors it has hired to list and sell each property. If you can't find a web site for a particular lender, try looking on Yellow pages.com (www.yellowpages.com), Skipease (www.skipease.com), or SearchBug (www.searchbug.com).

About Timing

Computers simplify your job and the jobs of those involved in the mortgage and foreclosure process, too. They also, theoretically, make the system much more efficient. When it comes to identifying and making foreclosure deals, you have two options: React quickly, or you're out! You must constantly be on your toes to anticipate particular properties, identify them, and move on them.

Remember foreclosure investor Alf from earlier? He didn't succeed at buying Sondra's property pre-foreclosure, but he kept his eye on the property listing and, with the help of his paid, online foreclosure-listing service, saw the notice of auction, followed up on it, and was able to successfully bid on the property at auction.

On Achieving Your Dreams and Goals

Keep in mind that you must be committed to working hard and learning much if you want to achieve your goals and dreams in foreclosure investing, as in life. One of my favorite business philosophers is Brian Tracy (www.briantracy.com). He's a world-renowned speaker, consultant, and author of *The Psychology of Selling* (Nightingale Conant, 1995).

Tracy suggests that the most successful people in the world have seven important qualities:

1. *Ambition*. These people see themselves as capable of being the best at what they do. Many of us, instead, have feelings of inferiority that often translate into believing we don't deserve certain things, including success. In reality, you deserve 100 percent of everything you make and enjoy as long as you get it from serving other people. Your rewards are in direct proportion to your service. If you serve better and serve more and serve at a higher level and serve more enthusiastically and serve a higher quality, then you'll have a wonderful income and you'll deserve every penny of it. You must see yourself as capable of being the best.

2. *Courage*. Successful people make themselves confront the fears that hold others back. Your two biggest enemies to success are fear and doubt. Eliminate those, and you're home free. Act courageously when boldness is called for, and develop the habit of courage. To overcome fear of rejection in your business dealings, you must recognize that rejection in selling is not personal. As successful salespeople realize, a "no" means you're that much closer to a "yes."

3. *Commitment*. Top people in their field believe in themselves and what they do. There's a direct relationship between the depth of your belief and what happens in your reality. A corollary is that caring is the critical element in modern selling—whether you're working with a big lending corporation or a homeowner in pre-foreclosure. If you have a passion for what you do, you're that much closer to success. If you have compassion for people, you're closer still.

4. *Professionalism*. Think of yourself as a consultant, a problem solver. The most successful consultants in America are the very best salespeople of their services. People will accept you at your own evaluation of yourself. As a consultant, you can build rapport with those people you work with. Their perception of you determines how much they recommend you to other customers.

5. *Preparation*. Successful people review every detail in advance. Make the effort and do those things the average person is not willing to do. Review every detail of every call or situation before every business meeting. Prepare for every contingency. Anticipate every objection or roadblock, and counter it. The difference such preparation makes is extraordinary.

6. *Continuous learning*. Recognize that if you're not getting better, you're getting worse. Read, listen to CDs, and take additional training like the top successes do. Professionals never stop learning.

7. *Responsibility*. Top performers see themselves as president of their own personal services corporation. The top people in our society have an attitude of being self-employed. We are presidents of our own personal corporations. You work for yourself. You are the president of your own company, your own career, your own life, and your own finances.

TAKEaway

- Understanding advanced types of foreclosure investing—buying deeds of trust, at courthouse auctions, REO properties from lenders, at REO auctions, and more—offers you flexibility to capitalize on almost any opportunity.

- Working closely with homeowners in default is generally *not* part of advanced foreclosure investing.

- The dollars and cents of a deal are primarily what count in advanced foreclosure investing.

- Get e-connected. Count on technology to save you time and streamline your ability to succeed in this business.

CHAPTER 2

Essentials That Seal the Deal

Ignorance is not bliss when it comes to foreclosure investing. It can cost you tens of thousands of dollars in one wrong deal.

—Alexis McGee

A s with any type of investing, the success of a foreclosure deal depends on much more than simply paying the dollars-and-cents price tag. If you want to buy an REO property from a bank and fail to do your math correctly or don't secure the proper financing in time, you could lose the deal or, worse yet, substantial cash. If you don't or can't see the interior of a property before you buy and you miss the mark on your assessment of rehab and repair costs, you're out of luck. And what if, no matter the approach you take to buying a property, its title isn't clear? As an investor, you could be out of luck and out of cash in this situation as well.

Consider what happened to Macy N., a relative newcomer to foreclosure investing. Macy wanted to bid on a $280,000 house at a foreclosure auction. Bidding opened at $80,000, and Macy was beside herself with excitement at the prospect of getting a property worth so much for so little. Unfortunately, she had failed to properly research the home's title. It turned out that she bid on the property's second mortgage, which was in default. She ended up paying $80,000 cash for the property and then automatically assumed the senior loan's debt. That first mortgage on the property was $280,000, so Macy actually paid $360,000 for a house worth $280,000. Ouch!

In this chapter, we take a closer look at how Macy should have thoroughly checked out the title. We also examine other important issues that foreclosure investors must understand to ensure the success of a deal.

Understanding the Data: A Review

The secret to successful advanced foreclosure investing, like pre-foreclosure equity-investing, starts with the ability to identify prospective purchase targets quickly and easily. To do so demands that you know how and where to get up-to-date information from reliable sources and, in turn, use that information to your best advantage.

The good news is that information and sources are plentiful. Unfortunately, the quality of foreclosure data varies widely. It can be inaccurate, out of date, and often flat-out wrong. Even if you're looking to buy properties at REO auctions, you'll want accurate information on a property's history. (Property listings with simple descriptions and sometimes photos are generally available online from the largest, reputable auctioneers.)

"e" Is for Easy

To assemble your lists of prospective properties, you could trek to your county recorder's office and start searching all the listings for Notice of Trustee's Sale or REO (Trustee's Deed) filings. That's wasting a lot of time up front. Instead, spend your time wisely by looking to online listing services as a primary source. Your time is better spent talking to motivated sellers. Spring for the fee that good services charge; it's money well spent for the e-ability to sort properties by the numbers and more. (See the examples in Figures 2.1 through 2.3, from www.ForeclosureS.com.)

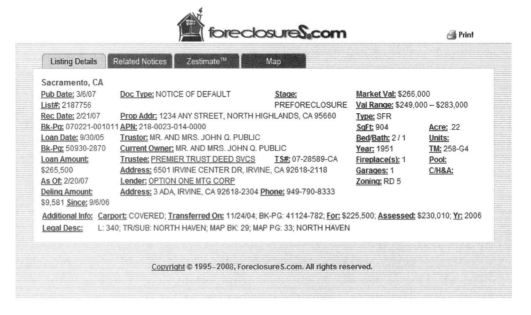

FIGURE 2.1   Pre-Foreclosure Listing

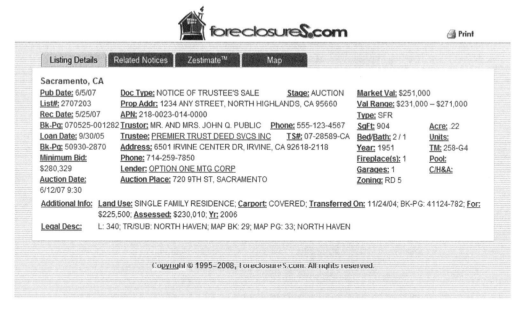

FIGURE 2.2   Sale Notice Listing

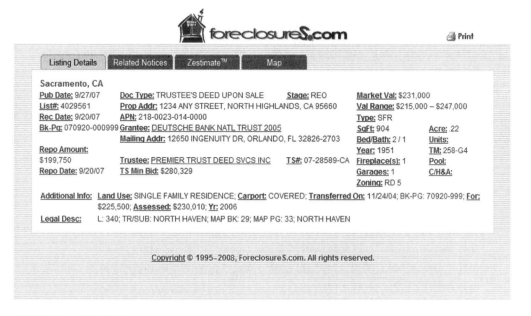

FIGURE 2.3   REO Listing

The Basics of a Good Foreclosure-Listing Service

A good foreclosure list should, at a minimum, provide you the following to get started:

- Property address.
- Current owner(s) names and mailing address (if property is REO, this would be the foreclosing lending institution's servicing agent).
- Estimated market value of the property.
- Estimated equity in the property (if pre-foreclosure or auction lead), based on one loan in foreclosure and estimated market value.
- Type of property—single-family residence, multifamily, duplex, etc.
- Size of property—square footage, bedrooms/baths, lot size.
- Amount and date of original loan in default.
- Default record date (when foreclosure began).
- Minimum bid for trustee sale auction.
- Trustee sale reference number.
- Location of trustee sale.
- Trustee's name and address.
- If REO property, amount paid at auction (either foreclosing lender or an outside bidder, winning amount).

A Primer on Key Numbers:

- *Equity:* The difference between debts on a property and property value; the owners' untapped savings in a property.
- *Loan date:* When the loan in default originated.
- *Default record date:* Day the default, Notice of Trustee's Sale, or REO filing became public record.
- *Trustor's name (if applicable):* The person who originally signed for the loan; may also be a different "current owner" if the trustor sold the house but the new owner did not pay off the trustor's loans and is now in default on those loans not in the current owner's name.
- *Trustee's name/address:* No reason to contact the trustee because he can't sell you the house.

- *Delinquency amount, loan amount, and loan document number:* All of the original information on the loan in foreclosure; this does not represent all the loans on the property.

- *Minimum bid and date of auction:* In Notices of Trustee's Sale, these are the current balances of the loan in foreclosure.

- *Loan document number:* Used to find the original loan document at the county recorder's office to see the terms of the loan.

- *Property details:* These include lot size and the year in which a property was built, number of bedrooms and baths, and more; you'll need these as a way to help determine market value and eliminate properties that don't fit the criteria you're looking for.

More Considerations

Again, online sources and services are a great and efficient way to get much of the information you need to do business. A few other issues to keep in mind include:

- *Legal forms.* Specific contracts, deeds, mortgages, notes, leases, and other legal instruments used in your area. Solid sources include LegalWiz (www.legal wiz.com) from author and attorney William Bronchick, and FindLaw (www .findlaw.com), as well ForeclosureS.com (www.foreclosures.com).

- *Recording rules.* Know where, when, and in what format documents must be recorded along with the fees associated with them. You can get that information from your state or county recorder's office.

- *State and local disclosure and licensing laws.* Check with your state licensing agency for more information. If you are rehabbing homes, pay attention to building regulations and licensing rules for contractors, too. That information is available from your state Secretary of State's office or building code division.

The Visual Factor

Seeing is believing. And seeing is essential when it comes to foreclosure investing. Never invest in a property without first seeing it, even if only from the outside. Whenever possible, see inside a property, too. Some foreclosure-investing experts may say it's fine to buy an unseen property. But if you're in pursuit of excellence in this business, doing what others do doesn't cut it.

Clues from the Exterior

As with pre-foreclosures, advanced foreclosure investing demands that you know what you're buying in order to determine how much you can pay for it. Affordability numbers, remember, include hard costs such as repair, updating, and the cost of carrying a property until you flip it—it can take longer to do that in a cold market—as well as soft costs such as marketing and your profit margin.

If a property is slated for foreclosure auction, drive past it and check out the property and the neighborhood. Does the home obviously need a new roof? That could be a hefty but not always unexpected expense in purchasing a foreclosed property. Homeowners in default generally can't afford new roofs. Even if Mother Nature is the culprit, as with hail damage, an insurance check is likely to go toward the homeowner's bills, not a new roof.

Are windows crooked or frames and shutters falling off? That could indicate potential structural problems. Or it might be a sign that the area is prone to vandalism, which could limit the property's resale potential or mean a longer hold time and more expenses. What about the yard? Is it overgrown, the fence collapsed? All these are clues to what's happening with a property.

Pay attention to the condition of other homes in the neighborhood, too. Are they well kept or run-down? Again, the answer to that question could affect resale time and value if you plan to flip the property.

A big secret that sounds like a no-brainer but absolutely isn't: Pay attention to the property's legal description and check it against an actual address. In other words, know a property's physical details and exactly where it's located on a particular plot of land. You want to make sure the house you're driving past actually is the one you're trying to purchase. More often than you'd think, investors purchase a property they didn't intend to buy.

Jon C. culled his lists, ran the numbers, and singled out two REO properties of interest. He drove by both, liked what he saw, and purchased them from the lender for what he thought were greatly discounted prices. Turns out, though, he didn't get what he thought he'd paid for. One of the properties, which Jon had assumed was the condo at the address listed, turned out to be a basement efficiency unit. The other was a tiny alley house behind a property facing the street at the same address. In both cases, the moral of the story: *Caveat emptor*—let the buyer beware.

Tales from Foreclosure Investors

Even seasoned investors can trip up on property locations. Christian Rooney, who has done close to 200 successful property flips, recounts a lesson learned a while back:

> I was interested in a particular property scheduled for courthouse auction in Rio Linda, California. I backgrounded myself on the property, including driving past the property at the street number indicated, then headed to the auction. It was a great property in beautiful condition with great equity, or so I thought.
>
> When I got to the auction, I ran into several other regular bidders and we began talking about our potential properties, including the *brick* house I wanted. It turns out I had made a big mistake. I had driven by the house at the right number on Seventh *Street*, but the house up for auction was on Seventh *Avenue*.
>
> If it hadn't been for the discussions with my colleagues, I could have had a major loss on my hands.

A Look Inside

Ideally, your goal before you bid on or buy any foreclosed property is to see its interior. You usually can do that when buying REO properties from banks or at REO auctions. Take advantage of that opportunity. Contact the bank or lender, and make an appointment to walk the property. Ask if there are any problems with the property. The lenders could say no automatically but, conversely, they could be helpful and point out the problems they're aware of. Bring your contractor for the walk-through, if possible, so that together you can more accurately estimate repair and rehab costs.

With trustee auctions you rarely are given the advantage of seeing the interior, so it's doubly important to pick up clues to the inside from the outside and by talking to neighbors as well as doing your records search.

Title Work

Big on that to-do list is reviewing a property's title. You don't know what you don't know, so get busy and find out. That applies to many areas of foreclosure investing, but it's especially true when it comes to making sure the title is clear on any property you're considering buying at trustee sales. In case you don't think it's worth your effort, consider this: A total 36 percent of all real estate transactions in 2005 had problems with their titles, up from only 25 percent in 2000, according to a survey by the American Land Title Association (www.alta.org).

You don't know what you don't know. Remember that!

—Alexis McGee on the importance
of paying attention to a property's title

You need to know if a property's title is encumbered by another lien, so ask questions and dig for the answers. If a loan in default seems too small for a big property, it could be the second mortgage. That's what happened with Macy, mentioned earlier. She spent her money, took title, and then discovered that her title to the property was *subject to* the first mortgage. She ended up responsible for that mortgage, too. Keep in mind that in some states—Colorado, for example—public notices of foreclosure must state that the lien may not be a first mortgage.

With REO auctions and REO sales, however, banks virtually always have clear title because the foreclosure sale wipes out all junior liens on a property.

Something else to consider is that even though you do the initial title searches—whether on pre-foreclosures or foreclosures—if you have the option, it's generally a good idea to spend the 0.5 to 1 percent of the property's purchase price, and maybe even less, to buy formal title insurance before any deal is final. (If you plan to resell the property within a year, ask your title insurer for a hold-open policy. The cost is perhaps an additional 10 percent, but it will save you 90 percent on the title insurance you'll need when you sell.)

Consider what happened to Sally J. when she tried to buy a home. She thought the property's deed was in order, but it turned out that it had been forged at the time of the previous sale, voiding any subsequent deed transfers. Needless to say, that was a quick deal that wasn't.

More subtle issues that may not torpedo a deal but can cloud a title include incorrect property descriptions or misspelled names.

Banks and lenders generally warranty title on their REO properties, but properties bought at trustee auctions are as-is and without warranties to their title. Again, think about Macy. You absolutely, positively must make sure no irregularities in the chain of title will cloud its integrity. That means getting online to your county recorder's office, if possible, and checking the chain of title on a specific property. If you can't do it online, head down to the office in person, hire someone

Tales from Foreclosure Investors

ForeclosureS.com coach Daryl White recounts a story from one of his coaching clients that shows the importance of knowing the business before you try to buy at auction.

The client, Andrew C., decided to check out a foreclosure auction strictly as an observer. While there, he met a couple who recently had attended an everything-you-ever-wanted-to-know-to-get-rich-quick seminar on auction investing. The couple told Andrew that they planned to bid on a property with its junior loan in default. They had absolutely no idea that if they won the bidding, they also would inherit the senior loan on the property. It turned out that their seminar hadn't bothered to address the importance of running a title search or in what situations they would take a property subject to existing liens.

If not for Andrew and his words of warning, the couple would have learned a very costly lesson. Bottom line: Learn the business before you put your cash on the line.

else to do it for you, or make use of a close relationship you've developed with a particular title company.

Why do the initial title work yourself instead of paying someone else to do it? You can get an uninsured title search report online (fee-based sites include http://www.titlesearch.com/ or http://www.americantitleinc.com) or pay for a preliminary title report from your local title company (average cost around $400). That's likely a very costly approach to doing business, especially when there are no guarantees you'll be the successful bidder on a property at auction.

Finances

With advanced foreclosure investing, you will do more deals on your own and need more money to finance them. So get over any initial butterflies brought on by the thought of spending all that cash. This is, after all, senior class, not Foreclosures 101. You're a veteran by now.

However, as with pre-foreclosure equity-investing, if you run the numbers and they don't add up, walk away from any potential deal. This is your business, not your hobby.

Risk and Reward

Risk can be greater in advanced foreclosure investing, and with greater risk comes the possibility of greater reward. With pre-foreclosures, your numbers should include a minimum profit of 12 to 18 percent of the resale value of a property after it's fixed up. That's double to triple a real estate agent's standard 6 percent residential deal, but those agents aren't taking the big gambles or risks.

You are, and you do, especially with advanced foreclosure investing. Consider a few of those risks:

- What if the property bought at a trustee sale isn't structurally sound? You can't know that if you don't go inside, and you usually can't get inside before a trustee sale.

- What if that property has problems with its title or you bid on a deed of trust assuming it's the primary only to learn too late it's a second or third note?

- What if that REO auction property doesn't resell quickly or within the time you expected and on which you based your numbers? That can be a real concern in cold markets.

- What if repair and rehab costs spiral beyond your estimates? And they will!

- What about the cost of spending your own cash? That's your only option with some types of advance foreclosure investing.

These are only a few of the risks faced by advanced foreclosure investors. You'll need to purchase any property at a minimum 30 to 40 percent discount— 15 to 25 percent of that to cover your actual costs (depending on current market conditions) and 15 percent profit to cover your risks as well as unforeseen problems that inevitably crop up. One problem with title, one major overlooked repair, or a market slowdown on top of an overly optimistic home value conceivably can wipe out your investment. It is, in most cases, your money at risk. With deeds of trust purchases or trustee auctions, you can't flip or hand off a property deal before closing to someone else because there are no purchase contracts to assign.

Options Available

Later we show you step-by-step how to figure the numbers associated with various foreclosure-investing deals, but right now let's look briefly at the different approaches and the financing available for each type. Of course, there are always exceptions and variables, so make sure you know what they are up front.

- *Pre-foreclosure.* Can be done with or without any of your own money. You sign a *subject-to* purchase contract and then close on it yourself or turn it over or flip the deal/property to another investor for a finder's fee at closing. *Subject-to* financing means you (or another investor) take over the property owner's existing loans (without asking permission of the lender) and bring them current. The purchaser gets a grant deed signed by the seller and then owns the home and is responsible for the prior owner's mortgage payments (which remain in the prior owner's name).

- *Deed of trust or note buying.* No financing available here. It's all cash up front, and there's no contract to flip.

- *Trustee sale auctions.* Pay for property purchases with cash or certified funds in accordance with specific state guidelines. For example, in California you must show up at auction with a cashier's check for 100 percent of the amount you plan to bid. Again, you have no contract, so you can't flip the deal to someone else.

- *REOs.* Plenty of financing options are acceptable, ranging from all cash to a hard-money loan (remember, those are higher interest rate, short-term interim loans), REO lender financing, and conventional mortgage financing. You cannot flip these contracts to other investors because most banks strictly prohibit assignments in their contracts. Most REO lenders use their own internal sales contracts, which don't tend to be buyer friendly, so you'll need to have a qualified lawyer review them. Watch the small print!

- *REO auctions.* Participating lenders and the auction house set the terms for financing. Make sure you read the fine print in the auction catalog, too, which will detail the financing, including what happens to your deposit if your financing does not come through or the REO holder rejects your bid. Auction houses, like banks and lenders with REOs, use their own internal contracts, so pay attention to the fine print. Again, the contract will most likely prohibit it being assigned to another investor.

Eviction: Doing It Right

No one wants to force someone out of their home, especially someone who has nowhere else to go. But vacating a property—eviction by force, if necessary—is the very real consequence of defaulting on a mortgage to the point of foreclosure. When we buy a home and sign the mortgage or deed of trust papers, we are agreeing to abide by certain rules and regulations or face the penalties. Don't be too tough on yourself if you must evict someone from a property after foreclosure. Eviction is not a surprise ending.

That said, there's a right way and a wrong way to go about evicting someone from a property after foreclosure. Rule number one: If you purchase a foreclosure property with the intent of flipping it, and the former owner still lives there, recognize that he must vacate the property, and that you must immediately take steps to make sure that happens. The former homeowner must know up front that he can't stay on the property.

The Legalities

Laws regarding eviction procedures are very specific. Entire books are devoted to the ins and outs of how to do it right, what to avoid, and why. No matter what some people say as part of their scare tactics, the sheriff doesn't simply show up one day and kick a former homeowner out in the cold. The laws in some states heavily favor homeowners, so you, as a property owner, can have your hands tied unless you know the laws specific to your area.

Basically, following default, sale, and subsequent legal recording of sale (perfecting of deed) in the county recorder's office, the steps to eviction—with state variations—include:

- The former owner is served with a notice to vacate within a certain time frame.
- If he doesn't vacate, the new owner files a complaint for unlawful detainer (lawsuit), and the eviction process moves forward in the courts.
- Eventually, however, the sheriff will physically remove the person if the courts side with the new homeowner and force the former owner to leave.

If this is your first time dealing with an eviction, it's generally a good idea to talk to a qualified attorney to make sure you know the ins and outs of your state's eviction laws. An attorney can also help you understand the right way to structure your negotiations with the former homeowner so that hopefully you can avoid going to court over an eviction order, says Gary Link, an attorney with Sacramento, California-based Rosenberg & Link. A specialist in eviction proceedings—his office has litigated more than 10,000 trials and filed over 35,000 eviction lawsuits—Link is also legal adviser to the Sacramento Rental Housing Association, a director of the California Apartment Association, and a former commissioner for the Sacramento County Human Rights and Fair Housing Commission.

Sources for Eviction Information

Eviction expert Gary Link, an attorney with Sacramento, California-based Rosenberg & Link, suggests more sources of information on the ins and outs of eviction in your state:

- National Apartment Association (www.naahq.org).
- California Apartment Association (www.caanet.org).
- Your local and state apartment association.
- Rental Housing Association (www.gbreb.com/rha/about_us/).

Possible Solutions

Gary Link advocates the *ABC* approach to evicting a former homeowner after a foreclosure auction:

- Ask.
- Bargain.
- Contract.
- If all that fails, just do it.

"Talk to the former owner first to see what can be done," says Link. "Ask the person to go. . . . Surprisingly, a lot of times the [former owners] will actually vacate the property. Typically, if you bargain and they agree to it, I find that the former owner vacates earlier than through the process of an eviction lawsuit, and fewer times they trash the property than if you actually evict them where the sheriff goes out and posts a notice to vacate. If payment of money to the former owner is involved, the real estate business calls this the cash-for-keys approach."

But Link takes the concept one step beyond. "I also add the *C*. I put it in writing so that the new owner receives the extra enforcement rights of a *contract*," he adds. "Then I have this contract, called a 'Mutual Written Agreement to Vacate and Surrender Real Property,' that I can use as the foundational basis for the eviction lawsuit, and I can show the court if necessary (if complications occur)."

The contract should call for the property to be vacated within a certain time that it be left in good condition, free from debris, trash, garbage, and all personal property that belongs to the former owner; that no fixtures or appliances be removed; that the property not be damaged; and that the keys be turned over without incident. In effect, says Link, the contract takes away most of the potential legal objections an irate former homeowner could raise if he decided not to vacate and you, the new owner, were forced to square off against him in court.

The extra-cash-for-keys approach also serves as positive reinforcement for the former owners that life isn't over just because they've lost their home. The cash literally is a former homeowner's second chance. How much cash you offer depends on your deal's numbers. We talk more about that later.

Of course, you also may run into the occasional hardship eviction case. Perhaps an elderly widow, a disabled individual, or even a struggling homeowner has been misled or duped out of substantial amounts of cash, believing it will cancel the foreclosure. Unfortunately, in these cases often unscrupulous people have basically sold them out with no apparent rights, says Link. In substantial hardship cases the courts will often give the former homeowner extra time to vacate, he adds.

As an investor, that extra time means you can't get access to or rehab the property until it's vacated, so your deal may lose its luster—and lose you cash—if you haven't planned for all contingencies. As an alternative, you may want to concentrate your efforts on properties that are already vacant.

Repair and Rehab Costs and the Numbers

Before you make an offer on a pre-foreclosure or foreclosed property, you must have a pretty solid idea of the cost to repair and rehab it. Your numbers—and your profits—depend on it.

Successful Approaches

As discussed earlier in this chapter, ideally, you want to see inside a property, walk it with your contractor (or bid it yourself), and then get an accurate, itemized rehab proposal. Of course, that's not always possible and often only a pipe dream in advanced foreclosure investing. Don't count on knocking on the door of a property set for foreclosure auction and expect to be greeted by a friendly homeowner graciously inviting you in for tea. You're pretty much out of luck when it comes to an inside view in these situations, and must count on the alternatives we've discussed to assess rehab and repairs.

Another approach is to figure into your costs some ballpark estimates for standard updates and upgrades. A good rule of thumb is to count on $15 to $20 a square foot in repairs if a house is in average condition and increase that if it appears run-down. With a 1,200-square-foot home—the size of an average starter home—that means $18,000 to $24,000 in rehab costs, which is a hefty chunk of cash.

(The first ForeclosureS.com guide, *The ForeclosureS.com Guide to Making Huge Profits Investing in Pre-Foreclosures without Selling Your Soul*, addressed many details of repairs and rehabs that offer the best return on your money, as well as how to get it all done.)

Top-Notch Condition

Keep in mind, too, that if you want the best price for a property, it must be in cherry condition—as good as the top comparable properties (comps) in the neighborhood.

A typical home should have the following fixes:

- *Termites and dry-rot*. Repair any damage already done to a property. Also, to make your property compare favorably to others in the neighborhood, fix any issues that could lead to future problems. A small water leak, for example, might in the future lead to dry rot. Clumps of dirt near the foundation could indicate termites.

- *Roof*. Repair or replace so that it has, at minimum, a three-year, watertight guarantee.

- *Landscape*. Clean and spruce up the yard, and fix any broken fences, sprinklers, or other outdoor features. Think curb appeal.

- *Paint*. New paint inside and out.

- *Flooring*. New carpet, padding, and vinyl/linoleum.

- *Kitchen*. New appliances, new faucet, new or reglazed counters, cabinets cleaned up or painted.

- *Bathrooms*. Reglazed tub/shower, new or reglazed sink/vanity, new toilet or at least toilet seat.

- *Heating and cooling system*. Clean vents; repair or replace condenser unit.

Some cosmetic additions to increase curb appeal and enhance the all-important first impression include a new front door, foyer flooring, and perhaps a new mailbox.

More Information on the Value of Repairs

Here are a few good sources of comparative data on the value and cost of specific home repairs:

- Contractors.com (http://www.contractors.com/h/info/resources.html). Detailed listings from a comprehensive online contractor directory for the United States and Canada.

- All Bay Home Inspection Incorporated (http://www.allbay.com/cost.htm). Thorough comparisons of the cost of various repairs by a northern California home inspection company.

- First American Home Buyers Protection Incorporated (http://homewarranty.firstam.com/HRenewHomeWarranty.aspx). Includes a helpful guide on typical home repair costs.

The All-Important Property Valuation

In addition to knowing the cost of fixing up a property, to realistically work your numbers in any potential deal, you must have an accurate valuation of the property in its cherry or fixed-up condition. Different types of foreclosure investing may add or subtract costs, but the basic approach to valuing a property is the same.

Use conservative numbers in your estimates of a property's resale price—especially in slower or colder markets—so that you don't get stuck with a house that eats up your profits, either through excessive repairs, languishing too long on the market, or the result of some other unforeseen issue (more on the importance of that in Chapter 12).

Determining the Resale Value

You'll need a market value range for the property to help determine its resale value once it's fixed up. That amount should be based on comps—prices of comparable property sales, pending sales, and active listings—in the same neighborhood for no more than the past six months (three months is better). Keep in mind, though, the comps are strictly a starting point to help you weed your leads. The real value of a property will depend on market conditions at the time of sale and more.

Finding Data on Comps

Good sources for finding prices on current sold properties to use in figuring a property's resale value include:

- ForeclosureS.com (www.foreclosures.com).
- SiteXdata (www.sitexdata.com).
- First American Real Estate Solutions (www.firstamres.com).
- DataQuick Information Systems (www.dataquick.com).
- Local Realtor multiple listing services.
- Local title companies.

Ballpark estimates won't do, either. It would be great if you could take the time and money to hire a professional appraiser to do the work for you. But you don't have the luxury of time (generally your window of opportunity is short) or money—it can be a costly proposition to pay for appraisals on every potential deal. So the job is yours. Make the most of it.

Start your figuring by getting values of comparable fixed-up properties in the area. Premium foreclosure-listing services are a good source for comps and generally can provide them for minimal fees. You can also turn to subscription databases such as SiteXdata (www.sitexdata.com) from Fidelity National Data Services (FNDS), First American Real Estate Solutions (www.firstamres.com), DataQuick Information Systems (www.dataquick.com), local Realtor multiple listing services (MLSs), or local title companies.

Any comparable sales report should list all houses that have sold within the past six months within a quarter-mile radius (up to one mile if necessary) of the property you're interested in. The sold houses should be similar in size, age, and style to the house you are appraising. Eliminate fixer-uppers with low market values because you're interested in the top dollar you can get for your house when it's in cherry condition after it's repaired and rehabbed. Then check your local MLS using Realtor.com, Metrolist.com, and other sites for all active properties on the market and for pending sales—both on the market and in escrow—with the same criteria to see what your current competition is doing.

Next, take your best comparables from among this data (solds, pending sales, and actives) and drive by them. Eliminate any comps that you cannot replicate in your property. Your remaining comparables will give you your resale price range.

Once you have that number, you then subtract your estimated cost of repairs and rehab. That's the appraised value starting point from which you will subtract your costs and more when determining any offering price in a deal.

The Last Essential: One Step Beyond

Set yourself up for success and apart from everyone else by committing to maximum effort for maximum success, says ForeclosureS.com coach and retired real estate broker Tim Rhode. The set formula for your success comes down to the old adage that you get out what you put in.

Rhode suggests laying out specific key performance indicators (KPIs) with a specific timetable for achieving them. This then becomes your own formula for success and the plan to achieve it. Work the plan and you'll get your desired success and beyond.

Consider the following example of one foreclosure investor's KPIs. This investor primarily concentrated on working with homeowners in pre-foreclosure, but you can use it as a basic framework to build your own KPIs, no matter the type of foreclosure-investing, says Rhode.

- I will purchase two properties at 70 percent of market value less repairs by November 30.

- I know that 200 seller contacts nets two deals. I must contact 100 sellers (talk to and build a relationship with them) in the first 45 days.

- I know that 20 relationships built helping people solve their stuck situation nets two deals. That breaks down to 17 seller contacts per week, given the November 30 deadline. So I will make a minimum of 17 new seller contacts per week.

- I know that I must connect and build a relationship with a minimum 3.5 new leads per week in the first 45 days (it takes time before someone facing default is ready to take action). So I will build a relationship with a minimum of 3.5 leads per week and work with these leads until they sell to me or otherwise solve their situation.

- I absolutely commit to doing all follow-up calls, research, and legwork necessary in order to accomplish these goals.

- I hereby commit to constantly improving my ability to convey my sincerity in helping folks solve their default situation. I will always do what's best for *them*.

- I know that follow-up is another critical component in my success and I hereby commit to doing all the follow-up necessary for me to maintain my relationship with folks who need my help.

- I know that distractions are a part of life and I hereby promise that *nothing* will stop me from achieving the KPIs I've laid out here.

Specific actions = Specific successes

—Tim Rhode, ForecloureS.com coach
and successful foreclosure investor

TAKEaway

- Advanced foreclosure investing, just as working with homeowners in pre-foreclosure, starts with subscribing to an accurate, reliable, and thorough foreclosure-listing service.

- Always look at a potential investment property yourself and, if possible, see the inside, too. You'll have a more accurate picture of the true value—as in re-hab and resale—of the property.

- Pay close attention to the chain of title on any potential investment. Too often investors don't and get taken.

- Always, always, always include your 15 percent profit in any potential deal. You earn it!

- There's a right and a wrong way to evict someone. The right way starts with understanding completely your state's laws as they relate to eviction, and then carrying them out to the letter.

- Pay careful attention to determining the value of comparable properties in the neighborhood. Make sure those you use are of properties that are the same size, age, type, and that can be replicated. Keep in mind, too, that your goal is to determine the value of your property when it's fixed up and in cherry condition.

- Lay out your formula for success with the help of personal key performance indicators—specific steps to achieve—and a timetable for achieving them.

PART II

DEEDS OF TRUST

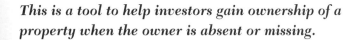

This is a tool to help investors gain ownership of a property when the owner is absent or missing.

—Alexis McGee

CHAPTER 3

A Primer on Buying Deeds of Trust

 *When you can't get the deal through the front door, buying the deed of trust and then foreclosing is an alternative backdoor approach.*

—Alexis McGee

You've found the perfect property in the perfect location and figure you can pick it up for the perfect price. The only problem: The owner has skipped town and can't be found. Does this spell the end for your perfect deal? No way.

Instead of taking the front-door approach to buying the property—which involves going to the owner (in this case absent and nowhere to be found) to work a pre-foreclosure deal—try the back door instead. That is, buy the mortgage note, or deed of trust. This alternative approach lets you gain ownership of a property by buying its note for a discounted price, foreclosing on that note, gaining ownership to the property at the foreclosure auction, and then flipping (rehabbing and re-selling) the property for a profit, or allowing an outside bidder to buy you out at the auction. With the latter, you make your profit on the difference between the amount you paid for the note and its face value.

This is not, however, a system you use when you can't get a pre-foreclosure deal with a homeowner in default. You're the good guy, the white knight. You don't threaten a homeowner with the backdoor approach if he nixes your front-door advances!

Don't confuse buying a deed of trust with making money on mortgages, either. This isn't a primer on the how-to-buy-notes business. Neither does this approach mean heading to court to battle a desperate homeowner on the verge of losing the roof over his head, or jostling with a crowd of bidders on the court-house steps.

"I love buying deeds of trust because they're fun; they're easier than dealing with the homeowner, and less emotion is involved," says Sarah Garlick, Forclo-sureS.com coach and successful deeds of trust buyer. "It's just the numbers— they're right or they're not."

Let's look more closely at what this backdoor approach to foreclosure invest-ing really is all about.

A Valuable Tool in Foreclosure Investing

When buying a deed of trust, you do not buy ownership of the property. You are, as we mentioned, buying a tool to help you gain ownership when the owner is absent or missing. This should not be your primary approach to foreclosure investing be-cause the process is loaded with dead ends and often is more frustrating than ful-filling. As an advanced foreclosure investor, however, you should understand note buying as an option in case a situation requires it.

The White Knight Rides Again

This backdoor approach to obtaining a house can also be a last resort by you as a white-knight foreclosure investor to help totally uncooperative homeowners avoid losing their home. By buying the note, you then can approach the home-owners with the reality that you truly don't want to foreclose, but they *will* lose their home if they don't cooperate. "You buy the note and you still get the oppor-tunity to help the homeowner," says Daryl White, ForeclosureS.com coach and successful foreclosure investor. "You put yourself in a position to help them, and they won't turn you down. My number one go-to is the homeowner. This is their home; they're losing it; this is a bad situation; what can I do to benefit them, if anything?"

> *When other investors see deals that are overleveraged*
> *(without equity), I see a still very viable deal.*
>
> —Sarah Garlick, ForeclosureS.com coach,
> successful foreclosure investor

Alternatively, if a homeowner has no option but to lose his home and has no equity, you can still help. If you understand deeds of trust buying, in some cases you can approach the homeowner to buy the home contingent on whether you can get the second or junior note holder to sell you that note at a significant discount. This is not the same as a short sale—when a lender agrees to take less than the amount of the debt and forgive the remainder—because there is no forgiveness of debt. Instead, the note holder simply takes a loss and sells the note for cash today rather than go through the foreclosure process. The size of the discount you negotiate on that debt, says Garlick, in effect creates the room for profit just as a homeowner's *equity* would.

Breaking Down the Numbers

Are you thoroughly confused by the idea of buying deeds of trust? Don't be. Let's break it down piece by piece. For example, let's consider how a deed of trust purchase might work on a property with a $300,000 top market value that's facing imminent foreclosure. A pre-foreclosure deal doesn't make sense because the homeowner has two notes on the property, a first for $180,000 and a second or junior note for $100,000. That's $280,000 in notes against a $300,000 property—not enough equity for a deal.

Home market value	$300,000
Primary/first deed of trust	$180,000
Junior/second deed of trust	$100,000
Total of both deeds	$280,000
Equity in the property (too little to buy pre-foreclosure)	$ 20,000

But let's assume that, as a deed of trust buyer, you can purchase the junior note at a discount—perhaps a $90,000 discount, or $10,000 total cost. That's not at all far-fetched. If the senior note ends up foreclosed, the junior note holder is wiped out at the trustee sale auction. He gets zip, nada, nothing!

Instead, you buy that note from the lender directly for $10,000; you get an assignment of deed of trust. You then reinstate the first deed that was in foreclosure and take that amount onto your deed of trust. That *advance* to the first lender then gives you the right to start your own trustee sale auction on your deed of trust. You then wait out your trustee sale auction. If no one shows up, you get the house with a trustee's deed. You're now its sole owner. You can now pay the former homeowner $10,000 to walk away (cash for keys). "I always give someone moving money at least," says Garlick.

Deed Differences

A deed of trust or trust deed is a mortgage.

An assignment of deed of trust is when the mortgage is sold to another lender.

A grant deed conveys title to a property.

Your cost to date for the property now totals $200,000. That leaves plenty of *equity* to take care of repairs and rehab, carrying costs, and a minimum 15 percent—or $45,000—profit on the $300,000 home.

"When other investors see deals that are overleveraged [without equity], I see a still very viable deal," Garlick adds.

The Details

A *deed of trust* or *trust deed* is a note that obligates its holder, the *trustor*, to pay a set amount for a property to the lender or *beneficiary*. A *grant deed* actually conveys the title to the property. An *assignment of deed of trust* conveys title of the loan from one lender to a new lender.

People often mistakenly interchange the words *deed of trust* with *mortgage*. But they are different. A deed of trust—those words will be at the top of the physical document—gives the trustee the power of sale in the event the note is in default. That means foreclosure is by nonjudicial means—it does not require court action. Home loan documents technically are known as mortgages in states that require judicial (court) involvement in foreclosure.

Think of the steps to buying a deed of trust as very similar to buying a property in pre-foreclosure, only with a few more line items added. Both processes start with identifying potential deals. You do that by data-mining and identifying solid sources of foreclosure property leads (that's how Garlick found her deal described earlier), and then culling those lists of properties. Parameters by which you can limit your lists include:

- Geographic area. You'll want only those properties in your target geographic area.

- Property type. Concentrate on starter-size homes (about 1,200 square feet) because there's always a ready market for them no matter the economic conditions.

- Homeowner equity. You don't need this filter when you buy a note because you create equity when you pay less for the note than its current balance.

- Related notices. Check your foreclosure listing service. It should include information on past loans in default at no extra cost. Often if someone is in default on one loan, they're in default on all the loans on a property, too. (Here, if a homeowner has more than one loan on a property, you'll also quickly find all those loans in default and junior note deals, too.)

- Contacting neighbors, friends, and the property owner: Only by talking to these people will you be able to unearth the reality of the foreclosure situation. If you discover that the property's owner is absent, obviously there will be no pre-foreclosure deal, and you have a possible candidate for the back-door approach.

For the deed of trust buying approach to work, however, all of the following criteria must be met:

- The house is in foreclosure and is going to auction.

- The first, or senior, note is in foreclosure, and a second, or junior, mortgage exists on the property. (Check out "Related Notices" on ForeclosureS.com listings.)

- The junior note is at risk of being wiped out—which is what happens to secondary loans when a senior note forecloses.

- The junior note's face value is high enough that you can buy it at a discount. In this deal, you make your money on the difference between the discounted price you pay for the note and the note's face value. If, for example, you pay $20,000 for a $60,000 note, the difference—$40,000—can be worth your time and effort. (Garlick bought that $100,000 junior note for just $10,000!)

- The property has title problems. Perhaps someone with a half interest won't sell, is deceased, or can't be found. The only way you'll discover such problems is by culling your lists and trying to contact the neighbors, relatives, and the homeowner.

Ideally, that second or junior note should be held by a private party or small investor. That's because mega investors or mortgage giants aren't interested in selling a single deed of trust at a discount to you, the lone investor. They prefer, instead, to bundle millions of dollars worth of notes at a time and sell them to giant corporate investors.

Julian wanted desperately to buy his first home. He could afford the monthly payments easily enough—or so the overzealous lender told him, insisting that Julian would coast through the payments with a 2/28 interest-only adjustable rate mortgage (ARM). The "2" refers to the first two years of a 30-year ARM, which would start with an artificially low interest rate and then, after the two years, adjust upward. That would give Julian plenty of time to increase his income—or so he assumed. The only problem was that Julian couldn't come up with the down payment for the deal. Then he found a property he liked, whose owner—we'll call him Tom—was willing to loan him cash for the down payment. Bingo! The home's seller, Tom, becomes a small private lender holding a second mortgage on the property. Technically, it's a deed of trust rather than a mortgage because Julian's home is in California, a nonjudicial foreclosure state.

Fast-forward to two and a half years later. The first note on the home is in foreclosure, Julian has skipped town, and a foreclosure auction on that original first note is scheduled. The sale will wipe out the second note, and Tom will be out of luck. But another option presents itself. An advanced foreclosure investor comes along before the auction and buys the junior deed of trust from Tom. No doubt anxious to salvage anything from the dead loan before the auction, Tom very likely would be willing to sell the note at a deep discount—pennies on the dollar—in order to walk away with at least a portion of his investment.

Investor Profits

How does all that translate into profits for the foreclosure investor—whom we'll call Roger C.? Won't Roger have shelled out tons of cash? Yes, this deal takes cash up front—no credit allowed here. However, if done properly—in other words, if

Roger's Deal by the Numbers

Here's why Roger's deal for Julian's house makes great sense:	
Market value of Julian's home	$320,000
First/primary deed of trust	$200,000
Second/junior deed of trust	$100,000
Total debts	($300,000)
Amount Roger will pay for second/junior deed	$10,000
Moving money for Julian, who eventually surfaces	$5,000
Total purchase costs for home (all loans plus costs)	($215,000)
Profit of 15 percent on $320,000 house	($48,000)
Cost of rehab/repairs	($17,000)
First reinstatement costs	($10,000)
Amount left for fees, holding, and other soft costs	($30,000)

you've studied and figured the numbers correctly—you can earn a fair and equitable profit and then some, depending on what happens.

> *Everyone thinks foreclosure actions on deeds of trust*
> *are expensive, but they're not. It's easy, and you don't*
> *have to understand every detail about the process.*
> *You just hand it over to the trustees and they*
> *do everything up through the auction.*
>
> —Sarah Garlick, ForeclosureS.com coach

After buying the note at a discount off its face value, Roger immediately pays off the back payments on the senior or first note. That brings the senior note current and cancels the first lender's foreclosure. Next, Roger forecloses on the junior or second note—which he now owns—even though Julian hasn't missed any payments and, technically, is not in default on it. Roger can foreclose on that note because of something known as a *lender's right to advance funds* when a loan is threatened. Roger *advanced* the money—paid off the default on the first note—because he felt his interests in the second note were at risk. Theoretically those interests are threatened by the initial foreclosure action on the first note.

> *Bottom line: The price you pay for a property—including*
> *costs associated with buying its junior deed of trust, curing*
> *the default on its senior deed, expenses incurred with*
> *foreclosure, holding costs, selling costs, and more—should*
> *not exceed 60 to 70 percent (the exact amount depends on*
> *current market conditions) of a property's fixed-up*
> *value minus the cost of repairing and rehabbing it.*
>
> —Alexis McGee

When Roger forecloses on the second note, the amount of the default/foreclosure equals the face value of the note (not the discounted amount Roger paid for it) plus escrow, title, and foreclosure fees. Even if the holder of the first note on Julian's home again decides to foreclose, that lender's new foreclosure action will occur after Roger's foreclosure and therefore won't affect Roger's auction. When the foreclosure on the loan held by Roger goes to auction, three outcomes are possible:

- An outside bidder comes to the auction and wins the top bid, the home sells to that bidder, and Roger walks away with a profit—the difference between the face value of the note and the discount price he paid for it plus reimbursement for foreclosure and other costs.

- The home doesn't sell at auction, Roger wins the property, and now owns it. His junior deed of trust is wiped out, and he is responsible for keeping the senior note current as long as he owns the property. He then will rehab, repair, and resell it for a profit. If he's done his figuring correctly (including the cost of purchasing the note, rehabbing the property, holding the property, and selling it, plus his holding costs—usually longer in colder markets) he walks away with at least the same 15 percent profit on the deal had he bought the property via the front-door approach.

- The absentee owner of the property suddenly reappears and pays Roger the face value on the note he holds (remember, Roger bought it at a discount) plus reimburses him for foreclosure costs incurred. Roger walks away with a profit—the difference between the face value of the note and the discount price he paid for it plus reimbursement for foreclosure and other costs.

We delve more deeply into the numbers in Chapter 4. But keep in mind that magic *30 to 40 percent* discount number for any foreclosure or pre-foreclosure deals. To make financial sense, your purchase price—whether it includes buying a junior note or not—must be at least 30 to 40 percent off the market value of the fixed-up property minus your costs to rehab and repair it. That 30 to 40 percent—closer to 40 percent in today's colder market, which means longer hold times before resale—breaks down to approximately 15 to 25 percent for the cost of buying and holding the property, and 15 percent profit for the time and risks you take.

Looking at it another way, the total cost for a property should never exceed 60 to 70 percent of a property's fixed-up value minus the cost of repairing and rehabbing. Don't forget, too, that you'll incur other costs with this backdoor approach to obtaining a property, including the cash to buy the note, title, escrow fees, and foreclosure fees.

Olivia, an advanced foreclosure investor, put together a list of potential properties/investments, then did her background work on those properties. In talking to neighbors of one particular property, she found what she thought might be the perfect property for a deed of trust purchase:

- First note in default.

- Secondary note held by a private lender.

- Missing property owner.

Looking more carefully, however, Olivia discovered that the junior note amounted to only $20,000, too little to allow her to purchase it at the discount needed to make enough profit on the deal. (A good rule of thumb is to look for a minimum $30,000 profit to make the deal and its risks worthwhile.) So, no matter how appealing the deal, Olivia crossed the property off her list and moved on to the next one.

Deed-of-Trust versus Mortgage States

Laws, processes, and timelines related to foreclosure differ in each state, making it vital to know *your* state's laws up front so you're not blindsided by a legal nuance that can torpedo a deal at the last minute. Check the Appendix for a summary of your state's foreclosure laws, then visit ForeclosureS.com (www.foreclosures.com/ www/pages/state_laws.asp) and read your state statutes carefully. If you have any questions, talk to a qualified real estate attorney.

Key Terminology

Judicial foreclosure: A foreclosure that involves a court action or lawsuit.

Nonjudicial foreclosure: An action to take and sell a home, made possible by a clause in a mortgage or deed of trust that grants the lien holder the right to take the property if the terms of the lien are violated.

Lis pendens: A lawsuit that must be filed to begin a judicial foreclosure; the term means "litigation is pending."

Power of sale clause: Portion of deed of trust or mortgage in which borrower preauthorizes sale of property to pay off loan balance in case of default.

Source: ForeclosureS.com.

First and foremost, however, for note buying to be a viable foreclosure-investing option, the property must be located in a deed-of-trust state, which means the state must recognize nonjudicial foreclosures. In contrast, judicial foreclosures involve a court action or lawsuit, a process that can be far too time-consuming and drawn out for note buying to make financial sense. Some states allow both.

Fortunately, the majority of foreclosures are nonjudicial. The property in question then can be sold at a trustee's sale or courthouse auction because the borrower has signed a document, such as a deed of trust, which includes a *power of sale* clause preauthorizing a trustee to sell the real estate to pay off the debt if the note is in default.

In most states, a nonjudicial foreclosure is initiated by a *notice of default*. If applicable, the notice of default must also contain a borrower in default's reinstatement rights—what he can do to stop the foreclosure proceedings. A borrower has the right to bring his account current and avoid foreclosure by paying the past-due amounts plus certain permitted expenses within a certain number of days (it varies by state) prior to the foreclosure sale. That's what Roger did after he purchased the second note, so that he then could foreclose on that note.

What Prompts a Junior Note Holder to Sell?

Even if all the numbers add up for you in a potential deed of trust purchase, the deal won't materialize without the cooperation of the initial holder of the junior note on the property. If that private lender doesn't agree to sell the note to you, you're out of luck, period. Therefore, pay careful attention to the approach you take and how you communicate and deal with note holders as well as potential property buyers and sellers.

No Surprises

Why would someone holding a second or junior note on a property in foreclosure bother to take you up on your offer to buy the note at a discount? After all, the *trustor* (the person who borrowed the money) may not even be in default on the note. The answer to that question is plain and simple dollars and sense. Before you arrive on the scene, the private lender may, at the least, already be aware that his financial investment in a property is at risk, and have, at most, been reconciled to writing off the loan as a loss. Too, that lender may not know how or want to get involved in bringing the defaulted loan current and then initiating his own foreclosure action. Even if you surprise the lender with word that his investment is in jeopardy, a look at the numbers clearly conveys the situation.

In that case, whatever amount you offer for a note is likely to be more than the lender would realize if he were to lose the balance of his investment—which generally is what happens to a secondary note when the first note forecloses. It doesn't hurt your negotiating position to gently remind the lender of that. You should also point out that to count on recouping losses through an overbid at foreclosure auction is a pipe dream. Very few properties ever sell for much more than the cost of the loan in foreclosure at auction.

Of course, there's a right and a wrong way to communicate all this to the lender.

Beyond the Money

The right approach pays dividends and generally expedites the entire process. A lender holding a junior note that you're interested in buying should be treated the same way as a homeowner in default you're trying to help: with dignity, respect, and concern. It's the ForeclosureS.com white-knight approach to foreclosure investing. You are the good guy, not the vulture. Act that way. It will go a long way toward separating you—and your offer—from other investors.

Be open and up front and don't belittle or berate—either the homeowner in default who's facing foreclosure or the private lender who may have made an iffy loan in the first place. Pay attention to your body language, too. Don't be confrontational or accusing; opt for cooperation and understanding instead.

How We Communicate

The message you convey in everything you say and do results from much more than the words themselves. Among factors that affect your message:

- Tone of voice.
- Body language.
- Your physical appearance.
- Your eye contact or lack thereof.
- What you leave unsaid.

> *When you approach holders of junior notes that you would like to buy, keep in mind that it's a business deal. If they don't know what they can and can't do, that's not your problem. It's not your responsibility to educate them.*
>
> —Sarah Garlick, ForeclosureS.com coach,
> foreclosure investor

Both you and the holder of the note you wish to buy know he will be wiped out by a foreclosure on the property's first note. As an investor, your responsibility is to demonstrate the numbers plainly and simply, make a fair and equitable discount offer on the second note, and then wait for the lender's response.

> *Buying a junior deed of trust is a business proposition. Does the junior note holder want nothing or does he want to walk away with something from a loan gone bad?*
>
> —Sarah Garlick, ForeclosureS.com coach

Hone Your Communications Skills

To avoid confrontation and potential conflict in your dealings with others, including private lenders, pay attention to how others perceive you.

- If you're meeting in person with the lender, keep your body relaxed, arms at your sides. Crossing your arms is confrontational.

- In conversations on the telephone, be aware of the tone of your voice. It should be neutral and businesslike, not condescending or critical. Ask in a professional tone if the note holder is interested in selling. If the answer is no, don't badger and simply move on to your next prospect.

- Be attentive, both in person and on the phone. That means listening to what's being said and responding accordingly.

- Don't try to impress others with how much you know. Introduce yourself, get to the point, listen, and then make your offer.

- Once you've made your offer, keep your mouth shut, and wait for a response. The next person to speak will have the upper hand and likely end up owning the deed of trust.

What's fair and equitable? "It's basically pennies on the dollar. But would they rather have ten grand or nothing?" asks Garlick.

How much you can afford to pay someone for a junior note depends on how the numbers of your deal shake out. We reemphasize the importance of the 30 to 40 percent minimum depending on current market conditions: You must always have a cushion of at least 15 percent of the fixed-up market value of the home minus the cost of repairs, and 15 to 25 percent to cover your holding and other costs.

We go into more about how to figure those numbers in Chapter 4, but, as we've mentioned, your profit in purchasing a deed of trust is the difference between the discounted amount you pay for a note and its face value at foreclosure sale. Or, if the property doesn't sell at foreclosure sale, your total costs should not exceed 60 to 70 percent of the rehabbed value of the home minus repair costs. This is, after all, your business, and you're not in it to lose money. You must be compensated fairly.

When you make an offer for the note, include how your offer benefits the noteholder so that you can get an immediate acceptance. Time is of the essence here. You need the lender to make a decision quickly so that you can get to work on your closing and stop the foreclosure on the first loan.

The Need for Speed

Fast and clean is the approach to take in buying deeds of trust. If you don't play the negotiating game, it's more likely the lender won't, either. Make your offer so appealing that the lender can't resist.

If a lender counters your offer with a much higher one because, he says, the property is worth so much more, ask him how he is going to get that much for a wipeout note? It's only worth the higher amount *if* the property were fixed up and sold to a full-market-value buyer. This is not the case here. Instead, he's going to get zero at the auction of the first loan. Anything over zero should make him jump. Now make it worth his while to jump really high because you are giving him cash for his worthless note.

Once you've sealed the deal, the purchase entails the normal sale procedure, including opening escrow with an independent third party, getting the necessary title insurance, documentation, signatures, and cash transfer, and formally recording the assignment of deed of trust documents.

Keep in mind, too, this isn't about making friends or enemies. It's about negotiating a deal that's a win-win for both of you. The note may have a face value of $40,000. But if you can make the numbers work only by paying $4,000 (10 percent of its face value), then that's your ceiling offer. The lender needs to know that. He may very well take you up on your offer, especially when he considers that zero percent of zero is zero.

A Time for Outside Help

As we've touched on, you initially should identify potential deed of trust deals yourself by culling your list of leads and following up on them. This is, after all, an alternative approach to foreclosure-investing, not a career in making big bucks off mortgages, deeds of trust, or destitute homeowners.

"As I track properties on my lists of potential deeds, I come across private note holders," says Garlick. "I network with them not only about buying the current note, but also to build a relationship as a possible source of a future note purchase and even of a future hard-money loan."

When you network with these and other private lenders, don't hesitate to ask who is brokering their loans. The answer to this question can yield a valuable source for future note-buying deals.

Title Company

After you've identified a property for a potential deed of trust deal (that means running the numbers to make sure they add up to your minimum 15 percent profit on top of all your costs) and reached an initial agreement with the lender to buy his note, you will want to hire a *title company* to verify the details of the title on the property. Beware of any senior liens or encumbrances other than the first mortgage in default. A property tax lien, for example, takes precedence over all other encumbrances and could wipe out any potential profits you might make in your deal.

If a deed of trust holder is willing to cooperate, you may be able to save time with the title by asking to see a copy of the title policy he received when the loan was initiated. The sooner you can get a copy of the policy (or do a title search yourself), the easier your job of ascertaining any encumbrances on the property. Any other liens or third and even fourth notes secured by the property will show up there.

Escrow Assistance

You'll need an *escrow company* or *attorney*, too, as the independent third party to handle the transaction of cash for assignment of deed of trust between you and the lender selling the note. After the transaction is complete, you'll also need to hire a qualified company or attorney to serve as trustee and initiate and handle the fore-closure proceedings on the deed of trust you now hold.

Make sure that whatever company or companies you choose are qualified and reputable, with track records in their particular business. Check them out online through the Better Business Bureau (www.BBBonline), look for comments about a particular company on various real estate blogs, and talk to your local Realtors, bank lending officials, and others for feedback. You may opt for a company such as ForeclosureLink (www.foreclosurelink.com), for example, that can handle all aspects of default servicing. Other companies, including Chicago Title Company (check out its web site for helpful information, www.chicagotitle.com), can handle not only foreclosure and related proceedings but title and escrow, too. Or you may have your own cadre of experts you can count on, especially if you've been in this business a while.

Final Word on Outside Help

When in doubt, get the advice of a qualified real estate attorney. A professional's fee is a small price to pay to avoid what could end up costing thousands of dollars if the law and legal proceedings aren't followed. Remember, states have different rules and regulations pertaining to foreclosure. (Check out ForeclosureS.com for a look at some of those rules.)

To find a real estate attorney, check out DSNews' Black Book (www.dsnews blackbook.com); Lawyers.com (www.lawyers.com) from the well-respected Lexis-Nexis Martindale-Hubbell; the American Bar Association (www.abanet.org, click on "Lawyer Locator"), or your local bar association. ForeclosureS.com offers an-other good reference source (http://www.foreclosures.com/www/forecast/ff_aug03/default.asp?topic=reference).

Recognizing Your Risks

Profits from buying deeds of trust can be hefty, but don't salivate just yet. The process is fraught with potholes, including your state's laws and limitations, mone-tary requirements, legal catch-22s, and more. Apart from the uncertainties associ-ated with buying a secondary deed of trust, you as an investor face myriad other risks in buying and flipping a property, especially in today's colder markets. Fortu-nately, if you know what to expect ahead of time you can plan for contingencies and perhaps avoid most of the potholes.

First, let's look at some risks inherent in foreclosure investing itself. They include:

- Cost overruns associated with repair and rehab of a property.
- Costs associated with previously unnoticed or unknown defects and damage to a property.
- Overzealous market valuation.
- Changing local real estate market conditions that affect the time needed to re-sell a property as well as its selling price and profit, if any.
- If a property isn't vacant, getting the former owners out quickly and without their trashing the property.
- If a property is vacant, vandalism can be an issue.
- Variables related to costs of holding a property, including closing costs, mortgage payments, carrying costs, and selling expenses.
- Possible increased cost of cash required to complete deals.
- A property owner filing bankruptcy. Any type of bankruptcy filing halts all foreclosure proceedings.

Now let's look more closely at the added risks when you factor in buying a deed of trust on a property:

- *Taxes*. Talk to your tax adviser for the lowdown on the tax ramifications of your investments in trust deeds. Keep in mind that any income you earn from trust deeds is considered ordinary income and therefore fully taxable.
- *Predators*. As with other forms of foreclosure investing, buying trust deeds has its share of sharks—those hungry investors circling victims for tasty deals. But this is neither your approach nor your goal. If your numbers add up properly and are fair and equitable to all parties, you will develop a reputation for excellence, fairness, and equitability. You will make the deals others can't get.
- *Military protections*. Federal laws protect active members of the military from foreclosure without judicial consent. That means a lender must go to court in order to foreclose on such a property. It's not enough for the owner in default to be absent. Translation: Make sure that any absent property owner is *not* in the military on active duty. Otherwise, you could face potential complications and a long-drawn-out procedure that's generally not worth the effort.

Bottom line: Using the backdoor approach to buying a property in foreclosure isn't easy, but it can be lucrative for you as a foreclosure investor if you understand the process, pay attention to potential pitfalls, and plan appropriately for any contingency.

TAKEaway

- Buying a deed of trust is the backdoor approach to gain ownership of a property. You do *not* buy ownership of the property when you buy the deed of trust note. You purchase the leverage to possibly gain ownership through a future foreclosure trustee sale auction.

- For a deed of trust purchase to work, a property must have a private-party junior note that's behind a senior deed of trust in foreclosure.

- The junior note's face value also must be high enough so you can buy it at a discount. The money you make is the difference between the discounted price you pay for the note and the note's face value.

- Zero percent of zero is zero! No matter the size of the second or third note that a private lender holds, if the senior note forecloses, the junior lender likely will end up with zero. Don't forget that.

- Money *is* the issue here.

- Foreclosing on a property does not have to be expensive.

- Get outside professional help to protect your interests. That means hire a title company, set up escrow, hire a trustee to handle the note foreclosure, and talk to your real estate attorney if you have any questions.

- Make sure any absentee owner is not a member of the military. Federal law prohibits foreclosure on a property owned by active military personnel.

CHAPTER 4

Finding the Deal That Adds Up

Note leads come from your garbage stack of "no-equity" leads with multiple loans on one property.

—Alexis McGee

f you think all you have to do is hang up a shingle reading "I Buy Deeds of Trusts" or blast e-mails announcing "Fast Deeds of Trust Buying" and prospects will beat down your door, you're sorely mistaken. Alternatively, poring over the plethora of web sites that list notes for sale and then following up on each vague reference won't yield much business, either.

Instead, to make buying deeds of trust work—as with any approach to foreclosure investing—you must hunker down, find your own deals, research them, and then take the next step that most investors either don't recognize, don't understand, or don't bother with. They see only that the first deed on a property is in foreclosure and the numbers for a pre-foreclosure or straight auction don't make sense, and that precludes any deal as far as they're concerned. Lucky for you they give up so easily.

Consider the following scenario: A $200,000 property is scheduled for foreclosure auction/trustee sale because its first loan, taken out years ago, is in default. The loan's current balance: $95,000. That means the home's owner has a ton of equity, or does he? On closer examination of the documents, it turns out the property also has a second deed of trust—a junior note for $40,000 held by a private lender. The foreclosure auction on the senior $95,000 note, remember, wipes out junior notes. Depending on whether the final auction bid exceeds the minimum amount owed, that junior note holder could receive all, some, or none of what's owed him. Is it worth your time and efforts to take the next step and contact that junior lender to try to buy his note at a fraction of the $40,000 debt, and avoid the crowds that possibly could bid up the price at auction? You bet!

Success in this business is about going beyond the obvious and differentiating yourself from other investors. In case you haven't noticed, hordes of them are beating the bushes for deals. A simple Google search with keywords "deed of trust" turns up more than 1 million hits—not including advertisements! Remember, the *average* foreclosure investor makes zip in this business. You must be above average and go the extra mile to win, win consistently, and win big.

Instead of walking away from the less-than-obvious deals like the one just described, take a closer look. Figure out what it takes for a note sale to make financial sense for you and that junior note holder, and create a win-win equation for all parties. Your own financial gain will handsomely reflect your efforts.

Locating That Right Property

Before you can identify a property with a junior deed of trust that has potential written all over it, you must first find those solid candidates with senior notes in foreclosure or scheduled for auction. That means you must collect and mine the data.

Foreclosure-Listing Services

Your data-mining efforts, as discussed in Chapter 2, start with finding the right source of foreclosure listings. Plenty are available, although their information and quality of service vary drastically. You'll find an occasional outdated property listing on even the best listing service, but abundant and ongoing outdated information costs you, the investor, time and money. You don't want a listing service that charges a bundle but provides little, so choose wisely. Because you can count on getting nothing for nothing, forgo the free lists and spring for paid subscription services.

National providers such as ForeclosureS.com (www.ForeclosureS.com) generally include more searchable information in their databases than do free or localized services.

A good foreclosure-listing service should offer a free trial before you plunk down your money. Use that opportunity to check out the list, and don't overlook what real estate bloggers are saying about a particular service. If many people are complaining about it, you're likely to run into similar problems, too.

Weeding Your Leads

Once you find your source of foreclosure lists, you're ready to weed those leads. Among the criteria that should be used to find your basic leads:

- *Property type*. Cull or eliminate any properties that are not one- to four-unit residential. That generally means concentrating on single-family homes, duplexes, triplexes, quadplexes, townhomes, and condominiums.

- *Location*. Limit your search to those properties in your entire county. If you turn up too many leads, filter them by zip code to get a more manageable list. If you don't turn up enough leads, try adding a neighboring county to your search.

- *Equity of 30 to 40 percent or more*. Equity is the difference between the loan amount in foreclosure and the property's estimated market value. To determine if a property owner has at least 30 to 40 percent equity—the exact amount depends on current market conditions that dictate how long you'll have to hold a property before resale—compare a property's market value with the amount of the loan in foreclosure. You should be able to get market value information free from your listing service, or check it out online on free sites such as Zillow (www.zillow.com), Yahoo's What's Your Home Worth (www.realestate.yahoo.com/Homevalues), and Trulia Real Estate Search (www.trulia.com), as well as other sites around the web.

- *Timeliness*. If the notice of default publication date is more than several weeks old, you'll need to check the county recorder's office to make sure a canceled notice of default hasn't been filed.

- *Target resale value*. Determine the range of target resale value for your area of coverage. It generally should be near or a little above the median home price in that county.

> *Equity is the difference between the loan amount in foreclosure and the property's estimated market value.*

Potential Deals

You should now have a culled and more manageable list of leads. Let's look more closely at which properties might be a good candidate for a deed of trust purchase. Remember, you're not searching only for deed of trust purchases. You're looking for pre-foreclosure deals with solid investment potential. If, in the process of searching public records, you can't locate the owner of a prime property, or you find a junior deed of trust and missing owner that fill the bill for purchase, you have the option of pursuing the backdoor approach to obtain that property.

Next, search your culled list for notices of default or auction on first deeds of trust. That search is easy with the help of your premium foreclosure-listing service. (See Figures 4.1 and 4.2 for examples from ForeclosureS.com.)

To find out which properties have junior deeds of trust, you'll need to check your county's grantor-grantee index. (A *grantor* is the seller and a *grantee* the buyer.) Usually located at the county recorder's or registrar of deeds office, this index is the public recording of property deed transfers within the county and includes encumbrances associated with those deeds. By law, the recordings also include a property lender's name and address. Some counties post their indexes online with easy and extensive search capabilities that let you search by name, business name, document category, document number, date of recording, and more.

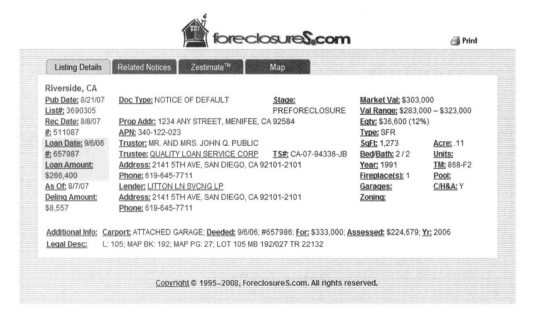

FIGURE 4.1   Sample Notice of Default, Senior Deed of Trust

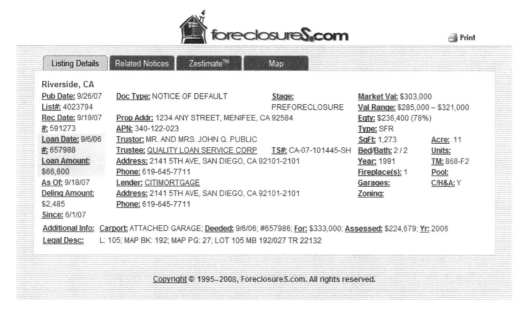

FIGURE 4.2   Sample Notice of Default, Junior Deed of Trust

Grantor-Grantee Indexes

What: The public recorded index of all property deed transfers in the county.

Information included: Types of documents recorded; names of grantors (sellers) and grantees (buyers); the document book and page numbers; sometimes cross-referenced document numbers (reconveyance documents will list which deed of trust was paid off by document number).

Pros: Many county indexes are online and easily searchable.

Cons: Other counties have the indexes on their own local networks but not on the Web, which means you'll have to visit those counties yourself to see their indexes. Still other counties record the information the old-fashioned way—by hand—so you'll have to look up the indexes in paper binders or on microfiche machines.

Steps to Find a Deed of Trust Deal

- Find the right foreclosure-listing service that provides accurate, up-to-date, and thorough information.
- Mine the foreclosure listings it provides to determine a list of potential properties that meet key requirements:
  - In default/slated for auction.
  - Equity of 30 to 40 percent or more.
  - Located within your target area.
  - Meets maximum dollar requirements.
- Identify properties with junior deeds of trust held by private lenders by searching a county's grantee-grantor index.
- Make sure the junior deed of trust meets certain essentials, including having a value high enough for you to buy it at a substantial discount.
- Gather the names, addresses, and other contact information of those lenders by reviewing the actual deed of trust document at the county building. The grantee-grantor index will not give you this information so you'll need to dig further to get the details.
- If all the criteria are right, contact the lenders.

If the county where a property is located doesn't have its records online—and, unfortunately, not all do—you can either do the title search in their local office or pay a professional *reader* to do it for you. I prefer the latter, which lets me make better use of my time. You're looking for beneficiary names—note holders—who are private lenders as opposed to conventional lenders, which are the large institutions. The big guys, as we discussed earlier, haven't time for you.

Note, too, that if a property has multiple deeds of trust—first, second, even third or more—it's not always clear which one is in foreclosure. A county's grantor/grantee index helps clarify that.

Contacting the Lender

Suppose you now have the name and address of a private lender—the beneficiary named in the deed of trust filing. Don't think for a minute that you're home free.

First, a lender's phone number rarely is included in the filing. Addresses aren't always listed, either, and if they are, they're often incorrect. This is, after all, a small, private lender—possibly a former homeowner who holds the note, just as Tom did in the case of young homeowner Julian in Chapter 3.

The name and address given are only the starting point. Next, try searching online for the person by name and/or address using some of the sources we mentioned earlier, including:

- Google (www.google.com), DogPile (www.dogpile.com), and ZabaSearch (www.zabasearch.com).

- Information directories, including reverse directories, such as Skipease (www.skipease.com), Yahoo's People Search (http://people.yahoo.com/), AnyWho (www.anywho.com), White Pages (www.whitepages.com), 411.com (www.411.com), and SearchBug (www.searchbug.com/peoplefinder/).

- Court and county records online (Nationwide Environmental Title Research, at www.netronline.com).

Once you find the beneficiary of the deed of trust, try contacting him. With your help (read "cash offer") the note holder can be assured of walking away with money in his pocket and without undue hassles.

This is the prime time to employ some of those communications skills we discussed earlier. This is a business, and your job is to make the deal. Think about who the note holder is and even, if possible, the circumstances under which a loan was made—personal links, a property seller carrying a down payment, or some other situation.

Mimi Z. was a foreclosure investor who wanted to buy a $75,000 second note on a vacant prime property valued at $435,000. Studying the documents, she ascertained that the note was held by Will R. It turned out Will was an elderly, widowed retiree who took pride in helping families in his church by making loans to them in the form of second and third notes on their homes. Not all the loans had worked out, but those that did made it worthwhile for Will. From what Mimi could gather, Will was extremely well off financially. Mimi discovered all this because she did her research.

After she initially identified the property as investment potential, Mimi talked to a few people in the neighborhood and learned about the "private benefactor" who "more than once" had bailed out the property's now missing owners. Mimi concluded there might be a second or third note on the property, and the county's grantor-grantee index confirmed her suspicion, listing Will as the beneficiary on the note. Still not convinced she had enough information to clinch the deal, Mimi spent a little extra time and Googled Will's name. Her search turned up

The Lingo

Beneficiary: The lender you contact about buying a deed of trust.

Trustor: The owner—in this case, one who can't be located—of the property in foreclosure.

Trustee: The person named in the deed of trust or other mortgage to conduct any foreclosure proceedings and sell property to pay off the mortgage loan balance.

some newspaper articles written about him and the fact that he was well-known as a private benefactor in the community.

What's the best way for Mimi to approach Will? Should she wave the cash, let the numbers speak for themselves, or take some other tack entirely? Armed with her background information, Mimi opted for a businesslike yet benevolent approach. She decided to let the numbers be her best argument and demonstrate how, by accepting her offer to buy the note at a discount, Will could then use the cash to help someone else. The deal went through because Mimi's approach made the difference. Had she coolly offered the cash that Will probably didn't need anyway, he might not have taken her up on the deal.

Of course, private lenders often aren't as public as Will in their lending, and you won't always have as much information as Mimi did when you approach them for a deal. Whatever you do, though, don't be the bull in the china shop, blundering and blustering your way in. Be observant, deliberate, concise, and businesslike. Make the extra effort. It will pay off.

How Much Should You Pay for the Note?

Successful deed of trust investing, like successful pre-foreclosure investing, depends on the numbers. Before you can determine your costs, you need to know what's right with the property and what's wrong with it, what needs repair and what can't be repaired, how much the updated property is likely to sell for, and how long you'll have to carry its costs before resale.

If you know or have access to the correct numbers, if you accurately figure your hard and soft costs, understand the various ways you can make the numbers work, recognize the benefits of your deal, and can persuade others to see them, too, it's a win-win for everyone. Hard costs include those associated with repairing

Your Potential Costs in a Deal

Costs to you in a deed of trust deal can include:

- Cost to buy a secondary note (associated title, closing, escrow fees).

- Foreclosure fees.

- Cost of your time if, after the deal goes through, the homeowner resurfaces and wants to pay off your loan.

If a property doesn't sell at foreclosure auction, more fees include:

- Reinstating the first mortgage again.

- Rehab and repair of property.

- Holding costs (including taxes, utilities, ongoing mortgage payments).

- Reselling costs (including marketing, Realtor, title, closing, escrow fees).

and rehabbing a property, while soft costs include buying the note; fees for closing, title, and escrow (when buying and selling) as well as foreclosure fees; costs to hold the property (taxes, utilities, mortgage payments); and more.

Your aim is not to take a note holder to the cleaners—to cheat him out of vast sums of money. Your goal is to make a deal that makes sense given your numbers, and one that is worthwhile for both you and the note holder.

Dissecting the Equation

As you can see, your costs to do a deed of trust deal can add up—and the money comes out of your pocket. The financial rewards, however, can more than make up for the trouble and cost of using your cash. Nonetheless, always start by figuring the basic numbers.

Even if your plan is simply to buy a junior note on a property at a discount, bring the senior note current, and then foreclose on your note and collect your profits, there are a lot of numbers to figure. What if the owner gets the money and wants to pay you off? Have you figured out those numbers, too, so you don't lose money in the process? A deal must make financial sense taking into account all the contingencies. Plan on them.

Mimi's Costs

Here's a glance at some of the costs Mimi faced in buying the junior note from Will on the home with a fixed-up value of $435,000:

Cost to buy $75,000 junior note held by Will	$40,000
Cost to bring $225,000 first note current	$10,000
Associated title and escrow fees (about 1% of loan)	$750
Foreclosure fees (as set by state law)	$2,500
Total costs to buy and foreclose on junior note	($53,500)
Sold to outside bidder at auction (minimum bid plus amount paid to bring first note current, plus foreclosure fees)	$87,500
Profit from note deal	$34,000

If there are no bidders at the auction and Mimi ends up with the house, here are her additional expenses:

Total costs to buy and foreclose on the note (above)	($53,500)
Cost to take over first note subject-to at the auction	($225,000)
Expense of bringing first note current again (four months)	($10,000)
Rehab and repair property (1,500 square feet at $15/square foot)	($22,500)
Holding costs for six months due to slow market (including taxes, utilities, ongoing mortgage payments)	$20,000
Reselling costs (including marketing, listing, title, closing fees)	($38,000)
Total potential costs if held for resale	($369,500)
Resale of property	$435,000
Profit total	$65,500

The formula is simple: Figure the resale value of your potential property, and then deduct your expenses—which include buying the note, paying current the first mortgage in default, foreclosure and accompanying costs, potential property holding expenses, fix-up costs, and the cost of your profit. If the numbers add up, go for the deal. If not, walk away. That's an absolute.

A few of the variables in figuring the numbers include the following:

- *Rehab and repair costs.* We talked about how to determine rehab and repair costs in Chapter 2. Remember, $15 a square foot is a good starting number for minimal repairs. Whenever possible, though, fine-tune those rehab numbers by walking a property with your contractor before you figure your costs.

- *Your profit.* Don't forget to figure for your profit. That's the difference between the face value of a note and the price you pay for it plus foreclosure costs if the property then sells at foreclosure auction. If it doesn't, your total purchase price (including note and foreclosure costs) should not exceed 60 to 70 percent of the fixed-up value of the home minus the cost of the home's repair and rehab (remember, in today's slower market that number should be closer to 60 to 65 percent). That leftover minimum 30 to 40 percent breaks down as 15 percent profit and the rest for property holding and reselling costs. Generally you should look for a minimum $30,000 profit to make a deal worth your while. That's your insurance for what can—and will—go wrong.

- *The property appraisal.* To know whether a particular deal makes financial sense, you must, of course, know the value of a potential property after it's fixed up and rehabbed into top-notch condition as compared with other houses in its neighborhood. That number is not based on guesstimates or what's in the foreclosure documents but on you doing your own appraisal. After all, if the numbers are wrong, the cash comes out of your pocket. Let's examine the appraisal process in a potential deed of trust purchase.

Delving into the Appraisal Process

As mentioned in Part I, no matter the type of foreclosure investing involved, it makes the most sense financially to do those appraisals yourself. (As an aside, you'll then know for sure the accuracy of your numbers.)

Here's a quick review of the appraisal process:

1. Start by determining a market value range for the property once it's fixed up, based on comps—prices of comparable property sales—in the same neighborhood in the past three months. The comps are available from subscription databases like SiteXdata (www.sitexdata.com), First American Real Estate Solutions (www.firstamres.com), DataQuick Information Systems (www.dataquick.com), local Realtor multiple listing services, or local title companies.

2. Use numbers related only to similar houses that have sold in the past three months (you can extend that to six months if necessary) within a quarter-mile radius (up to a mile if necessary).

3. Do not use properties tagged fixer-uppers with low market values.

4. Use the same criteria to search the local MLS using Realtor.com, Metrolist .com, and other sites for all active properties on the market and for pending sales, in order to assess the current market.

5. Pull the best data from among the sold properties, pending sales, and actively selling properties; drive by them; and then cull your list of those you can't duplicate.

6. What's left is the resale price range.

Always opt for conservative numbers in your estimates of a property's resale price. This is particularly important in today's uncertain housing market. Plan for the costs of longer hold (selling) time in a buyer's market (slow periods) and shorter hold times in a seller's or hot market. You can always add to the bottom line, but if you have to subtract from it, your profit margin suffers. Never get caught holding a house that doesn't break even or better, even on rental income.

But do estimate a property's price so it will sell. A good rule of thumb is to estimate any property's resale value at the mid- to low-range resale price. That way you don't price your property out of the market at either end and lose out on deals or reasonable profits.

The Rest of the Equation

That resale price range is the starting point in your equation to determine whether a deal makes financial sense. The next steps are these:

1. In normal markets, subtract 30 percent from your estimated resale value. That represents 15 percent for the cost to you of holding the property and 15 percent profit for your risk. For colder markets, that 30 percent increases to up to 40 percent.

2. Subtract from this new amount your estimated cost of repairs and rehab on the potential property. The result becomes the starting point for your deed of trust purchase profitability equation.

3. Deduct the cost to you of purchasing the deed of trust, including transaction costs such as escrow, closing, title, and more.

4. Now deduct the cost of foreclosure on the note once you own it.

Sarah's Tips and Hints

ForeclosureS.com coach Sarah Garlick, a successful deeds of trust buyer, shares a few essential tips:

- Do your research. You must understand how to get the most out of the position of the potential note you want to buy (first/senior, second/junior, third in order of succession, or beyond).

- Do the preliminary title research yourself via the county's grantor/grantee index. But do have a good relationship with a title and escrow company so you can make a quick call to verify your findings or to check out something unusual or that you're uncertain about.

- Don't rely strictly on your own research or what a homeowner says about a property's title. Work with a title company to get it right.

- Figure the cost of title insurance—a percentage of the purchase price (usually $500 to $800)—as part of the cost of doing business.

- Give a homeowner moving money, at least. It's also a cost of doing business.

What's left is what you can afford to pay the note holder for his investment. As mentioned earlier, that magical 30–40 percent number represents a 60–70 percent loan-to-value (LTV) ratio. You derive the "loan" part of the LTV by adding your actual purchase price for the note (not its face value), plus the cost/value of any senior loan on the property, plus your costs to foreclose, fix up, and hold the property.

All this may make it sound impossible for the numbers to work. But they can and do, in large part because of the tremendous discounts associated with buying a note from a lender in what often is, without your intervention, a no-win situation.

In doing his data-mining, Art K. flushed out what he thought was a prime property for a deed of trust purchase. The property, he determined, had a market value of $399,000 (the mid-range cost of a starter home in the geographic area where he concentrated his foreclosure investing); the $211,000 first mortgage was in default (plus the $10,000 owed to bring it current), and a second, $52,000 mortgage on the property was privately held, for a total of $273,000 in outstanding debt. The property's owner had left town, and the foreclosure auction was scheduled in four weeks.

If the home's owner had been available, Art would have looked at his numbers and then made an offer. He would have determined that 70 percent of the resale

Art's Deal by the Numbers

Property's market value (fixed-up condition)	$399,000
Less 30% for buying, holding, selling, and profit	($119,700)
Less estimated cost of repairs	$14,300
Maximum purchase price	$265,000
Total outstanding debt	$273,000
First loan in default	$211,000
Amount to bring first loan current	$10,000
Second loan	$52,000
Added costs to buy the note	$6,000
Title and escrow fees	$500
Foreclosure fees	$1,500
Carrying costs (first mortgage payments)	$4,000

The Full Equation

Maximum offer price	$265,000
First mortgage costs	($221,000)
Subtotal	$44,000
Less costs to buy note	($6,000)
Maximum offer price for note	$38,000
Face value of note	($52,000)
Net profit spread (difference)—too little to make the deal work as is	$14,000

Conclusion: Instead, factoring in the minimum recommended $30,000 profit, Art should offer only **$22,000** for the note and *not* the **$38,000** as determined in this outline.

---

value of the fixed-up home was $279,300. Subtracting fix-up costs of $14,300, Art would have figured that the maximum he could offer for the property was $265,000—less than the $273,000 owed against the house.

Rather than do a *short sale* with the owner (whom he couldn't locate anyway), Art had to add some line items to the equation and then subtract those numbers from the $265,000 to determine his maximum offer for the note. Those items include:

- Cost of first note: $211,000.
- Cost to reinstate first note on property: $10,000.

- Title and escrow fees to buy note: $500 (1 percent of note value).

- Cost to foreclose on second note (varies by state): $1,500.

- Carrying costs for first note (four months times $1,000): $4,000.

Subtracting the line items from the $265,000 leaves $38,000, the maximum Art can offer for the $52,000 junior note. However, factoring in the minimum $30,000 recommended spread on any note purchase, Art can offer only $22,000 for the $52,000 note. Considering the note holder will get nothing if the first note goes to auction, this $22,000 is a good deal for him and a good deal for Art. It's win-win for both parties.

Richard C. was sifting through his foreclosure lists when he came upon an absolute gem of a deal, or so he thought. The property was a starter home—easy to sell if he had to flip it—valued at $350,000. The value of the first note was $115,000, so that meant plenty of equity in the property. The default amount was $9,000, with another $1,000 in penalties.

Further research disclosed that the owner had died, leaving no heirs, and the first loan was slated for foreclosure. The property also had a second note from a private lender for $45,000. The house was in good shape and needed a minimal $10,000 in repairs. Running the numbers (see the box on the following page), Richard realized that even if he structured the deal right, it was too risky unless he could buy the note for $15,000.

About the Cash

Of course, to make these or any deeds of trust purchases, you must have a source of ready and immediate cash. It can be in the form of an investor who writes you blank checks or your own cash. Financing is not available. That reality alone is enough to scare off the timid investor. On the bright side, however, the need for cash cuts down on your competition for the best deals. Profits can be exceptional on trust deed purchases if a note is purchased at a big enough discount.

When Financing Works

If you end up owning the property—that is, you purchase a junior deed of trust, cure the default on the primary loan, foreclose on your loan, and then the property fails to sell at auction and you end up with it—you can take title to the property and its first mortgage through *subject-to* financing.

Subject-to is quick and efficient interim financing that allows you to take over

Richard's Deal by the Numbers

Property's market value (fixed-up condition)	$350,000
Less 30 % for buying, holding, selling, and profit	($105,000)
Less estimated cost of repairs	($10,000)
Maximum purchase price	$235,000
Total outstanding debt	$170,000
First loan in default	$115,000
Amount to bring first loan current	$10,000
Second loan	$45,000
Added costs to buy the note	$8,000
Title and escrow fees	$500
Foreclosure fees	$1,500
Carrying costs (first mortgage payments)	$6,000

The Full Equation

Maximum offer price	$235,000
First mortgage costs	($125,000)
Subtotal	$110,000
Less costs to buy note	($8,000)
Maximum offer price for note (well above the note's face value)	$102,000
Face value of note	($45,000)
Net profit spread (difference)—negative spread; too risky	($57,000)

Conclusion: The deal is too risky given these numbers. Although the numbers point to a huge profit if Richard gets the house through foreclosure, he would lose $57,000 if he doesn't get it! What if the owner steps up to pay his note off, or an outside bidder gets the house at Richard's trustee sale auction? Richard could lose big. To reduce his risks, Richard should approach the note holder with an offer to buy the note for $15,000 to ensure his $30,000 profit as a contingency. *Plan for the unexpected.*

an existing loan on a property without asking permission of the lender. You bypass the time-consuming and anxiety-ridden approval process. You, the purchaser, get a trustee's deed from the trustee of your foreclosure sale, and you own the home and are responsible for the senior mortgage payments (which remain in the prior owner's name). Subject-to differs from loan assumption because the mortgage remains in the original homeowner's (trustor) name.

If you are the winning bidder at your auction, the house is now yours. You will need to make sure the first loan that you took over subject-to is current and fully reinstated. Call the first lender to make sure. Keep the payments up to date, too, even though the loan isn't in your name until you sell or refinance the property.

More Red Flags and Cautions

Just because the money and numbers add up, though, doesn't mean your deal is done. Last-minute snags are commonplace and can sink a deal if you, as the investor, haven't done your due diligence, can't recognize potential pitfalls, and aren't prepared for every contingency ahead of time.

Don't be scared off by the legalities and nuances of the rules and regulations—we've addressed some of them. Instead, learn them, understand them, and use them to your advantage. That, after all, is an important aspect of the backdoor approach to obtaining a property through foreclosure, and it separates you from investors who aren't in senior class.

Tales from Foreclosure Experts

Mark and Ann had been investing in pre-foreclosures for more than a year when they bought their first junior deed of trust on a property in foreclosure. It was a great property in a great location that needed minimal repairs/updates—a great investment to flip. They bought the $52,000 second note at discount for only $22,000.

As planned, after they closed the deal on the note, they cured the default on the first note in foreclosure, then turned around and foreclosed on their note. With their expenses, the foreclosure amount was $63,500.

At the auction, an outside bidder turned up, eager to pick up the property for considerably more than the $63,500 starting bid. Mark and Ann decided not to invest more money in the property, so they let the bidder have the property.

Their gross pay: $63,500 (they do not get the overbid that goes to the next in line on the property's title—possibly other lien holders or the owner) less $1,500 fees, less $10,000 paid to bring the first note current, less $22,000 they paid for the note.

Their net: $30,000 that day.

Remember, once you obtain a junior note, you're able to foreclose on it because of a simple nuance in your deed of trust. It's a junior lender's right to advance funds to protect their interests. That is, you as the junior lender can bring the senior note in default current, and then add that amount to your junior note and begin your own foreclosure action.

The average foreclosure investor doesn't know about or understand these legal nuances and, therefore, can't capitalize on them. You do, and you can!

Following are some other issues of concern.

- *Mechanic's lien.* Because it's secured by the property in question, check to see when the work was done as compared with when it was recorded. If it's before your junior note, it becomes your responsibility to settle it. To be certain, though, check with a local real estate attorney for advice on how this lien might affect you.

- *Document inconsistencies.* As with any real estate transaction, watch for inconsistencies in the documents. Is the legal property description on your assignment of deed of trust different from that on the original deed of trust or initial title documents provided by the note seller? Do the names and signatures match? If the private lender selling the deed of trust is not the original holder of the deed of trust, you are dealing with the wrong person. You need to find the current deed of trust holder by reviewing the original documents and any subsequent assignment of deeds of trust, and contact the most current holder of the note as listed on the documents.

- *Paying for nothing.* Be aware, too, that not all information—paid for or otherwise—is complete or accurate. Some web sites will charge you an arm and a leg for scanty information they've compiled by scanning free web site listings. They're not using county recorder's filings, and so they have only a small fraction of the information.

How do you know if you're being duped? Before you pay for any lists, thoroughly check out the provider. Look for mention of the provider on real estate blogs. Remember, what's on a blog is someone's opinion. But if you read the same thing again and again from various sources, that could indicate problems or an issue to consider.

TAKEaway

- Mine the data right and you're on the right track to finding potential deeds of trust deals.

- Find the name of the beneficiary of the deed of trust by reviewing the actual documents recorded at the county.

- Offer the note holder all cash as a way to walk away with money—as opposed to a loss—from a loan gone bad.

- Pay close attention to the property's title to make sure other liens can't torpedo the deal.

- For a deal to make financial sense for you, the numbers must work out so that your costs amount to no more than 60-70 percent (depending on current market conditions) of the fixed-up market value of the home minus the costs of rehab and repair.

- Be conservative in your estimates of a property's resale price and time on market. It's particularly important in today's uncertain housing market.

PART III

TRUSTEE AND COURTHOUSE AUCTIONS

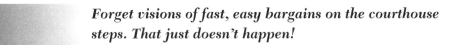

Forget visions of fast, easy bargains on the courthouse steps. That just doesn't happen!

—Alexis McGee

CHAPTER 5

The Reality behind the Hype

You're playing with the big boys at courthouse auctions.
You had better know what they know.

—Alexis McGee

Despite efforts by government, industry, and private investors to stop the bleeding, the United States is hemorrhaging foreclosures by the tens of thousands. In the first nine months of 2007 alone, 5 out of every 1,000 homeowners—or almost 400,000 households across the country—couldn't work out their mortgage default problems and lost their properties to foreclosure, according to numbers from ForeclosureS.com.

Before those properties officially ended up as REO or lender/bank-owned real estate, they went on the auction block at a courthouse auction or sheriff's sale, where the lender hoped to recoup the cost of the loan in default.

Forget the idea of picking up fast, easy bargains at an auction on the courthouse steps—and, yes, that's where they're usually held—without investing the time and effort to learn the nuances of successfully buying foreclosed properties at auctions. Many of these foreclosed properties sell to outside bidders; many don't, and end up REO. Those that do sell to outside bidders sometimes go at prices well below market value, a few above, and the rest for close to their actual market value.

Hype versus Reality

No matter how you look at it, foreclosure auctions are not a realm for neophytes. The bargains can be few and far between even in today's overwhelmed foreclosure market. Ignore the hype. Those flashy ads for many web sites that tout "Fast deals on properties for pennies on the dollar" or "An easy way to get started in real estate, no experience required" are come-ons that bear little resemblance to the reality of buying a property at a courthouse auction.

> *Attend a foreclosure auction strictly as an observer at first to get your feet wet and pick up a better understanding of the process and its nuances.*
>
> —Alexis McGee

If you think a courthouse auction or sheriff's sale is a quick and easy way to buy foreclosed properties, check out an auction on the courthouse steps strictly as an observer. (Some of these auctions will be listed in the "Legal Notices" section of your local newspaper, albeit with very little information about the property. To get the full information on an upcoming auction, you'll want to subscribe to a solid foreclosure-listing service.)

In fact, an excellent way to start your education is to attend an auction. It will help you gain a better understanding of exactly who and what you'll be dealing with. One caveat, though: Don't believe all you hear, especially what the bidders around you are saying. Not all is as it seems at a foreclosure sale!

Get to know some of the regulars who bid at these auctions, suggests Tim Rhode, ForeclosureS.com coach and longtime successful real estate investor. "Buy some of them lunch and take the opportunity to learn more about what's going on so you don't go in there green and buy properties from day one."

A Primer

A courthouse auction—it's known as a sheriff's sale in some states—is another way to transfer ownership of a property. In this case, the loan on the property is in default and the auction is the culmination of the foreclosure on that note.

The auctions themselves are held, by law, on the courthouse steps or, in the case of sheriff's sales, on the lawn of the property for sale. They're handled by the *trustee*, an independent third party such as ForeclosureLink (www.foreclosure link.com) hired and paid for by the holder of the foreclosing note to take care of the foreclosure process and run the actual auction. The trustee's fee is set by law and varies by state. The trustee is supposed to ensure that all the required documentation, filings, and steps in the foreclosure process are performed in accordance with that state's laws (see Figure 5.1). The length of time a notice of foreclosure auction

Different states have different rules, regulations, and requirements associated with foreclosure and sheriff's sales. Here are a few of the requirements in some states with the most auctions:

- **ARIZONA:** Sale conducted by trustee at a designated location at the county courthouse; all cash offers. The successful bidder must make payment to the trustee's satisfaction by 5:00 P.M. on the day following the sale unless that day is a Saturday or a legal holiday.

- **CALIFORNIA:** Sale conducted by a trustee at the courthouse or at designated location. All offers to be made by cash, check, or cashier's check. Trustee requires that every bidder show evidence of the minimum bid of required funds.

- **COLORADO:** Sale conducted by public trustee official. All bids are in cash or cashier's check. The highest bidder must tender funds for the total amount of the bid to the office of the public trustee. Call the county to find out when the funds are due, what forms are required, and if there are additional rules for bidding.

- **FLORIDA:** Sale conducted by an officer of the clerk's office in the courthouse. All sales much be paid in full by cash or cashiers check. Deposits are accepted on day of sale, and must be left with the clerk. The final payment as well as registry of court fees is due before 4:00 P.M. on the day of the sale.

- **GEORGIA:** Sale conducted by an appointed official from the county sheriff's office. Bids require all-cash or cashier's checks in increments for the full amount of sale. The sale is final and binding from and after the moment of the sale.

- **ILLINOIS:** The sale may be conducted by the sheriff or by any judge in the subject county, and held at the sheriff's office. Investors must deposit 10 percent of their bid amount in cash, and must pay the balance within 24 hours.

- **NEVADA:** Sales are held by an agent/trustee and conducted at a designated trustee location. Bidding requirements vary by trustee so call the trustee prior to sale. The winning bidder must pay the full bid amount in cash or cashier's check to the trustee.

- **NEW JERSEY:** Sale conducted by an appointed official from the county sheriff's office. Bidder must pay a 20 percent deposit in either cash or a certified or cashier's check after the sale. The successful bidder must pay all settlement charges to the sheriff within 30 days of the date of sale.

- **TEXAS:** The sale may be conducted by the sheriff or an officer of the sheriff's office. Winning bidder must pay by cashier's check, money order, or cash. The trustee may allow highest bidder to pay the full amount the same day. Contact the sheriff's office for more specifics as well as an unexpired written statement from the county tax assessor-collector that the purchaser does not owe any delinquent taxes.

- **UTAH:** Sale conducted by the trustee or attorney at a designated location as stated in the notice of sale. The purchaser pays the price bid as directed by the trustee. Call trustee/attorney prior to sale for specific requirements.

FIGURE 5.1   Bidding Details
Source: ForeclosureS.com.

must be posted, and where and when, for example, are specifically addressed in state statutes. If those laws aren't followed, the foreclosure can be voided. The sale itself can also be handled by an attorney hired by the foreclosing lender or trustee.

The trustee or lawyer is supposed to ensure the impartiality of the bidders and bidding on a property. Unfortunately, though, they can't always detect or don't always recognize unfair bidding practices that can and do occur at auctions. Collusion between bidders—generally an agreement on how much to bid for a particular property—prior to the actual sale does sometimes happen.

Don't look to trustees for guidance, either. That's not their job, and they don't provide it. They are, however, required to tell you the date, time, and minimum bid for a specific scheduled auction. You must have the correct trustee sale number (reference number for the auction) when you contact the trustee for an update. Each trustee manages his communications with the public a bit differently. Some trustees use automated phones systems, others post information on their web sites, or you may have to speak directly to a representative.

The proceeds from the foreclosure sale pay off the note and its *delinquency*. That's why minimum bids are set at the amount of the note in default plus expenses, penalties, and fees associated with the loan and the process. Because the bid is for the amount in default (the unpaid loan balance plus penalties and fees) and not the full market value of a property, a bidder theoretically could pick up a property at a sizable discount. If no one offers the minimum bid or no one shows up for the auction—which happens quite often—the property becomes REO and reverts to the holder of the loan in default. (More on REO buying in Chapter 7.)

Risks and Variables

Sounds simple enough, but, as always, buyer beware. The road to picking up a solid deal on a courthouse auction property is rife with potholes, ranging from the right of a homeowner to resurface and reclaim the property to big unknowns about the properties themselves.

*Trustee sales are riskier than pre-foreclosure purchases
because you don't usually get to inspect the property,
so there's a chance it could have a serious problems,
including mold in the walls. That could
mean a very expensive cleanup.*

—Christian Rooney, former Alexis McGee student,
successful foreclosure investor

Variations by State

Foreclosures are governed by the law, and you must follow it or risk losing your investment opportunity and your cash. Worse yet, if the legal system determines that your violations of the law are willful, you could face criminal penalties.

Keep in mind, too, that legal requirements and timelines related to foreclosures and the process vary dramatically by state. In Texas, for example, the foreclosure process—from initial default filing to auction on the courthouse steps—is short: 30 days. In other states, such as Ohio, it's five times as long at 150 days. South Carolina does not allow homeowners the right to reclaim a property after foreclosure sale (a process known as *redemption*); North Carolina does. Different states require different documents, procedures, and time frames as well, all of which must be followed exactly to ensure the integrity of your investment.

In California, for example, the Notice of Sale is recorded no sooner than 90 days after the Notice of Default is recorded, and stipulates that the property's auction will occur in no less than 21 days. In Colorado, after following strict rules for publication of the Notice of Scheduled Sale, the trustee must—at least 21 days before the date of sale—mail to the borrower a notice containing instructions on how to redeem the property. The sale itself must take place 45 to 60 days after the Notice of Election and Demand (foreclosure) is filed. (Visit ForeclosureS.com and click on "Tools" and "Foreclosure Laws" to learn some of your state's stipulations.)

An absolute in this business: Know your state laws. Your efforts will be rewarded with every deal you make.

Schedule Changes

The date set for a sale or auction can change. Merely because a notice of foreclosure auction or sheriff's sale on a property lists a specific sale date doesn't mean the auction will take place as scheduled, or even at all. The notice is simply public notification that a homeowner is in default on his mortgage and faces the possibility of losing the home to foreclosure if the delinquency on the loan is not paid off (*cured*).

Many homeowners cure the default or sell their property pre-foreclosure before the scheduled sale date. In the latter case, probably someone like you as a white-knight pre-foreclosure investor worked with the homeowner in default to understand his options and, in some cases, bought the property and then flipped it for solid profits. (Learn how by checking out *The ForeclosureS.com Guide to Making Huge Profits Investing in Pre-Foreclosures without Selling Your Soul*, Alexis McGee; John Wiley & Sons, September 2007.)

The lien holder who files the foreclosure or the home's owner in default may request, with mutual consent, that the sale be postponed. You must call the trustees and track trustee sales individually to find out exactly what properties are being auctioned on any given day. Check with the trustee before an auction to make sure a Canceled Note of Default has not been filed on the property. In many cases, the auction will be canceled or postponed. "On a given day there might be twenty properties scheduled for auction at the courthouse," says Christian Rooney, successful foreclosure investor and former Alexis McGee student. "But when I call the trustee the morning of the sale to reconfirm which ones are not canceled, maybe only four are actually going to sale that day."

Keep in mind, too, that the initial Notice of Foreclosure Auction must be published but not the subsequent rescheduled auction. You'll have to call the trustee or attorney handling the auction on the day of the sale to again verify that it actually will go ahead as planned. In many cases you can check on their web sites, too.

Right of Redemption

In some states, the sale of a property at foreclosure auction is not final until the right of redemption expires. *Right of redemption* is the home's former owner's right for a specific time following the auction to reclaim the property and reinstate the mortgage or note by paying off the default and reimbursing the winning bidder for his or her expenses.

If you do business in a state that allows redemption after a foreclosure sale, you as an investor must simply learn to live with it. Just don't put any money into your purchase until after the redemption period is over. Generally, none of your expenses can be recouped if the former owner decides to redeem the property.

Tales from Foreclosure Investors

James J. had high hopes of picking up a particular property at its foreclosure auction. The home's location was right, the numbers added up, and if things went the way he hoped, James figured he'd be able to flip the property for a sizable profit.

Better yet, James didn't think he'd have much bidding competition at the auction. Unfortunately, things didn't go as James planned—but not because of any bidding competition. The original auction was postponed, and James neglected to follow up with the trustee to find out the rescheduled date.

The result: James missed the auction entirely and the opportunity for sizable financial rewards. As he had expected, only one bidder showed up, and the property sold for $1 over its minimum bid.

The Jargon

Auction: Process of selling a property to the highest bidder.

Beneficiary: Lender on a security of a note and deed of trust.

Beneficiary's statement ("benny" statement): Written statement of conditions and remaining balance on the loan secured by a deed of trust.

Certificate of sale: Document indicating a property has been sold to a buyer at foreclosure sale subject to right of redemption for a set period after the sale.

Credit bid: Bid made at auction on behalf of the lender holding the foreclosed note; lender is not required to produce the cash for the bid.

Power-of-sale clause: Portion of deed of trust or mortgage in which borrower preauthorizes sale of property to pay off loan balance in case of default.

Right of redemption: The right of a homeowner in some states to reclaim his property lost to foreclosure by paying off the debt within a certain period of time after the sale.

Trustee: Independent third party hired by the lender on a foreclosing note to handle the foreclosure auction and associated details.

Trustee's deed: Type of deed issued to winning bidder at the trustee sale; used both when the winning bidder is an outside bidder or when there are no bidders and the deed reverts to the beneficiary (and ends up REO).

Rather than wait out the redemption period, consider contacting the owner directly and offering him cash to deed you his home and waive his redemption rights. A lot is involved in this process, so check with a local real estate attorney first if you're considering this purchase option.

Special Procedures

Upset Bids

With less common judicial foreclosures, certain states allow bidding on a property to remain open until 30 days after the foreclosure sale. During that time, an *upset bidder* may make a suitable deposit (it's refundable if the deal doesn't go through) and outbid the highest bid on a property made at the foreclosure sale. Generally that upset bid is 5 percent higher, though a lesser amount may be acceptable to the court.

Right-of-Redemption States

The following states are among those that, in at least some cases, allow a homeowner the right of redemption—the ability to reclaim a property for a certain length of time after foreclosure auction:

Alabama

Alaska (nonjudicial foreclosures only)

Arkansas

California (nonjudicial foreclosures only)

Colorado

Connecticut (at the court's discretion)

Florida

Georgia

Idaho

Illinois (limited)

Indiana

Kansas

Kentucky

Maine

Massachusetts (in foreclosure by possession)

Michigan

Minnesota

Missouri

Nebraska (none after confirmation of sale)

Nevada (judicial foreclosure only)

New Jersey (limited)

New Mexico

North Carolina

North Dakota

Ohio

Oklahoma (none after confirmation of sale)

Oregon (judicial foreclosure only)

Rhode Island (varies by process)

South Dakota

Tennessee (nonjudicial only)

Utah

Vermont

Virginia (varies)

Washington (judicial foreclosure only; very rare)

Wisconsin (if no court confirmation of sale)

Wyoming

Source: ForeclosureS.com (www.foreclosures.com).

Deficiency

In some instances, if the debt on a property exceeds its value at foreclosure, the lender may sue and the court may in turn order the borrower to pay the *deficiency* or shortfall. Also in some instances, the borrower within a specified period of time may ask the court for an *order of appraisal*. If it is granted, the borrower appoints an appraiser, the lender appoints another appraiser, and the court yet another one. If their appraised value of the property after subtracting the foreclosure sale proceeds is more than what remains owed on the loan, there's no deficiency. However, if it is less, the borrower gets credit against the judgment for the appraised value of the property, and the lender can only collect what's left—the difference between the appraised value of the property and the amount of the deficiency.

Cash Concerns

In order to bid at a courthouse auction or sheriff's sale, you are also required to produce a certain amount of money (it varies by state law) in the form of cash, a cashier's check, or certified funds. Personal checks and lines of credit are not accepted. (Contact the sale trustee before the sale date to find out how to make out the check.) Note holders on the property, however, are allowed to *credit-bid* up to the amount of their note plus penalties and fee charges—they're given credit for that amount and not required to produce the cash or cashier's check.

Be aware of your state's rules for payment procedures. For the sale to be valid, some states require that you immediately produce a cashier's check to cover the full cost of your bid. Other states accept a portion of the payment with the balance due later.

A further variable: If a property has multiple notes on it and the senior note is in foreclosure, you could end up bidding against the junior note holder—or someone representing the junior note holder—who hopes to buy the property to protect an interest that otherwise would be wiped out by the auction. In such a scenario, it's still possible to pick up a property, but gird yourself for competition in the bidding.

Title Glitches

Absolutely, unequivocally understand a property's title documents prior to a courthouse sale. Otherwise, you could be blindsided by unforeseen complications. We explain more about title in Chapter 6 because it plays such a major role in figuring the actual cost of buying a property at auction. But for now, make sure the title documents are accurate. Longtime foreclosure investor Christian Rooney recalls his own horror story in which he relied strictly on the property tax rolls at the tax assessor's office. "The tax roles told me the house was 1,100 square feet and had three bedrooms. After I bought the property, I found out it was really a two-bedroom house, which lowered the estimated value by about $15,000," he says.

Luckily, Rooney still ended up ahead on the deal because he bought the property at a deep discount, but not everyone is as lucky. Sometimes errors are made and never corrected at the tax assessor's office. That's just one more reason to be prepared, check the details, and then double-check them.

The Ultimate Catch-22

Beyond the bidding and title issues, you must also recognize that the successful buyer at a courthouse auction or sheriff's sale takes the property *as is*. Neither the physical condition of the property nor the title to it carries a warranty, so you can't know the state of either for certain. The property becomes yours, plain and simple, including any and all problems, issues, and costs associated with it. You may end up being forced to evict the former owner, who, if unhappy about the situation, could trash the property on his way out the door.

Let's look closer at some of the less obvious as-is potholes.

Tax Liens and Senior Encumbrances

A successful bidder takes the property subject to all senior liens and notes, so pay attention to title on any potential property. (As mentioned, we discuss title further in Chapter 6.) Property tax liens are senior to all other debts—including first mort-gages. The notion that you can pay pennies on the dollar sounds good, but you must tread carefully. Often in a tax sale the senior note holder will come in, advance the money to pay the delinquency to protect his interests, and stop the sale. In turn, he will add that advance money to his tab, and foreclose on the property for that total amount.

Time after time an unsuspecting and untrained investor will think he's picked up a hot deal at a courthouse auction, only to discover a tax lien afterward or that he purchased a junior note—and the senior lien along with it.

Conversely, in the good news column, the successful bidder at a courthouse auction takes the property free of all junior liens—with some exceptions, of course, like property taxes and some mechanic's liens, for example.

Property Problems

Faulty plumbing, broken heating or cooling systems, worthless appliances, trashed interiors, leaky roofs, rusting underground fuel tanks, mold in the walls, and more—these are a few of the headaches you can and will buy at courthouse auctions. That's why it's essential to talk to neighbors, review the records (mechanic's liens, for example, could indicate a larger problem), get as near the property as possible with your contractor, and do whatever else it takes to get a feel for the condition of the house and how it's been maintained.

Again, realize that in many cases a disgruntled, displaced homeowner may trash the property before leaving. One way to forestall that possibility is the cash-for-keys approach we discussed in Chapter 2. Alternatively, plan for the unexpected by figuring your numbers with room to spare. That's how Rooney avoided financial disaster with his supposedly three-bedroom purchase that ended up only a two-bedroom deal.

Your Work Pays Dividends

By now you're beginning to see the importance of thoroughly checking out a property and the documents relating to it. Don't be scared away from this type of investment opportunity, but do learn how to deal with the problems and issues that are likely to pop up. As with any other foreclosure investment, you start by culling your lists of potential properties, talking to neighbors, driving by the properties, determining property market values and potential repairs, making sure the title is clear, and knowing your state's laws. If you do all this and more ahead of time, you can come out a big winner at courthouse auctions or sheriff's sales.

The Sale at a Glance

What happens at the sale:

1. Auctioneer reads the legal notice.

2. Auctioneer begins to take bids on the property, asking for the minimum bid to start.

3. Bidding ends when the auctioneer takes the highest price.

4. Purchase and trustee's deed papers are drawn up for the winning bidder. The documents may be tentative if the state allows for redemption (homeowner reinstatement of foreclosed loan) or upset bidding (further bidding after auction).

5. Some states allow a time period before the total amount of purchase is due.

6. Final closing.

Call the auction trustee or lawyer handling the sale the morning of the sale to get the final minimum dollar amount you'll need to bid on a particular property. Remember, the dollar amount you're required to bring to the sale depends on that minimum and your state's laws regarding the method of full payment—whether all at once or a certain amount up front with the rest paid at a specified later date.

When you call for that dollar amount, make sure you have the trustee sale number, says Marsha Townsend, vice president and co-founder of ForeclosureLink Inc., Fair Oaks, California-based foreclosure trustees. New foreclosure investors sometimes fail to recognize that a courthouse auction trustee and his staff conceivably could be handling hundreds of foreclosures at once, so it's no easy task for them to pull up the information on one particular sale. Don't forget your communication skills here. Do what you can to make someone else's job easier and you'll separate yourself from the other investors. You'll reap the rewards of your consideration over and over.

The Sale Details

The day of the sale arrives. Let's assume you've done all your work and are poised to dig in and come out a winner. Consider the following details and tips.

Last-Minute Review

Just before the sale, recheck a property's title to see if anything new has been recorded that could create a problem. If you're unsure about something, get legal advice from a qualified real estate attorney if you haven't done so already. Don't forget to make sure a property hasn't been red-tagged for code violations, either. It's not so far-fetched that a house at foreclosure auction might have been used as a methamphetamine lab or that its owners had dumped oil (toxic waste) on the property or, especially in the East and Midwest, a buried fuel tank had leaked. You should check this out at the city or county building department. All these scenarios cost big bucks to clean up.

Double-check with the trustee or attorney handling the sale to make sure the auction hasn't been delayed. Don't forget to verify the time and place of the sale, too.

At the Sale

Typically the sale is on the steps of the courthouse in the county where the property is located. When you arrive, immediately register to bid with the trustee or attorney's representative. They'll want to see the full amount of your certified funds as required by state law so they know you're a serious bidder. Most bids are oral, although—as with upset bids—they don't have to be. Again, check your state laws to make sure of the requirements *before* the sale.

Bargain Hunters Abound

As the number of foreclosures across the country soars, so does the number of bidders out to make a buck. Some may think that by starting the bidding high, they can cut down on the competition, but auctions don't work that way. Keep in mind that your opening bid cannot be less than the amount owed the foreclosing lender. It can, however, be more. If you have no bidding competition, absolutely don't bid more than a dollar over the full credit amount, although a foreclosing lender has the option of rejecting a bid for less than that amount (more on this in Chapter 6).

Be Alert

Always pay attention to what's going on around you at an auction, too, because just when you think you're on top of it, something else happens. Tampa, Florida foreclosure investor Alvin J. got a quick lesson in that while observing a recent foreclosure auction.

Despite what seemed like rampant collusion on the part of bidders and the auctioneer, a great property at a great price went unsold and ended up back in the lender's hands. Consider what happened.

Four bidders showed up at this scheduled courthouse auction. All knew each other, and prior to the auction, the group—auctioneer included—went over the list of properties, indicating which ones interested them.

Later at the auction, as a property came up, the bidders openly would say to each other, "This one is yours. I'll get the next one."

When the "great" property came up for auction, no one was interested. The auctioneer even told the bidders how much over the minimum bid the lender was prepared to *bid up* the property (pay over and above the minimum bid to get the property). Nonetheless, the group of four wasn't interested, and the property remained unsold.

If Alvin had done his homework, and been ready to bid, he could have picked up a profitable deal.

The deals are there. You just have to know where and how to find them, and then be prepared for whatever comes up.

After the Sale

When the sale is finalized—after the upset bid period, if applicable—the trustee will issue the winning bidder a trustee's deed, noting the winner (the investor) as the new owner. Usually the balance of funds for purchase is due if the full amount wasn't required at the sale itself. Again, no personal checks or credit cards are accepted. You need certified funds or a cashier's check.

If the property hasn't been vacated, now is the time to evict the home's former owners. As we've discussed, you must tread a fine line. Be firm about their leaving the property, but treat them with dignity and decency. Follow the letter of the law, and cross your fingers that they don't trash the property. The problem is you never know for certain until they've moved out and you visit your property.

Can You Back Out?

You've won the bidding for a foreclosure property at a courthouse auction, and the property is yours. Suddenly you realize you made a horrible mistake in your numbers and don't really want the house. Unfortunately, you're basically out of luck and out the cash you've put up—even if it's the entire amount of the sale. No money-back guarantees in this business. If you paid only a deposit or a certain percentage of the bidding price up front and you back out before you sign the final papers, you lose the deposit.

A Word about Fraud and Dishonesty in This Business

The warnings about fraud, collusion, and dishonesty at courthouse auctions are everywhere: "Don't throw away your money on auctions," "You can't win," "It's all a big setup."

The hype is based on the fear factor. If you know what you're doing, how to do it properly, and what not to do, you, as an honest investor, can come out ahead at these sales.

But you must know how to differentiate the right situation from the wrong one. You also need to understand that a great many bidders at these auctions represent professionals who buy literally hundreds and maybe even thousands of such properties a year. If they make a mistake and overbid on one property, they'll easily make up that money on the other properties they buy that week. They can afford to play a bidding game with you. You, however, can't afford and don't want to play their games. Before you go to the sale, know the local market, the situation behind the sale, the value of the property, and your top bid. Stick to that bid! Don't get sucked into a bidding war and bid more than your predetermined top-dollar amount. Control your emotions and walk away instead.

This is not a game. It's serious business. Don't be scared off by the professional bidders, but don't be pressured into making a bid you didn't intend to, either.

If someone approaches you at the sale and either casually or quietly suggests that you don't bid and that they'll give you a *piece* of the deal afterwards, immediately, without hesitation walk away. That's collusion, and that's against the law. In such a situation, I actually would consider getting far away from the sale, too. If that person approached you, he likely approached others, too, so the integrity of the sale might be at issue.

Others also may try to scare you away from bidding with comments such as "Oh, that house had a flood. You knew that, right?" or "That house would be a great deal if it wasn't for the mold." You get the picture. These people are trying to shake you up so you won't bid at auction. Don't listen to them. But do thoroughly check out a property and its related documents ahead of time.

TAKEaway

- Before you start bidding on properties at courthouse auctions, become familiar with the process by attending a few auctions first strictly as an observer.

- Don't always believe what you hear from bidders at an auction.

- Know your state's laws regarding foreclosure sales, timelines, whether the ousted owner has the right to redeem his property, and more.

- The initial Notice of Foreclosure Auction must be published—state laws are specific as to the details of how, when, and where—but not the subsequent rescheduled auction.

- Recognize that a property purchased at a courthouse auction is *as is*. That means no guarantees as to the state of its title or its condition.

- The day of the sale, check with the trustee or attorney handling the auction to verify the minimum bid, and to verify that the sale will actually be held and to confirm its location.

- Don't be unwittingly sucked into collusion. Willing or not, it's still against the law.

CHAPTER 6

The Dollars and Sense of Finding and Figuring the Deals

Take the time to figure your math correctly before you buy. You can't count on the market to make up for your mistakes when you sell.

—Alexis McGee

By now you know the routine. Successful foreclosure investing of any kind starts with identifying potential properties. Those properties end up on your list of possibilities.

With courthouse or sheriff's sales, you will probably start out by sorting through fewer property listings—hundreds instead of the thousands facing Notice of Foreclosure Sale in your area. Before we get started, though, consider the importance of picking the right properties on which to bid.

Choosing the Right Property

Why would anyone want to buy a property when they've never seen its interior, which might be a disaster? Worse yet, if for some reason you bid on such a property at a courthouse sale, how do you know you're not overbidding? How do you determine how much you can afford to bid? The answers to these questions depend on dollars and common sense, which can net you incredible financial success if only you heed them both.

The Role of Common Sense

Foreclosure investing is about making a reasonable profit, so obviously we don't go into the business or into a deal expecting to lose money. Neither do you want to spend your money on a dog of a property that will do little more than suck up your dollars and likely never produce a profit.

Beyond knowing how to make the numbers add up, success in the business of buying properties at courthouse auctions and sheriff's sales is a combination of paying attention to the details and to that red flag or gut feeling you get when something is not quite right. If you understand the business, and pay attention to every detail, you'll learn to recognize those deals with issues that seriously cloud the potential for success.

If the numbers add up but your drive-by reveals a ramshackle property in a terrible neighborhood with rampant vandalism, you probably don't want to bid on that property at a courthouse sale. Likewise, if the numbers add up and the property is in a great location but you worry about getting clear title—there could be a pending lawsuit on the property, for example—you won't want to bid on that property, either. Both indicate big headaches later on, so keep moving down your list of potential properties.

If you, as a foreclosure investor, have any doubts,
don't seal the deal until you resolve them.

—Alexis McGee

As blatant as these examples sound, investors, especially newer ones, sometimes overlook or ignore the obvious red flags. They blame their uneasiness on their ignorance instead of giving credence to their gut and intuition. If you have any doubts, don't do the deal until you resolve them. Too much cash is on the line in a foreclosure sale.

Rod K. has been investing in foreclosures for a number of years and is incredibly successful at it. He has what he calls a good "feel" for the deals that work and those that don't. But it wasn't always that way.

Rod recalls one of his first deals, when he thought he had found the perfect house. The numbers couldn't have been better. The junior loan was scheduled for sale and the senior loan was small enough that even paying it off, too, meant big profits from flipping the property. There was no way he could lose, or so Rod thought. The only possible glitch in the property's title was that the owner, now in default, had overlooked paying federal income taxes for several years, and the IRS had filed a lien against the property. The lien had been filed several years ago and was recorded prior to the junior loan with no subsequent mention or resolution that Rod could discover. The federal tax lien was for a very small amount—less than $13,000—so Rod was not worried.

Rod bought the property at the junior lender's foreclosure sale—in other words, *as is*—and shortly afterward contacted the IRS to pay the lien off, as well as the senior lender to make sure their loan was reinstated so that they wouldn't go to auction later and wipe Rod out. Unfortunately, the amount owed to the IRS now had ballooned to $88,000 from the many years of unpaid income tax. Rod had no choice but to pay it because it remained attached to the property. Lesson learned: Call on all senior loans and liens in advance of attending the auction to get their current balances instead of being surprised after the fact.

If you notice a red flag—especially one related to title on a property—pay attention to it, no matter how insignificant it may seem. "I came away from that deal a much poorer investor, but a much smarter one, too," Rod recalls.

An Outside Peek Inside a Property

In this business, the fewer the variables and the less left to chance, the more likely you are to steer clear of the unexpected hassles that can steal cash from your bottom line.

In general, successful foreclosure investing requires a clear-eyed view of a property, its numbers, its neighborhood, and the players involved.

The old adage claims "you can't tell a book by its cover"—or can you? Maybe you can't discern everything from the outside, but if you look closely, you certainly can deduce quite a bit. Examine the cover of this book, for example, and assume you're seeing it for the first time. The title hints at what you'll learn—foreclosure-investing techniques. The presentation and words set the tone for what's inside; testimonials give you a peek at the content, the author, and the quality of the writing and information. Turn over the book, and you'll even see a brief synopsis.

Now think about picking up similar hints from potential foreclosure properties. Look for the obvious signs first, and do so with your contractor, if possible. An expert at your side can eliminate many variables.

Does the house look run-down, with the grounds overgrown and out of control? Broken or boarded-up windows are a red flag indicating vandalism. Translation: You had better figure major costs—$25 to $35 a square foot and maybe higher—for interior repair and rework, at minimum. Do worry about the roof, and

Tales from Foreclosure Investors

Miguel R. had singled out a particular property for purchase at its upcoming foreclosure sale. He had checked out the title thoroughly, had run the numbers, and everything looked in order. However, he was troubled by several cracks along the walls that he noticed when driving past the stucco home. He thought he might be overreacting but wanted to be sure he'd figured his rehab numbers correctly, so he asked his contractor to swing by the property, too. The contractor had worked in the area for a long time and was aware of problems with the soil that often led to serious foundation issues.

Good thing Miguel heeded that nagging concern. On his drive-by, the contractor immediately noticed visible problems with the foundation, so he got out of his car to take a closer look. He saw what he considered severe damage to the foundation that would require major repairs—so major, in fact, that he recommended Miguel not buy the property.

Miguel didn't, but someone who hadn't paid as close attention to the details did. It turned out that the home's entire foundation had to be reworked and reinforced to the tune of more than $75,000! Miguel sent his contractor a check for $1,000 for his invaluable time and expertise.

look for structural sags, peeling shingles, several layers of roof, and decomposing debris that may hide what's underneath. Foreclosed properties often need roof work, so except in rare circumstances you may want to figure that into your equations. When a homeowner has financial problems, roofs generally are too big-ticket to replace. Even an insurance check for wind or hail damage is likely to go toward something other than a new roof.

Be prepared. You can't always know what's inside, either. ForeclosureS.com coach Tim Rhode remembers a million-dollar home that ended up on the courthouse auction block. From the outside it was a beauty, but the owners were so upset by the foreclosure that they literally took a sledge hammer to the interior. They pounded the carved oak staircase and beat in some walls, then covered the others with graffiti. The home sold at auction for $500,000—50 cents on the dollar.

Neighborhood Chitchat

Look around the neighborhood where a potential property is located, too. Are the other homes well-kept or run-down? Neighborhoods can change from block to block. Some streets will be filled with longtime residents who take pride in their homes, and it shows, while other streets host a more transient population who lack this pride and, as a result, the properties look run-down.

Talk to the neighbors in cases of foreclosure sales just as you would if gathering information on a pre-foreclosure or deed of trust property. What a neighbor considers small talk can provide big clues to your property's condition and resale marketability.

Ask about the neighborhood and your property owners and the condition of the house. Start with simple questions such as "How does the neighborhood look overall? How has it changed since you've lived here?" This can segue into a discussion of what's right and wrong with your potential property. When you ask a question, remember to let the other person answer it. Good listening skills are among the most essential and valuable tools for a successful foreclosure investor.

An Open Door

Before bidding on a property, learn as much about it as you can, advises Tim Rhode. "If you've previously talked with the homeowner about working out a pre-foreclosure deal, pick up some sandwiches and head back again. He just might invite you inside to eat those sandwiches."

While there, be observant, and look for clues to the condition of the house. Do you see water marks on the ceiling or walls in the bathroom or kitchen? That could indicate plumbing or roofing issues.

"One of the things I've learned over the years is that the condition of the house on the outside is a very good indication of what the inside looks like, too," says ForeclosureS.com coach Daryl White. "I've also learned that the average cost of the average wear and tear on a house—new paint inside and out, new carpet and flooring, new toilets, counters, and more—is about $15 a square foot. Even if you're walking through a house with your contractor, you're doing a guesstimation that starts at $15 a square foot for repairs and then trying to determine if a property requires more or less.

"Therefore, if you're going to an auction and can't see inside the house, if it looks decent on the outside, stick with $20 a square foot as the estimate for rehab costs for those *just-in-case* things that you can't see. On the other hand, if it's run down, estimate probably $25 to $35 a square foot or more for rehab and repair costs. Personally, though, I wouldn't bid on anything at an auction if I couldn't see the inside of the property and the outside doesn't appear in decent shape," he adds.

After all, he concludes, "Full disclosure or not, the seller isn't going to tell you what's wrong with a property, because he wants you to buy it."

Step-by-Step

No matter the numbers, and no matter the approach to foreclosure investing, the background detail work is basically the same. The first step, however, is particularly important with courthouse auctions: Know the laws of your state.

Before you start on anything related to courthouse sales, you must know and thoroughly understand the foreclosure timeline and process for your state. That lets you know how much time you have to prepare for the auction. As we discussed in Chapter 5, the time varies by state and could be very limited. (See the Appendix for more information.)

Property Criteria

Next, determine how selective you want to be with potential properties. What are the basic criteria your potential investment property must meet? Considerations include:

- Geography/location.
- Price range.
- Size with resale potential in mind; first-time buyer starter homes work best.
- Amount of equity; it should be enough to allow for that magic 30 to 40 percent discount (15 percent profit and 15 to 25 percent soft costs, depending on market conditions) off the full market value minus the cost of repairs.
- Condition/age of property.

In today's market with many overextended homeowners, you're likely to filter out the majority of properties because of too little homeowner equity. Without that equity, your numbers won't add up to any profit for you.

Review Filings

Review the foreclosure filing lists for courthouse and sheriff's sales in your county or area and pull those that meet your basic criteria. You can do that via your national or local foreclosure listing service, or through your own research by reading the legal notices in your newspaper and adding to that information from your county tax assessor's and recorder's offices.

Cull Your List

Once you've assembled your preliminary list, examine it closely to get rid of properties that don't specifically meet all your criteria. For example, no equity, no deal; five bedrooms, too big; $850,000 property, too high-end in some areas; and so on.

Title Time

You should now have a list of properties with relatively good potential as investment deals *if* their titles are clean and *if* their numbers add up. Run preliminary title on the properties (more on that later in this chapter). Keep in mind that this task is easier if you have a working relationship with a title company's customer service department so you can verify details with them via a simple phone call. Some title companies offer free customer service, some don't. Questions you need to ask include:

- What names affect the title? Get every possible name and spelling of the name.
- Since the date of purchase, what deeds of trust have been recorded? Get the date and amount of each additional one.
- Have any of those deeds of trusts been paid off? If so, which ones? A reconveyance should be recorded if a deed has been paid off.
- Have any general index liens or lis pendens (lawsuits) been recorded? If so, you'll need the title people to fax you a copy of each lien for your review.
- Have any of those liens been paid off and a release recorded? If so, which ones?
- When in doubt, ask a real estate attorney for advice.

Doing the Numbers

Eliminate those properties on your list with unresolved title issues, and now you're ready to determine the dollars and sense of the properties that are left. You'll have to drive by the properties for a visual inspection and more, if possible. Pay careful attention not only to the condition of the property—we've talked about some exterior clues to the interior—but to the neighborhood, and more, too. Remember Christian Rooney's close call with a near-bid on the wrong house in Chapter 2? He

Courthouse Auction by the Numbers

Property market value	$300,000
Mortgage in default	$200,000
Minimum bid at foreclosure auction (includes fees/penalties)	$220,000

Formula

Market value less 15 percent soft costs (buying, holding, selling costs)	$255,000
Less repairs ($15/square foot × 1,000 square feet)	$15,000
Break-even price (no profit included)	$240,000
At $220,000 minimum bid, gross profit margin	$20,000

Conclusion: Don't be fooled—$20,000 is not enough profit. This deal's penciled-in profit is 6.67 percent of the resale value. You might as well get a real estate license and work for 6 percent commission on your deals. That way you won't have to risk any of your own money in the deal.

confused a home on Seventh Street with one on Seventh Avenue. Pay attention to legal descriptions of property locations, too.

Talk to neighbors of a particular property to find out what you can about the property and its owners. That can help give you a peek inside the home and offer an indication of whether a homeowner might end up trashing the property before leaving, too. Make notes on the condition and needed repairs of each property.

Next, run the comps on each of the properties you've reviewed. Determine their market value based on comparable properties and then subtract the cost of repairs and rehab for each from the market value. Now factor in your 15 percent profit and 15 to 25 percent buying, holding, and selling (soft) costs. The latter, remember, will depend in part on the existing market conditions. In today's buyer's (slow) market, you'll want to factor in significantly more than the 15 percent soft costs for normal markets—perhaps up to 25 percent to take into account a longer hold time and the resulting higher out-of-your-pocket costs.

Keep in mind up front, though, you want to choose the right property in the right location at the right price so you can resell at the right price, too. If the numbers add up, that's your maximum bid. Don't go over it!

When it comes to researching title, most states are race notice states. That means the first to record a lien on a property takes precedence over all others.

Planning for Contingencies

When you identify a potential property, think about possible complications, and plan for those what-ifs ahead of time. Some variables to consider in finding and figuring the right deal include:

- What if the property you intend to flip doesn't sell quickly and you're left with prolonged holding costs?

- What if the ousted former owner refuses to move and you end up having to evict him? That can mean delays of 60 days or longer before you even start your rehab work.

- Worse yet, because you really don't know the condition of the property's interior, what if it needs a major structural overhaul (which it may) to the tune of tens of thousands of dollars that come out of your pocket and profits?

- Scariest of all, what if the title to the property isn't clear and a senior lien surfaces?

The cement trick is one of the worst offenses of very disgruntled homeowners evicted by foreclosure. They pour cement down the plumbing before they leave, and, as an investor, you have no way of knowing that until you get into the house.

—Alexis McGee

Don't think we're overreacting with all these cautions. An American Land Title (www.alta.org) survey found that 36 percent of all real estate transactions in 2005 had problems with their titles, up from only 25 percent in 2000.

Such potential problems are real possibilities with properties bought at a foreclosure sale as-is, no guarantees. Fortunately, you can avoid many of the snags. The more thoroughly you research a property, its title, and its condition, the less chance you'll be blindsided.

In Your Own Backyard

Open your eyes to your own neighborhood, too. Some of the best deals in foreclosure and sheriff's sales might be in your own backyard. You already know the neighborhood, the market, perhaps even the property's history and condition, and possibly some of the circumstances surrounding the foreclosure. That automatically erases those variables.

Mort and Louise were retired teachers who invested in pre-foreclosures and foreclosures. They shied away from properties sold at courthouse auctions, says Louise, because even though they were seasoned veterans in the business, they didn't want to deal with the unknowns associated with this approach to investing. But when they read on their foreclosures listings about a home down the street scheduled to go to auction, they were thrilled. If the numbers added up and the title came through clear, it would be an ideal situation. They were already aware of many details involving the property and consequently were able to eliminate many variables. They also appreciated the convenience of rehabbing and selling a home in their own neighborhood. The couple ended up with the property and flipped it for a handsome profit.

Taking on Running Title

Tracking or running title on a property, as Rod earlier in this chapter discovered, is serious work with serious consequences. Remember the American Land Title survey? It found that more than a third of all residential real estate transactions—new, resale, and refinances—had problems with their titles. Among the most frequent curative actions (resolutions), according to the survey, were these:

- Obtaining releases or reconveyances, or obtaining payoffs for prior or existing deeds of trust liens, unpaid child and spousal support, outstanding taxes, and other judgments against the property.
- Recording errors of names, addresses, or legal descriptions of the property.

Obviously not all of these issues will torpedo a deal, but any of them certainly can damage your investment profits—not to mention your mental state—if you discover them after the fact and become embroiled in seemingly endless hassles.

ForeclosureS.com coach Tim Rhode recalls watching an auction in which a novice investor apparently hadn't properly researched a property. The investor thought he was bidding on a second mortgage in foreclosure, but instead was bid-

Title Talk

Here are a few important terms related to tracking or following the title on a property:

Clear title: Ownership rights to a piece of real estate that are not diminished by liens, leases, or other encumbrances.

Cloud on the title: An outstanding claim or encumbrance that, if valid, affects or impairs owner's title.

Easement: A right that may be exercised by the public or individuals on, over, or through the property of others.

Encroachment: A building or obstruction that intrudes on the property of another.

Lot book report: A document from the title company that identifies encumbrances recorded against a particular property; it does not identify liens recorded in the name of the owner that may affect the property.

Title defect: An unresolved claim against ownership of property that prevents presentation of marketable title.

Title insurance: An insurance policy that protects the holder from any loss caused by defects in title.

Warranty deed or grant deed: Conveyance of land in which grantor guarantees title to grantee.

ding on a third. "The poor guy had no idea he actually was buying the property subject to two other liens—the first and the second. To make things worse, he was bidding against pros who knew what was going on and kept bidding up the property. Everyone (the bidders) just sat there and let him die on the vine. They thought it was funny."

The investor ended up paying $70,000 more than he should have.

Do It Right Yourself

If only the investor in the preceding example had run title on the property before the auction, he would have saved himself a great deal of money and embarrassment. In addition to being the practical approach to foreclosure investing and saving cash, running preliminary title yourself by tracking it through the county recorder's office also ensures you've caught every discrepancy. Of course, that's assuming you've done the job correctly.

Rhode recalls another auction in which a veteran investor slipped up and missed a $200,000 IRS lien against a property he bought. Remember, IRS federal tax liens are a general index lien with special rights. Even if the federal tax lien is recorded after your deed of trust going to auction, it isn't wiped out by the sale until 120 days after the auction. During those 120 days, the winning bidder should not do any repairs on the property because the IRS can redeem the property, only reimbursing the bidder for what he paid at the auction plus simple interest—repairs or other expenses are not reimbursed. After the 120 days, if the IRS hasn't redeemed the property, the lien is wiped out and the winning bidder can sell the property with clear title.

In the situation that Rhode described, luckily the investor (with the help of his real estate attorney) was able to negotiate with the IRS to settle for only $50,000 and get them to release their redemption rights so he could proceed without waiting the 120 days. Otherwise he would have lost $150,000 on the deal—certainly no small change and plenty of incentive to run your title right.

A fully insured, formal title report generally costs around $400 or so, but, as we discussed in Chapter 2, you can pay much less for an uninsured title search report online. (Two sources include http://www.titlesearch.com/ and http://www.american titleinc.com.)

If a county's property records are online, tracing a deed history isn't nearly as cumbersome as following a recorded paper trail. If the records aren't online, resign yourself to the fact that this is one of the most important aspects of foreclosure investing, and just do it. A shortcut: Pay close attention to each and every release or reconveyance recorded to see the liens and deeds of trust they reference. That's one more way to cut down on your research time.

Be aware that the note in foreclosure at a sale may not be the first mortgage on the property. If a deal sounds way too good to be true—well, you know the rest. Remember Macy in Chapter 2, who was thrilled to pay only $80,000 for a $280,000 property at foreclosure sale, only to learn that she had bought the home's junior note instead? With that junior note came assumption of the senior note as well, and Macy ended up paying $360,000 for a house worth $280,000.

In the state of Colorado, as mentioned earlier, public notice of a courthouse auction must caution buyers that the note in question may not be the first mortgage.

When checking out a property for a trustee sale, take your time with title. Research all the contingencies by checking that, among other things:

- Property taxes are up to date.
- The foreclosing note is the senior lien.

- No other senior liens exist, such as federal tax lien, a mechanic's lien, unpaid homeowners association dues, or something else entirely.

Pay particular attention to any mention of easement or zoning issues with the property, too. A disgruntled neighbor who is convinced that a property owner has encroached on his territory could mean migraine headaches for you if the issue isn't resolved. An easy way to identify problems like that is by talking to neighbors. You may want to investigate further if a related lien of some kind has been filed and then released. Make sure the lien does, in fact, have a recorded full release. If not, as we mentioned earlier in the chapter, you could face headaches similar to Rod's when the IRS lien snowballed from a relatively manageable $13,000 to big bucks.

More Details

Running a property's title means you trace ownership (chain) through public records until you find a grant deed that shows a *full value* transfer. That's the zero point in the title search. With a full value transfer, that means all previously recorded mortgages and other liens—from alimony to zoning—have been released.

Because the property in a foreclosure sale is sold as-is, you won't get a title guarantee (there's no escrow or title insurance at trustee sale auctions), so be thorough in your work. Of course, after you've rehabbed the property, when you resell it the buyer will have to pay professionals to run formal title and you will have to provide insurance on that title.

Running the title will also allow you to see the position of the loan going to the trustee sale. Knowing when the particular loan was recorded—its position compared with the origination dates of other loans and liens on the property—allows you to see which loans, liens, and encumbrances are senior (and will remain with the property and be transferred to the successful bidder) and which are junior and will be wiped out by the foreclosure sale.

Because most states are *race notice* states—the first to record becomes the first in line—typically the date of the original deed of trust, lien, or encumbrance reflects the position of that encumbrance. If, for example, you're bidding on a first deed of trust at auction, most liens, loans, and encumbrances recorded after your original deed was recorded are considered junior to your position and will be wiped out, except for property tax liens (some mechanic's liens and lis pendens).

If the deed you're bidding on is a second, the first loan recorded remains on the property and goes to the successful bidder *subject-to*. Most liens, loans, and encumbrances recorded after the second deed of trust will be wiped out. Of course, there are exceptions, too.

To Help with Your Title Search

- Review your title research to discover the exact positioning of the loan in default that's going to the trustee sale.

- Keep in mind that junior liens and encumbrances—other than property tax liens, some mechanic's liens, and federal income tax liens (until 120 days after the sale)—are wiped out by the deed of trust going to sale.

- Most states are *race notice* states—first to record becomes first in line—so the date the original deed of trust, lien, or encumbrance was recorded typically will direct you to the position of that encumbrance.

- If your deed of trust at the auction is a second, then the first loan recorded will remain on the property (and you will get the property subject to that existing lien). However, most liens, loans, and encumbrances recorded *after* your second deed of trust will be wiped out.

- Get legal advice on the state of title. It's easy for an amateur to miss a deed of trust, lien, or encumbrance that is senior to the position you're bidding on. If you want to invest in foreclosures at auction, get a good real estate attorney to help you with the title and keep you from losing your shirt.

Fast Title Cures

Simply because a property has issues with its title isn't necessarily cause to reject the deal. It depends on the problem and the circumstances surrounding it. With a small judgment lien, for example, curing the title may be as simple as writing a small check.

Lawyers Can Be a Good Thing

A missed deed of trust, lien, or encumbrance can bury you at a trustee sale. And often, it's not easy to catch all the liens, from mechanic's lien, to federal or state liens, property tax liens, judgment liens, subordination agreements (written agreements between lien holders to change the priority of certain liens), and more. That's why the wise investor looks to real estate attorneys for advice. They keep you from losing your shirt, so when in doubt, seek them out.

If you don't already have a qualified real estate attorney on your investment team, some helpful sources include DSNews' Black Book (www.dsnewsblackbook .com), Lawyers.com (www.lawyers.com) from the well-respected LexisNexis Martindale-Hubbell, the American Bar Association (www.abanet.org, click on

"Lawyer Locator"), California-based LawGuru (www.lawguru.com), or your local bar association.

Tips to Take Home

First and foremost, as with all other types of foreclosure investing, when looking for deals at auctions you unequivocally must know your state's rules and requirements for foreclosures. Your state's foreclosure timeline can limit your time to act.

Also, does your state recognize the right of redemption—a property owner's right to reclaim a property after its foreclosure sale? If so, a sale isn't final for a certain period of time, creating additional holding costs that can seriously affect the deal's bottom line.

Do laws in your state require the full bid amount or only a portion up front? You'll have to bring a cashier's check made out for the minimum bid amount as well as incremental checks for potential overbidding you plan to make. Because these deals can be all cash, the amount required up front means you will have to find a source for quick cash like a line of credit on other property or margin access on stock market accounts. This is not a time to find new financing or look for money. You need to have it already in place and be ready to go, in order to be a senior-class trustee sale buyer. Plan ahead so you know where the money is when you need it!

The All-Important Appraisal

An accurate appraisal of a potential purchase should reflect the property after it's fixed up in cherry condition. (We talked a bit about the requirements for that in

Tips for Appraisal Accuracy

- Use only properties comparable in age, building and lot size, and style.
- Comps should be in close geographic proximity to the property you're appraising.
- Forget the fixer-uppers. You want the value of a potential property after it's in cherry condition.
- Forget the properties that are overimproved and that you can't or don't want to replicate in your rehab efforts.
- Use homes sold in the past three months (you can include up to six months if necessary), recent pending sales, and those actively on the market. The source for the latter two is your local multiple listing service (MLS).

Chapter 2.) A major aspect of your appraisal comes from comparing values on comps (similar properties in the neighborhood).

Measuring the Costs

Because properties sold at courthouse auction and sheriff's sales are as-is and you can't see the physical and structural details of the interior before you buy, you will very likely face issues requiring expenditures. Beyond the basics of new paint inside and out, new flooring, termite clearance, a good roof, and general sprucing up, the ousted homeowner may leave you a surprise or two. Such surprises often involve plumbing or interior walls. Even if the ex-homeowner left the property neat as a pin, his financial difficulties could well mean you'll face expenses related to big-ticket items such as new windows, heating and cooling systems, fireplace repairs, or even foundations—as Miguel found out earlier in the chapter.

With all these financial uncertainties, how then do you figure whether a property's dollars and cents make financial sense? Check out a property as thoroughly as possible. Be generous when estimating the cost of repair and rehab, and conservative when estimating the time needed for resale. That sounds easy enough, and it can be if you do your homework.

TAKEaway

- Pay attention to the red flags. That includes a gut feeling you have that something isn't right; it probably isn't, so walk away.

- Do your research. The more you know about a potential property before the purchase, the fewer the variables and the better chance your deal will be a good one.

- Thoroughly verify a property's title. That means making sure that property taxes are up to date, the foreclosing note is the senior deed of trust, and that no other senior liens exist on the property. Or, if senior liens do exist, make sure you're aware of them and have made arrangements to pay them off. Watch for zoning easements and issues, too.

- Don't skimp on a property's repair and rehab cost estimate, especially if you haven't seen inside it. The variables are just too many in this type of sight-unseen foreclosure investing.

- A property's exterior can (but won't always) give clues to its interior. If it looks decent on the outside, stick with $20 a square foot as the estimate for rehab costs (normally it's $15 per square foot, but you need to be more conservative in your estimates when you can't see inside the home before you buy). But if it's trashed, $25 to $35 or more a square foot is a better estimate for rehab and repair costs.

PART IV

REOs AND SHORT SALES

This is a strictly dollars and cents approach to foreclosure investing. Show the lender the money and why it makes sense for its bottom line, and usually the deal is yours.

—Alexis McGee

CHAPTER 7

Another Option, Another Opportunity

Dealing with REO lenders is how I started my foreclosure investing career. It's all business and a totally different approach than pre-foreclosures.

—Alexis McGee

Properties by the tens of thousands ended up back in the hands of their lenders this year. Thousands more will likely share the same fate. All are properties that have gone through the foreclosure process, failed to sell at auction, and now are REO—lender-owned real estate.

The good news is that REOs represent yet another excellent opportunity for the savvy foreclosure investor to pick up properties at a discount, fix them up, and then flip them for profits. This opportunity, however, comes with one big condition: To succeed at REO investing, you must thoroughly understand the REO process and its ramifications for the bank or lender holding the property. Then you can put together a win-win deal for both of you.

Investing in REOs has nothing to do with emotion or working with a homeowner to make a deal happen. This is strictly dollars and cents—show me the money and why it makes sense for the corporation's bottom line.

Let's look more closely.

Properties by the Thousands

Consider first the amount of real estate in lenders' hands today, and how and why it got there. As mentioned earlier, in just the first nine months of 2007, there were nearly 400,000 REO filings in the United States. That's 5 out of every 1,000 households across the country that were lost to foreclosure, up from only 3.6 out of every 1,000 homeowners during the same time period a year earlier, according to numbers from ForeclosureS.com.

Subprime Fallout

This abundant supply of REO properties is only part of the economic fallout from the nation's subprime lending debacle. That morass, which includes the corpses of dozens of subprime lenders, is what's left of the one-time feeding frenzy of buyers and lenders clawing at each other to cash in on the nation's housing boom. At the height of the boom, lenders handed out home loans that in many cases defied financial sanity. Almost anyone could get credit and a big mortgage. *Stated income* and *low-doc* loans, requiring little or no documentation, were commonplace. Subprime borrowers (those with troubled or no credit) qualified for 100 percent financing, interest-only loans, and option adjustable-rate mortgages (ARMs) with artificially low teaser rates. When those loans adjusted upward, the buyers who never could have qualified under normal (realistic) loan standards simply refinanced.

> *The effects of the subprime lending debacle extend well beyond home buyers with little or no credit. Credit markets— and resulting liquidity—have tightened for everyone, even the nation's largest mortgage provider, Countrywide Financial, which was recently purchased by Bank of America.*
>
> —Alexis McGee

This skewed approach to financing homeownership worked as long as housing prices kept escalating. But when the housing market began to collapse in 2006, hundreds of thousands of homeowners were left with little choice but foreclosure. To make matters worse, the bottom fell out for even more overextended homebuyers as the lending world realized the error of its ways and began to tighten lending standards. (Freddie Mac, the congressionally chartered, private organization, led the way in early 2007 when it decided to no longer back ARM loans unless the borrower qualified at the fully adjusted interest rate.) Unable now to qualify for refinancing, those homeowners, too, were left with little choice but foreclosure. Even with Congress and public and private institutions and organizations offering *bailouts* for certain qualified financially strapped homeowners, many others still see little alternative to foreclosure.

Although the reality is that foreclosures represent a very tiny portion of the $10 trillion U.S. mortgage market, fallout from the past year's lender failures and foreclosures has reverberated across all credit markets. There's been an overall clampdown in liquidity—that's the availability of money to lend for housing and otherwise—for everyone. With credit harder to come by, even more homeowners are squeezed and struggling. Lenders, too, have been hit hard.

> *"The Alt-A market with no or limited documentation also is suffering from past shoddy underwriting practices. . . ."*
>
> —James B. Lockhart, director of the Office of Federal Housing Enterprise Oversight, August 10, 2007 (see http://www.ofheo.gov/media/letters/Schumer81007.pdf)

A Note on How Home Lenders Operate

Banks typically lend money for mortgages financed by the money they take in on deposits. But that's not how some mega lenders do business. Instead, they borrow money on Wall Street or from banks by issuing commercial paper or debt. They then repay the debt by closing mortgages and selling them quickly again and again. It's sort of a "borrowing from Peter to pay Paul" philosophy, but it can work well and profitably if everything goes as planned. When the system goes awry, however, as now, and there's no purchase demand for those mortgages, the lenders' liquidity dries up and the lenders come up short.

In fact, the nation's largest mortgage lender, Countrywide Financial Corporation (NYSE: CFC), sought additional financing in mid-August 2007 to shore up its cash position. The lending giant announced that, because of "lessened liquidity," it would tighten its underwriting standards primarily to only those loans eligible for purchase by Freddie Mac and Fannie Mae—both private, government-chartered agencies that buy mortgages from private lenders (see http://about.countrywide.com/PressRelease/PressRelease.aspx?rid=1041245). Then in January 2008, Bank of America agreed to buy Countrywide with its embattled loan portfolio (http://newsroom.bankofamerica.com/index.php?s=press_releases&item=7956).

Another bank-owning financial company is Capital One Financial Corporation (NYSE: COF). In August, the company pulled the plug on its GreenPoint Mortgage unit, although it said at the time that it will retain its $12.5 billion mortgage portfolio (see http://phx.corporate-ir.net/phoenix.zhtml?c=70667&p=irol-newsArticle2&ID=1042128&h).

Yet one more mortgage giant that called it quits was New Century Financial Corporation (OTC: NEWC). The Irvine, California-based company filed Chapter 11 bankruptcy protection in April 2007, and then sold off its loan-servicing operations (see http://investorrelations.ncen.com/phoenix.zhtml?c=73989&p=irol-newsArticle &ID=1004374&highlight=).

New York-based American Home Mortgage (NYSE: AHM), consistently ranked as one of the nation's largest home lenders, also filed for Chapter 11 (August 2007), citing "the sudden adverse impact on the Company's business with respect to its liquidity, due to the extraordinary disruptions now occurring in the secondary mortgage and real estate markets." (See https://www.americanhm.com/index.aspx.)

More lender casualties in just August 2007 included:

- BNC Mortgage LLC. New York-based Lehman Brothers Holdings Incorporated's (NYSE: LEH) subprime lending unit closed its doors. The parent company also cut jobs at another of its lending-related units, HSBC Holdings. Subsequently, in September, Lehman announced a "restructuring plan" for its residential mortgage origination business worldwide that included closing the company's Korean mortgage business and cutting back its operations in the United Kingdom (http://www.lehman.com/press/pdf_ 2007/082207_bncclosure.pdf). In January 2008, Lehman further scaled back U.S. mortgage lending operations, this time cutting approximately 1,300 jobs in its Aurora Loan Services subsidiary (http://www.lehman.com/ press/pdf_2008/0117_mortgage.pdf).

- Accredited Home Lenders (NASDAQ: LEND). The San Diego, California-based lender slashed its work force, closed more than 60 branches, and stopped accepting applications for home loans in the United States. Subsequently Loan Star U.S. Acquisitions tried unsuccessfully to withdraw its deal to merge with Accredited. But under legal pressures, in late September both parties agreed to the deal at a substantially reduced price-from $15.10 a share to $11.75 a share or about $295 million (see http://investors.accredhome.com/ phoenix.zhtml?c=132116&p=irol-newsArticle_print&ID).

- First Magnus Financial Corporation. The Tucson, Arizona-based company stopped funding mortgage loans or taking applications "in light of the collapse of the secondary mortgage market," then less than a week later filed for Chapter 11 bankruptcy protection, citing "the extensive and sudden liquidity crisis in the secondary mortgage market" (see http://www.firstmagnus.com/ PressReleases/08-21Bankruptcy.pdf).

- The financial sector, including mortgage/subprime lending institutions, cut 30,892 jobs in August 2007, according to global outplacement consultancy Challenger, Gray & Christmas Inc., which tracks daily job cuts. That compares with just 282 in August 2006. That sector cut 69,664 jobs in the first nine months of 2007, compared with 12,874 for all of 2006!

For the latest in lender casualties, check out the Mortgage Lender Implode-o-Meter (www.ml-implode.com).

Hot Opportunity

What does all this have to do with you as an investor in REO properties? In a word, discounts!

In a hot sellers' market—limited sellers and many buyers—few, if any, REO properties are available to purchase at discount prices. Most homeowners in financial trouble simply sell their properties pre-foreclosure. If a property does end up REO, the bank or lender fixes it up and then turns it over to a Realtor to sell for full market price. But, as you can see from the preceding synopsis of markets, this is *not* today's reality. We are in a strong buyers' market and—given surging numbers of foreclosures, REO properties, credit crunch, and more—lenders and banks are beginning to feel the squeeze, some more than others. On the one hand, they're caught in a credit crunch; on the other, they are overwhelmed by REO properties.

All this can mean opportunity for you *if* you know how to make the right deal and your timing is right (more on deal making in Chapter 12). Right now, the market is in flux. Some banks are beginning to deal and discount. It depends, however, on the lender, your local market, supplies, demand, near-term outlook, and more. For some investors, it may make more sense to buy and hold a property a bit longer until discounts are greater. For others, the discount may materialize and translate into a solid deal.

Don't ever forget, though, that banks are in the business of making money. Selling an REO property to you at a discount is by no means their only option, so don't think you can make out like a bandit and waltz away with huge deals on REO properties. In some cases, banks with deep pockets will simply hold on to REO properties until the market improves. Another especially popular option these days is the big REO auction—we discuss that in Part V.

Nonetheless, if you can structure the right deal with the right price, lenders may jump at the chance to sell to you at a discount. Don't be greedy, though. Be profit-oriented and practical, make the right connection, and you're home free.

It's a numbers game. Remember that.

The Pros and Cons of REO Purchases

For an investor, an REO property purchase can be a simple deal that doesn't require the emotional involvement of helping a homeowner work out his financial problems. Neither is an REO deal encumbered with the myriad uncertainties that can bog down pre-foreclosure, deeds of trust, and courthouse sale purchases. And, because we're likely near the bottom of an economic downturn in housing markets with a glut of houses on the market and a plethora of bank-owned properties, some banks/lenders are discounting, although not always deep enough or right away.

"With REOs, you're dealing with the financial institution with no emotion in the property. It's strictly numbers and lender guidelines for the parties involved," says Ian Maker, a specialist in REO and foreclosure sales since 1990. A co-founder of REO Deal Makers (www.reodealmakers.com), he's also a veteran of more than 2,500 REO sales. "It's either black or it is white, and there is no in-between," adds Maker, who does much of his work via Internet and e-mail communications.

Let's take a closer look at some aspects of an REO purchase.

Property Information Packets

If you hate variables in your foreclosure business deals, REO investing is just the ticket for your peace of mind. REO properties generally come with property information packets (PIPs). These include legal details ranging from land survey, title, and lien searches to radon and termite inspections, zoning, and property taxes. Lender/owners even provide buyers with their own internal REO sales contracts. But beware the fine print. It doesn't generally favor you, the buyer. Get a good real estate attorney to review it and, as always, find out all you can about a property ahead of time.

The Liens Issue

Once a property is back in the hands of its lender, most junior liens are wiped out. You as a buyer needn't worry about title or equity positions, either. If the bank/lender foreclosed on a senior loan, they will own the property free and clear. No need to worry about federal tax liens or property tax liens, either, because the lender most likely already took care of them before they put the property on the market. And with an REO purchase, you can buy a full title insurance policy guaranteed so you know exactly what it is you're buying.

If, after you purchase a property REO, Aunt Martha comes forward and says she loaned so-and-so the cash for a down payment and wants it back, she's out of luck. Same with the ex-wife who is owed back child support. Once a property is REO, those other liens are history.

Seeing Is Believing

No gambles or guesses inside or out, either, with REO properties if you go through the process correctly. You can make an appointment with a bank or lender's specialist and walk through the property to find exactly what's wrong and what's right with it. That's a big plus that some investors fail to take advantage of.

The physical condition of REO properties can vary dramatically, says Tom Daves, a longtime successful REO investor and broker. "You can find some homes neat as a pin where the homeowners even shampooed the carpets before they left. Or you can find others where the homeowner plays total victim, rips out the appliances and toilets, and damages and defaces every part of the property, and then refuses to leave," adds Daves, who has spent the past 30 years in the real estate business. "In this business, you can go from the height of exaltation to the depths of defeat in the same 60 seconds," he adds.

To hopefully avoid the latter, take the time up front to thoroughly check out a property. The effort will also signal an REO agent that you're serious about your deal. When you check out the property, take your contractor with you if possible—be sure to pay him for his time and efforts—and together assess what needs to be done to bring the property up to cherry condition and comparable to the best homes in the neighborhood. Your goal, remember, is to be able to flip the property for top dollar, and to do so quickly and easily.

As with other forms of foreclosure investing, in order to accurately determine your offer price for an REO property, you must know how much you can get for the rehabbed property when you're ready to flip it. That requires not only a solid market-value figure for the property—determined via comps and your appraisal—but also an accurate estimate of the cost to upgrade and repair it. We address the details of how to figure the numbers in Chapter 8, but keep in mind that your bottom line is the full market value of a property at resale minus the cost of your repairs, rehab, and holding time.

"We probably get 40 to 50 offers a week that are unrealistic from people who haven't done their (background) work, haven't seen the property, haven't looked at what the comps are in the neighborhoods, and make offers at 50 cents on the dollar—when it's already an incredibly good deal," says Maker. Needless to say, few if any of those offers ever get taken seriously.

Motivated Sellers or Not

In today's cold market (countless sellers and only a handful of buyers), some banks/lenders may be motivated sellers if they are swamped with REO properties that are nonperforming assets affecting their bottom lines. Your job is to capitalize on that situation with the right cash-only, as-is offer that relieves them of the non-performing asset and precludes their spending any more on the property for repair, rehab, or even resale.

If you move quickly and contact the right person, a lender may not even need to pay a Realtor to sell the property. The key, of course, is to have an accurate, up-to-date foreclosure-listing service that lets you be among the first to access data. You must also have a top-notch REO contact list that allows you to go straight to the point person with your offer.

On the flip side, however, not all lenders are highly motivated sellers. Some larger lenders with well-oiled REO departments and deep pockets with few sub-prime loans aren't overly interested in selling properties at steep discounts and will work to get the most money they can for their assets. "REO today is a very specialized niche in the business," says Maker. "Whereas you used to deal with financial institutions directly, today you're dealing with an asset management company that has put all the systems in place and the staff in place to handle these nonperforming assets. As a result, it's just another product in the inventory. It's a numbers game, and you just have to look at the numbers."

That doesn't mean the banks won't deal. It simply means you'll have to work twice as hard to find a lender who will accept your offer. That's where networking, professionalism, presentation, and work can pay off. Do it right, and you can get the deal.

Another consideration in REO buying, Maker points out, is that in today's marketplace REO properties can easily *age*—that's a reference to the length of time a property languishes unsold on the market while the lender continues to hold it as a nonperforming asset. The longer they age, usually the greater the discount, he adds. "Look for those properties with longer days on market. You'll likely get a better deal because the bank will be more likely to write down the asset."

The Profits Issue

As you can see, purchasing a property REO whittles down the variables in foreclosure investing. You still must deal with rehabbing and repairing a property, but you have the opportunity to know the property inside and out before you buy; you get clear title; and you get a done deal with 100 percent ownership.

This peace of mind comes at a price—you didn't really think it was a free lunch, did you? Your profits can be less than from other forms of foreclosure investing. That's why you must learn to deal and to create win-win situations. You could, for example, become an all-cash, as-is pocket buyer for a Realtor and get your discount anyway.

Although *pocket buyer* may sound sinister, it's not and is, in fact, completely aboveboard. If you're on a Realtors' list of pocket buyers, you're considered one of their best buyers and generally offered the first shot at well-priced listings not yet on the multiple listing service (MLS). Realtors will call you first and try to make a deal work.

You get on the list by developing relationships with Realtors. You develop relationships by schmoozing with them and making sure they know you offer an as-is, all-cash, quick-close deal. The latter can prompt them to call you first when the lender is ready to discount because the Realtors/agents need your quick sale now, and it helps put a feather in their cap in the eyes of their REO lender client.

Red Flags and Concerns

By now you're undoubtedly thinking that REO buying sounds like a foreclosure investor's dream even if profits aren't sky-high. Before you jump on the bandwagon, though, pay attention to the details. An REO property isn't always an easy purchase.

Realtor Loyalties

Many big lenders outsource their REO management to Realtors and other professionals. If you think you're set because a Realtor or an REO management company includes you on its pocket buyer list, think again. Keep in mind who pays the salary of the person peddling an REO property—the lender/bank who holds the property. Realtors and management companies are hired by these REO owners to get the most money they can for a property, so a Realtor's or manager's first allegiance is to their REO/lender boss. The higher the price paid and the quicker the sale for an REO property, the greater the likelihood of repeat business for that Realtor or company.

Therefore, if you take this route, realize that big discounts on REO properties are less likely than with other approaches to foreclosure investing.

Beware the "Big Sale"

Most of us at one time or another have participated in an online auction on eBay, or been to an estate sale or antiques auction. If the sale's marketing department has done its job and splashed ads everywhere, chances are the place was packed, prices were rising, and products moving off the shelves. After all, the law of supply and demand means that big demand pushes prices higher and lowers inventory.

It's the same when it comes to shopping for highly marketed REO properties. If buyers are plentiful, prices go up, too.

Repos as a Magnet

Never underestimate the value of the word *repo* in driving up the price on a property. For many novice buyers, *repo* translates to "big bargain" whether it is or not. Calling a property a repo is likely to attract plenty of inexperienced investors who inadvertently push up the price. It's that same law of supply and demand.

Novice investors also enjoy the bragging rights of being able to say they made a killing on a repo purchase, even if they actually paid more than necessary.

Banks and lenders who own these REO properties know all that and most likely will not be willing to take your discount offer on a property right away. Don't give up, though. If your timing is right, you have made the right contacts, and you have presented a win-win deal for both parties, they just may end up wanting to sell to you. After all, you do offer the all-cash, quick-closing approach to taking a nonperforming asset off their books, and to do it in a time frame that works for them. Patience is the key here.

A Note about HUD Homes

Many people tout HUD homes as the quick ticket to riches in foreclosure investing. Not I! These homes are REO properties that originally were purchased by first-time homebuyers with loans insured by the U.S. Department of Housing and Urban Development (HUD). These homes show up on the "free repo list" that Realtors hand out. There's that word *repo* again, which, combined with *free list*, should send up a giant red flag.

One big reason Realtors push these homes is that as a buyer's agent, they receive a full 6 percent commission on any sale (rather than the normal 3 percent they get in a typical sale where they split the 6 percent with a listing agent). Adding to the homes' popularity, HUD will finance its REO properties with only 3 percent down.

What then is wrong with HUD homes as an investment? Nothing but the dollars and cents of purchasing them. Their popularity is their downfall. Anything popular with the crowd means more competitive bidding and higher prices. It's rare that a homebuyer or contractor won't outbid me on a HUD home because they're willing to pay more than I am for the property. Because of the popularity of HUD properties, you'll seldom, if ever, have a chance at an exclusive deal at your price.

The moral? Don't waste your valuable time on a prospect on which you're likely to get outbid anyway. This is a case of "Thanks, but no thanks."

Beware Geographic Economics

Sure, the foreclosure tsunami has swept across the United States. And true, hundreds of thousands of homeowners have lost their homes to foreclosure. But, as a savvy foreclosure investor, keep in mind that not all areas of the country have the same housing economics. Some states, some counties, some cities, even some pockets in a hard-hit area may be experiencing a stable real estate market while their surrounding environs may be suffering the chill of a cold market.

Part of your job is to keep abreast of the economic condition of your target market so you can respond, deal, and invest accordingly. You can easily overpay for an REO property in a depressed area, and the lender will gladly accept the extra cash if you're not on top of the game.

Some of my favorite online sources to stay up-to-date on real estate markets and trends (you can sign up for free regular newsletters and reports from some of them, too) include:

- Bob Bruss's Real Estate Center (www.bobbruss.com). From nationally syndicated columnist Bob Bruss, this site offers real estate commentary, advice, and information, both free and fee-based. (Bruss passed away in September 2007, but his work will never die. I highly recommend his past reports and legal newsletters as additions to your real estate library.)

- DSNews.com (www.dsnews.com). The online counterpart to *DS News* (formerly *REO Magazine*), this site provides helpful information and news on the default mortgage–servicing industry.

- Inman News (www.inman.com). Solid fee-based resource for real estate news, information, advice, direction, blogs, and more.

- HSH Associates (www.hsh.com). Major publisher of independent mortgage and consumer loan information and statistics, much of it free.

- MarketWatch (www.marketwatch.com/personalfinance/realestate). This free site from Dow Jones includes news, rate information, real estate and personal finance resources, and more.

- Mortgage Bankers Association of America (www.mbaa.org). Industry organization that tracks real estate money trends including mortgages, delinquencies, refinancings, and more.

- Real Estate Consulting (www.realestateconsulting.com). John Burns, real estate consultant to builders and investors, helps executives make informed decisions. Sign up for his three free monthly e-mails on building marketing intelligence.

- Real Estate Journal (www.realestatejournal.com). From the publishers of the *Wall Street Journal*, a source of solid information, property listings, resources, remodeling direction, and more.

TAKEaway

- REO investing is strictly a dollars-and-cents proposition. You will need to make a lot of offers to get one acceptance. When the timing is right for the lender to discount, you will likely have your deal.

- An REO purchase removes many of the variables from foreclosure investing. You'll get clear title as well as see inside a property, but in exchange, discounts may be less.

- Pay attention to local and national real estate market economics. They play a big role in whether a bank/lender is a highly motivated seller (read "willing to discount significantly").

- Avoid overly worked HUD and VA properties. You're less likely to get a deal with a big enough discount because you'll be bidding against too many contractors, homebuyers, and other investors.

CHAPTER 8

The Deal: Find It, Figure It, and Win

Don't forget: no discount, no deal. That's an absolute.

—Alexis McGee

Numbers are the pivotal players in successful REO investing. Learn to make them work for you as well as for the lender/seller, and you're on your way to striking a deal that's a win-win for everyone. Of course, to seal the deal you must also combine the right numbers with swift timing, appropriate lender contacts, and a clear and concise presentation of your deal!

Sounds complicated but, as with other aspects of advanced foreclosure investing, it's fairly simple once you understand the requirements, the nuances, and the red flags. The big plus of REO purchases, as we've said, is that they offer lower risk and fewer variables than other forms of foreclosure investing, and solid profits to boot.

Yes, lenders in almost any market have options galore other than selling an REO property to you at a discounted price. We talked about some of the lender's options in Chapter 7. But holding on to a vacant REO property costs money—both out of pocket and as a nonperforming asset on the bank or lender's balance sheet. Don't underestimate the weight of a nonperforming asset and the lender's need for liquidity. Both are big line items for major lenders, especially as they struggle with the flood of foreclosures and stalled real estate markets in many areas of the country. Repairs and rehabs further subtract from the bottom line with an REO, as does hiring a Realtor to sell a property.

As an advanced foreclosure investor, your job is to show the REO property owner/lender and its REO management group why your all-cash, as-is, immediate-sale discount offer works for them. Doing it right, you can succeed. Plenty of investors have the deals to prove it.

Begin with the Basics

Your success at REO investing starts with the basics—finding the right property quickly and easily. With REOs, as with other types of foreclosure investments, you build on many of the already learned pre-foreclosure basics such as compiling and culling property lists, identifying potential deals, and running the numbers.

Unique Timing

With no other type of foreclosure investing, however, is speed quite as crucial. Being able to make decisions and move on them quickly separates REO investing from other types of foreclosure investing. REO investors must move fast. As soon as a property that meets your criteria shows up as REO, you should contact its lender to forestall him from starting a rehab or investing in sale preparations. Either will add to the potential selling price and generally torpedo any chance you have of a discount deal.

The other alternative is to wait it out and hope an REO property languishes on the market (i.e., *ages*) long enough so that the lender/bank willingly accepts a bigger discount. "The longer a property is aged and seasoned, the better the opportunity for the investor," says Ian Maker of REO Deal Makers.

Don't forget, though: As with other forms of foreclosure investing, no discount, no deal. That's an absolute.

Know What You Want and How to Get It

As always, you begin with foreclosure lists. And as with other types of foreclosure investing, before you can cull them you must know what kind of property to buy. That's essential in today's market with its glut of properties, stagnant selling prices, and liquidity (financing) issues for many buyers of new and existing homes. Knowing what sells will indicate what to buy and how to buy it at below-market prices.

Avoid expensive move-up housing. Even if it seems like a great *steal*, move-up and larger properties are the first to crash. Plus the cost of holding on to a $500,000 home can quickly suck up your profits and then some.

Also, pay attention to where and what the builders are building. When the market is slow, they discount and offer concessions you can't compete with or match for your buyers. Instead, look for older REOs (built in the 1980s and earlier) that are starter homes located in more-established neighborhoods. These properties are always in demand, which can cut down on your hold time and save you cash outlay. Don't bank on shorter hold times, though. If a property sells more quickly than you expected, consider it a little extra profit. The average buy, fix, and sell time in a hot market is about three to four months, while in a cold market it stretches to six to nine months. In today's market, figure on hold times of about six months and even more to be safe. That means you'll have to budget into your numbers the costs associated with carrying a property that long. You may want to consider other options, too, such as buying a property, fixing it up, and then renting it until markets change. (More on selling in a cold market in Chapter 12.)

Weeding Those Leads

By now, we hope, you've established a relationship with a foreclosure-listing service that meets your needs (read "provides thorough and up-to-date information for your property searches"). If you've had problems with the accuracy and timeliness of your list's data, now would be a good time to seek out a new provider. You will get nowhere fast in REO investing without up-to-date listings.

> *With REO-investing, you absolutely, positively must have reliable, up-to-date, and accurate foreclosure information or you'll end up spinning your wheels on worthless leads.*
>
> —Alexis McGee

Cull your list by notice type—specifically REO. These should be recently recorded trustee deed filings, which are the documents from the foreclosure auction that transfer ownership from the owner in default to the lender. Limit your search by geography, property type, size, and age, too. Because timing is important, look to the newest leads first. Then check to see if the property is listed in the local MLS. If so, is it listed as-is at a discount, or at full market value? If the price is high, leave it alone and allow it to age. Then, in three to six months, if it's still on the market, check with the sellers to see if they're any more motivated to sell—in other words, ready to discount it.

If a property isn't in the MLS, try to contact the lender directly. As we touched on earlier, they may be ready to deal.

Something else to consider: Don't worry about the amount of equity in an REO, because the foreclosure on the property most likely means it's now owned

Tales from Foreclosure Investors

Foreclosure investor Regina M. had been using a premium (that is, costly) foreclosure-listing service for almost a year. She had often run into outdated information on the site, but figured she could overlook the dead ends and misinformation as long as she continued to be successful with leads generated by the site.

Then Regina decided to try her hand at REO investing. It didn't take her long—about six instances of flagging a property only to discover it was no longer REO—to realize she needed a new information provider. She made the switch and, armed with accurate information to complement her persuasive approach and hard work, found REO investing to be extremely lucrative.

Moral of the story: If a provider doesn't measure up, make the switch sooner rather than later. You can't afford to waste time on obsolete leads.

free and clear, hence 100 percent equity. If a junior loan has foreclosed, however, that lender may take title subject to the existing senior loan and doesn't own the property free and clear. But in either case, you won't be filtering your leads by equity as you did with pre-foreclosure properties and auction notices.

More Sources of Leads

Beyond searching for property leads through your foreclosure-listing service, also network and mine your personal connections with banks, lenders, Realtors, agents, and others. Again, as we've cautioned, avoid HUD and VA repos—too much competition—and, in general, steer clear of MLS listings—also too much competition, and no discounts.

Outsourcers also can provide REO property listings. Ocwen Financial Corporation (www.ocwen.com), for example, a Florida-based outsourcing provider for the financial services industry, offers a "Properties for Sale" link off its home page that allows you to search by state and city for current REO listings.

Individual lenders/banks of all sizes also post REO property listings on their web sites. Downey Savings (www.downeysavings.com), for example, a small bank in Downey, California, and environs, has a "Properties for Sale" link off its home page. Giant CitiMortgage (http://www.citimortgage.com/Mortgage/Oreo/Search Listing.do) of St. Louis–based Citigroup also lists properties for sale in certain areas; the value of their data depends on where you live.

Be careful in your searches. If you simply plug "properties for sale" and "REO" into a Google search, you'll bring up plenty of "REO properties for sale" but not all of them are from reliable sources. Most are from middlemen who are re-selling another site's REO listings, and oftentimes the properties have already been sold. Buyer beware!

Although it doesn't provide direct links to properties, REONetwork (www .reonetwork.com), from ClearCapital.com Inc., is another option. It's an online direc-tory of real estate professionals who specialize in the remarketing of REO properties.

Contacting the Lender

Once you've identified the best potential REO properties, you'll need to move quickly to contact the lenders associated with each property to learn if they're will-ing to sell the property as-is and at a discount for an all-cash offer.

List Advantage

Preferably, make contact by telephone or e-mail, or both—it's quicker—which means you'll need a directory of key REO contacts. Good lists are updated regu-larly and provide web links to the REO departments of most major banks and lenders nationwide. In some cases, the lead's listing includes the bank's contact in-formation. In those instances in which neither is available, your listing service should provide a link to a Google search for the REO lender.

In case you think you don't need to pay for this information, keep in mind that the lending and banking business can be a revolving door, especially in today's here-today, gone-tomorrow lending environment. Remember those 30,892 jobs cut in August 2007 in the financial sector, which we talked about earlier?

In dealing with an institution holding literally thousands and tens of thou-sands of REO properties, getting to the right person can be a nightmare of com-munication or the lack thereof. Nonetheless, if you do opt to set out on your own, hunker down, and wait it out. Expect countless phone calls, transfers, disconnects, brush-offs, and more before you connect with the right person—if you reach him at all. This is a business where tenacity pays off. There are no shortcuts.

The Approach

When you reach the lender/property owner, begin by asking for the name of the specific REO asset manager handling the property you're interested in. If that per-

Tales from Foreclosure Investors

All is not always as it may seem, according to Daryl White, REO veteran investor and ForeclosureS.com coach:

> I had been calling banks with REOs to inquire about their plans for some of their properties. Many told me they were selling the property at 30 percent below market value. But when I did my own comps, it turned out that the market value they were stating was about 10 percent higher than the property likely could sell for. The properties were in very bad shape and needed a lot of rehab, too. Their 20 percent discount when you included the cost of needed repairs really was more like 5 to 10 percent off, and no deal at all.
>
> My advice to anyone who wants to invest in REOs is to learn to do your own valuations, and don't just accept the bank's or lender's numbers.

son tries to brush you off, don't become rude or defensive. Recognize that in these days of bulging portfolios and different outsource providers, lender employees across the board likely are overworked and overwhelmed by trying to keep up. Be polite and persistent. After all, your advantage here is your willingness to take a property off a lender's hands and its books *immediately*—no problem, no delay, and with minimal or no additional losses for the lender.

If a lender refers you to its Realtor, think *schmooze factor* and make friends along the way. Remember the pocket buyer list we described earlier? That's a worthy goal that will pay ongoing dividends for you as an REO investor.

Running the Numbers

For a deal to go through, it must make dollars and sense for the lender/REO property holder and for you. "See where an REO property is priced in relation to the rest of the market, then make a realistic offer . . . 50 percent of list price is a waste of everyone's time," says REO seller Ian Maker.

Whatever your offer, however, make sure that what you pay for the property doesn't exceed 60 to 70 percent of the property's fixed-up market value (minus your cost for its rehab and repair). Don't minimize your profits simply because REO investing has fewer variables. You can, however, as mentioned earlier in this chapter, adjust your offer for a hot or cold market, if necessary. Again, we are in the 60 to 70 percent market depending on your local market conditions.

Let's look at figuring the numbers and where, if anyplace, you have some negotiating/wiggle room.

Steps to Your Offer Price

1. Determine the resale value of a property. That's the maximum and realistic amount for which you can sell the property when it's in fixed-up, cherry condition. To figure that out, you'll need to look at prices of sold, pending sales, and active listings of comparable properties in close proximity. Make sure those properties are comparable in size, age, appearance, and more. You're not looking at prices of fixer-uppers or overly improved properties, only clean-cut comps in the area.

2. Deduct 15 percent of the market value amount for your profit.

3. Deduct another 15 percent in a normal market (20 to 25 percent in today's cold market) for your soft costs to purchase and flip the potential property. That includes purchasing costs like title, escrow, and closing; operating/holding costs like utilities, insurance, taxes, and maintenance on the property; money costs like monthly interest and points when applicable, as well as selling costs, which include marketing and more.

4. Determine, preferably with the help of your contractor, the rehab and repairs necessary and the cost to bring the property up to top standards. We prefer to avoid guesstimates, especially with REOs, because the more you can offer a lender/REO owner for a property, the more likely your offer will be accepted. You might be able to shave a little off the cost of rehab by matching your property to top comps in the area. If, for example, those properties don't have central air-conditioning, you won't need to install it in your property, either.

5. Subtract the total amount of repair costs from the fixed-up market value of the property.

6. You now have your maximum offer price.

Lyle K. meticulously and regularly reviewed his foreclosure and default property lists. That's how he found a particular entry-level home in a solid neighborhood. He knew timing was important, so as soon as the listing popped up on his list, he called the lender directly. He could do that because he had developed his REO contact list with names, addresses, and phone numbers of key REO personnel at many of the major banks and lenders nationwide, including the owner of this particular property.

The lender, it turns out, knew Lyle from other quick as-is, all-cash deals they had done together. When Lyle asked about the property, the property manager was very vague. The property needed some work, he said, but Lyle was welcome to take a look anyway. Undaunted, Lyle, along with his contractor, headed out to see the property. At first glance, it appeared pretty beat up. But closer, inspection showed the problems to be generally cosmetic—ruined carpets; some holes in the walls; missing fixtures; nicked doors, woodwork, counters, and sinks; broken appliances; and a trashed yard. Lyle and his contractor agreed that the property seemed structurally sound and didn't appear to need much more than simple rehab. The roof was nearly new, the plumbing was sound, and the window seals were in good shape.

The property was tailor-made for a quick as-is, all-cash REO deal. The 1,200-square-foot home would require approximately $20,000 in cash outlay to repair and rehab. But the lender might be willing to sell at a discount, precisely to avoid having to dump that $20,000 into the property, especially in today's cold market. After all, the property had already cost the lender more than $40,000 in delinquency and foreclosure costs, from the initial default and delinquency through the foreclosure process (see the chart in the accompanying box for foreclosure cost data, according to research from the Tower Group in Needham, Massachusetts), as well as $120,000 in the defaulted loan.

The Cost of Foreclosure

Foreclosure costs lenders big money, and so does taking a property back as REO and then reselling it. According to research from the Tower Group of Needham, Massachusetts, consider the following estimate of the costs:[1]

- Three months delinquency plus nine months foreclosure: $25,199[2]
- Six months REO holding: $16,460[2]
- Selling: $17,100[3]
- Total: $58,759

[1]Estimates based on a sample of loans for a specific period. Actual costs will vary by loan type, investor, guarantor, market conditions, state in which property is located, and other factors.

[2]Loss costs include unpaid interest, legal fees, taxes, homeowners insurance, utilities, home maintenance, and repairs.

[3]Includes the cost of sale, including title, escrow, commissions.

Source: "Servicing Default Management: An Overview of the Process and Underlying Technology," a report from the Tower Group (www.towergroup.com), © 2002 The Tower Group, Inc.

Lyle had already done his prep work to determine the fixed-up market value of the property—$200,000. He simply took 70 percent of $200,000 and subtracted his costs for the repair work ($20,000), which gave him the $120,000 offer price to present the REO lender.

Financing

With REO investing, your offer is all cash and as-is. The good news, however, is that your financing options range from a conventional mortgage to interim hard-money loans. REO property sellers may even have their own financing available. Shop around though, because hard-money loans carry higher interest rates and points with much less favorable terms.

Finder's Fee Not an Option

You most likely cannot flip these REO contracts to other investors in exchange for a finder's fee because most lenders use their own contracts and have built-in clauses that stipulate "this contract cannot be assigned." Instead, you will need to have a money partner or lender in place before you write your offer. Remember, REO investing is senior class investing! No contract assignments here.

Lyle's Deal by the Numbers

Fixed-up market value of property	$200,000
Less 30 percent (15% soft costs and 15% profit)	($60,000)
Less repairs	($20,000)
Maximum offer price	$120,000

Lyle's 15 Percent Soft Costs

Holding costs (soft costs include $1,000/month for five months, plus taxes, insurance, utilities)	$10,000
Buying and selling costs (soft costs include cost of hard-money loan, closing, title, escrow fees, real estate commissions)	$20,000
Lyle's 15 percent profit	$30,000

Fine-Print Cautions

Pay attention to the contracts. Many REO lenders have less than buyer-friendly internal sales contracts that should be reviewed by your attorney *before* you sign. Most likely the REO lender's contract will prohibit assignment to another investor. That little tidbit often can be buried in the fine print, so read carefully! Remember, again, that banks are in business to make money, and they seldom miss an opportunity to do so. It pays to be a smart investor.

As with other types of foreclosure investing, the deep pockets are out there if you know where to find them.

Where's the Cash?

If you're not flipping the deal to someone else, a hard-money loan is usually the best approach to an REO purchase. A *hard-money* loan is one that's funded privately (not through a banking institution) based on the equity in a property, not an individual's creditworthiness. It's quick, it's easy, and you don't waste your time filling out tons of documentation. Neither does it tie up your own cash.

Hard-money loans don't come cheap. If the going rate for a first mortgage is 6.8 percent, with perhaps 1 percent of the loan's value in fees, the rate for a hard-money loan is most likely double that (14 percent) plus 5 to 10 points (5 to 10 percent of the loan's value) in fees. Remember, though, this is only a short-term, interim loan until you flip the property or refinance, so you needn't sweat the fees—just figure the cost into your offer price, and make sure you account for your 15 percent profit. In today's market, you're more likely to refinance that interim hard money loan because usually—but not always—it will take longer to resell the property.

More sources of ready cash may include businesspeople you know. Ask them if they're interested in having real estate deals land in their laps that are at a 30 to 40 percent discount. Look in your local newspaper or its online classifieds, or Craigslist (www.craigslist.com) for "Money Available," "Investments Wanted," or "Cash for Real Estate."

Another way to find money partners is to Google "hard money" and your city, which will bring up a number of hard-money lenders and their web sites. Real estate message boards such as those on Creative Real Estate Online (www .creonline.com), ForeclosureS.com (www.foreclosures.com), Real Estate Forums (www.realestateforum.com), and BiggerPockets Forums (http://forums.bigger pockets.com) can also be solid sources of private investors and hard-money lenders.

The Presentation

Buying REO properties from lenders and banks is *not* a wing-it, fly-by-the-seat-of-your-pants proposition. You had better be well prepared for the contingencies—and present your deal with them accounted for—if you hope to come away successful.

> *How you present your proposed deal to the bank/
> lender of an REO property is as important as
> figuring the numbers properly.*
>
> —Alexis McGee

The Contents of Your Proposal

What's "well prepared" the ForeclosureS.com way? It's more than just a fast offer to buy a property, with a few numbers scribbled on a piece of paper. To come away a winner in the REO-buying business, you must take the time and make the effort to give the seller/corporation all the reasons it's in their best interests to sell the property today for your fair offer. Your offer should include a well-written cover letter that highlights the features, advantages, and benefits of your offer, and why the seller should accept it. Use facts and figures to back up your statements. Above all,

Lender Contact Info

Some good sources of contact information include:

REO Key Contact Directory (www.foreclosures.com/www/pages/mastering_deals.asp). An exclusive, newly updated in 2008, national contact listing of lender-owned property decision makers; includes their direct telephone and fax numbers, and web/e-mail addresses (where available).

REO Network (www.reonetwork.com). An online directory of screened real estate professionals specializing in remarketing of REO properties.

Working RE (www.workingre.com). Published by the nonprofit Organization of Real Estate Professionals, providing information and articles that can help you identify and locate lender contacts.

Organization of Real Estate Professionals (www.orep.org). Industry organization that has provided education and information to real estate professionals for more than 14 years; also a source to find lender contacts.

you want the lender/bank to take your discount offer seriously. Not only must your numbers be persuasive, but their packaging should attest to your professionalism.

Find out about the lender and its portfolio as well as the property, current markets, and pricing. Does the lender currently have a backlog of REO properties? Is the lender facing any funding, financing, or, in the case of a big corporation, shareholder issues? Is its nonperforming asset base getting too big? (You can check that with a publicly traded company by reading its financials that are sometimes accessible via its web site or via MSN Money at http://moneycentral.msn.com/home.asp.) Perhaps a lender might even consider selling more than one property at once or a package deal.

This is not a one-on-one purchase from a homeowner. You will initially present your proposal to an individual employee or agent of a lender/bank who will, in turn, present your offer to someone else and, quite possibly, to a committee to decide its fate. If the formal proposal addresses questions before they're asked, you stand a better chance of winning the deal. Some questions you can answer for the lender include:

- What's the current time on market for comparable properties?

- Among pending sales, what are comparable properties in the same area going for?

- What is the estimated cost of rehab and repair for the property?

In Lyle's case, even though he knew the lender representative handling the property and was pretty sure he had a deal, he put together an impressive package. It spelled out the advantages to the lender of an immediate, as-is, all-cash sale, including removing a nonperforming asset from the lender's already strained bottom line, the current slow market, and more. Lyle had checked out the lender and knew its REO portfolio was overflowing. He alluded to that in his proposal and used current time-on-market and selling statistics to bolster his statements. His goal was to make the deal easy for the agent and everyone else involved.

Dealing with Agents, aka the Schmooze Factor

To make a deal (and, it is hoped, subsequent deals) work, you must learn how to preserve the integrity and reputation of the bank/lender's agent or Realtor while achieving your own goal—to purchase the property at your discount. No matter what transpires, no matter how transparent or convoluted or crazy an agent's actions might seem to you, never burn your bridges. Make the agent/Realtor look good, and you will be rewarded many times over in the long run.

The agent or Realtor is simply one more person you have to sell on buying into the deal. Small talk is fine and part of the equation, but never lose sight of the fact that you're the salesman in an REO deal and the agent is your customer/buyer.

Dealing with Overinflated Values

Standard operating procedure for many Realtors or agents is to tell their employer—the bank or lender—that a property is worth more than it really is. It's a ploy to get the listing. If you research the property, you know that the agent has inflated the property's value, and the agent probably knows that you know. But rubbing that fact in the agent's face won't get you the desired results.

Instead, forget your ego and concentrate on your job, which is helping that agent sell your discounted deal—even more discounted, by the way, because of that initial inflated property value—in a way that upholds his reputation.

Persuasive Arguments

Be persuasive in your offers. This form of foreclosure investing is, after all, about creating win-win situations for both parties. A few things to keep in mind include:

- Although your dollar offer is lower than the initial asking price, it represents a *sold* property on the books versus an *expired listing*. In other words, sold is better than losing a listing.

- Don't submit lowball offers to agents without first asking the seller's bottom-line price. If the listing price is firm, don't write a lower offer or you'll earn a reputation as a lowballer and your offers won't be taken seriously. Word will spread among the industry, too, and you'll have trouble elsewhere.

- If an agent says the lender is ready for an offer and for you to "write something up," don't stop there. Ask more questions about what the lender really wants and needs. The more questions you ask, the more likely you are to make your offer close to what the seller really wants.

- A good rule of thumb in dealing: Never write an offer if the two of you are more than 20 percent apart on price.

*Don't count on REO investing as your bread and butter
because banks and lenders may not be motivated enough yet
to discount prices fairly significantly. But do build up your
cash flow to be ready to go, because, if foreclosure
inventories keep rising, banks likely will end up
with too many properties and will in turn accept
big discounts—maybe even selling REO
properties for 60 cents on the dollar.*

—Daryl White, ForeclosureS.com coach,
successful foreclosure investor

When presenting your offer, use market facts to help sell your case. For example, show how the market has changed since a property's initial valuation by using comps (prices on comparable properties in the area) and facts about the property or its geographic area. A property might not be located in a good school district, for example, and hence is unlikely to draw young parents. Or, as is common with older homes, the neighborhood could be in transition. An especially relevant selling point for your discount deal these days is the slow and stagnant home-sales market. Facts like these and more make it easier for an agent to defend accepting a discount offer for an REO property. Again, it's about preserving that agent's image and integrity. As a philosophy, "You scratch my back, and I'll scratch yours" works well in REO buying. You may even end up that agent's pocket buyer.

REO investor Cody W. identified a solid property, contacted the lender owner, and was referred to its REO agent—we'll call him Louie. Even before they met, Cody knew it was going to be a tough sell. Cody had heard of Louie, who had a reputation for being arrogant, obnoxious, and a know-it-all who didn't know much. From what Cody had heard, no one could understand why anyone would hire Louie to represent any property. But the property Cody had flagged was ideal for REO purchase and had solid profit potential if Cody could just get the numbers to line up.

So Cody prepped himself with all the facts and figures, determined his bottom line, sucked it up, and met Louie—who was exactly as expected. When Cody inquired about a discount, Louie reacted accordingly: "Under no circumstances am I in the slightest bit interested in a discount sale to a small investor who can't even afford to pay full price!"

Undaunted, Cody gently probed a bit further, calmly asking questions about the property, and lo and behold! Louie gave an inch. "What kind of an offer?" he asked.

Rather than simply throw the numbers out on the table, Cody prefaced his offer with some schmoozing. He gave Louie various solid (and factually supported) reasons why a discounted deal would make sense for the lender. He also pointed out that a fast, all-cash, as-is sale would be to Louie's credit in the eyes of the lender. He then gave Louie a full-blown presentation of the numbers and how they worked to the advantage of both sides. Impressed with Cody's professionalism and demeanor, Louie agreed to take the thorough, formal proposal back to the lender. Louie also conveyed Cody's persuasive arguments to the lender, who eventually gave Cody the deal.

As an aside, Cody ended up on Louie's pocket buyer list. The point is, if you leave your ego at home and replace it with persuasive facts and figures, you can come out a winner no matter whom you're dealing with.

TAKEaway

- REO property owners—lenders and banks—generally have an efficient REO property management team.

- They don't have to sell to you. However, holding on to an REO property costs them money out of pocket and keeps a nonperforming asset on the bank or lender's balance sheet. It also cuts into their liquidity, which is the ability to lend money to others. Capitalize on that.

- Target the right person at the bank/lender to pitch your deal. To make sure you do that, pay a reputable provider for its up-to-date REO lender/bank information with links to the REO lender's team.

- To sell your deal, make sure your presentation to the lender/bank representative is thorough, professional, and answers as many of their potential questions as possible.

- Know the right way to deal with the bank's agent. If he has exaggerated numbers to get a listing and you know it, don't rub it in his face. Learn how to capitalize on that to your advantage. Work with him and you may end up a pocket buyer.

CHAPTER 9

Short Sales

*Don't believe the hype. Short sales are **not** your way to get rich quick. There is much more to them than meets the eye.*

—Alexis McGee

n today's charge-it world of maxed-out credit, plenty of homeowners end up with multiple liens on their properties. The mess gets stickier when you stir in the subprime loan debacle, in large part the result of overly zealous loan officers pushing creative financing on overextended consumers who couldn't afford those mortgages. And it was all done in the name of the American dream— homeownership.

Add deflated home prices to the mix, and you have a recipe for disaster: property owners with negative equity who owe more than the value of their property. Unfortunately, that's a harsh reality today. Many of these homeowners can't sell their properties to a third party or even refinance because the proceeds won't cover what's owed. Even factoring in bailouts from government, industry, and private organizations for certain qualified homeowners, many are still left with few options but foreclosure.

Fortunately for some, the lender may buy into a compromise in the form of a short sale. In a short sale or short payoff, the lender agrees to write off the portion of a mortgage balance that's higher than the value of the home. The seller must have a proven financial hardship, and a buyer must be on hand and ready, willing, and able to purchase the property at the fair market value. Many other variables and ramifications are involved. But done right, a short sale can be that all-important win-win for all parties:

- The seller gets rid of the property and its crippling debt pre-foreclosure, thus preserving his credit.
- The bank/lender's loss is mitigated.
- You, the buyer/investor, can add equity to a deal that initially didn't have any so that you can flip it for a profit.

No Free Lunch

Buying a property for less than is owed on it sounds like a great deal—no problem, no sweat. The come-ons are everywhere. All sorts of people may tout making fast, easy money with short sales. But you know better. The business of foreclosure—all aspects of it—takes hard work and a thorough understanding of the issues and their ramifications. Banks *aren't* in business to give away money, and neither are you. Of course, neither one of you wants to set yourself up for huge losses, either. But keep in mind, too, a bank is under no obligation to accept a short sale offer even if a homeowner in default owes more on the property than it's worth.

Why Bother with Short Sales?

Aside from the fact that a short sale helps a homeowner in default walk away from crippling debt with his credit intact, the right short sale with the right discount and the right numbers can net solid profits for an investor interested in flipping the property.

Why would a bank even consider forgiving part of the debt if a homeowner can prove hardship? There could be several reasons:

- A sale allows the bank to avoid the cost of foreclosing and managing a property REO, if necessary.
- As markets move downward, a short sale enables a lender to immediately quantify a loss as opposed to waiting for an even lower price with an REO sale.

- Selling off the property, even at a discount, reduces the drain on a bank's liquidity by freeing up funds from its required nonperforming assets reserves.

- Divesting the property allows the cash to be reinvested sooner than if the lender waited for the foreclosure process to run its course or for an REO sale to be held.

With today's glut of subprime foreclosures and trouble-plagued subprime lenders, savvy investors may want to reexamine the short-sale approach if a subprime lender is involved, says Ian Maker of REO Deal Makers. A lender may want or need to liquidate its portfolio, and you may be able to pick up great deals at a discount.

Keep in mind, though, bank asset managers must follow specific guidelines on what they can and cannot accept in terms of a deal or discounted sale. Although guidelines vary depending on the financial institution, many are not allowed to accept less than 80 percent of the loan balance, says Maker. If, for example, a loan is in default for $100,000, the lender may take no less than $80,000 for it. But if that $80,000 is for a home with $150,000 market value and needing few repairs, the property can be worth your while as an investor.

I don't bother with short sales because there's too much paperwork and too many headaches. Many times you go through all their hoops and paperwork, and then the bank will say no anyway.

—Christian Rooney, successful foreclosure investor

Your profits, however, may not be as great as with other forms of pre-foreclosure and foreclosure investing. That's precisely why ForeclosureS.com coach Daryl White stays away from short sales. "I don't do them because it's lots of work and little profit. I can negotiate a short sale deal with a homeowner and the whole process may take a couple of months, but the bank/lender won't accept my discount, and instead approves a price that nets me only $30,000 (6 percent) on a median-priced $500,000 home in Southern California. Whereas if I worked with that same homeowner in default on a pre-foreclosure deal that involved equity, my profits likely would be closer to my 15 percent or $75,000."

Navigating a Bumpy Road

It sounds simple. But we know better. Like an REO, a short sale means you must negotiate with the bank and homeowner in default. But unlike an REO, the road to this kind of pre-foreclosure sale is loaded with obstructions. Let's look at a few.

> *Job loss alone doesn't qualify as hardship when it comes to a lender forgiving a portion of a mortgage debt with a short sale.*
>
> —Ian Maker, REO Deal Makers

The Hardship or Not

To begin with, a lender rarely has incentive to take less than full value for a loan and will not accept a short sale unless the homeowner in default can prove hardship. The homeowner must have significant issues that prevent him from meeting the mortgage obligation. No hardship, no sale, says Maker of REO Deal Makers.

Generally, a lender will try to work with homeowners who end up in default because they have lost their job. Some workout options to avoid foreclosure include:

- *Forbearance.* A lender may opt to allow the borrower to pay back the money through installment payments over six months or to pay a reduced monthly payment until he can get back on his feet financially. The borrower can then pay any remaining outstanding loan delinquencies in a lump sum.

- *Loan modification.* The terms of the original note can be changed and can include a cut in the loan's interest rate, reamortizing the remaining balance, extending the term of the loan, or other options.

- *Refinancing.* If a borrower has an outstanding past credit history, a lender may allow him to refinance the existing mortgage, wrap in any late payments and fees, and cash out part of his equity in the home so that he can regain control of a debilitating financial situation.

Unfortunately, these days the latter—refinancing—is no easy thing, no matter how good your credit is, because the nonconforming loan business has all but evaporated in the wake of the subprime debacle.

On the good-news front, however, the Federal Housing Administration (FHA) has stepped up to the plate to fill some gaps. With proposed and existing reforms, qualified homeowners facing or already in default have more ways to hold on to their homes. Among those new options is FHASecure, an affordable refinancing alternative for qualified homeowners already in default. To qualify, homeowners must meet specific criteria, including the following:

- A history of on-time mortgage payments before the borrower's teaser rates expired and loans reset.
- Three percent cash or equity in the home.
- Sustained history of employment.
- Sufficient income to make the mortgage payment.
- Temporary tax relief to ensure cancelled mortgage debt on a refinancing mortgage isn't counted as income.
- Interest rates must have reset, or be scheduled to reset, between June 2005 and December 2008.

As an investor, that means that if you can work with qualified homeowners still in pre-foreclosure, you may be able to steer them toward what could be another solid alternative to foreclosure.

Stay tuned, too. At press time Congress was considering more FHA changes that will greatly help homebuyers find financing when we as investors sell our properties, including:

- Raising the ceiling on the dollar amount of its loans so they're more accessible to those living in areas with higher-cost homes.
- Greater flexibility to set down-payment requirements.
- Extending maximum loan maturity to 40 years to reduce borrower's monthly mortgage payments.
- Revising the often burdensome FHA requirements for condominium loans.

In December 2007, the federal government also announced an agreement with mortgage lenders and loan servicers designed to help ease the nation's foreclosure crisis. The voluntary program would allow certain qualified homeowners with crippling ARMs to refinance or freeze the interest rates on their loans for five years. Lenders aren't required to participate, and the plan affects primarily a limited number of borrowers who can afford to pay their low teaser-rate mortgage, but not the higher resets.

Proving the Hardship

A job loss alone isn't enough to declare hardship unless you can't get another job, says Maker. "Being over your head is not a reason to walk away from your financial obligation. It's like going out and buying a Ferrari when you can only afford a Capri."

As crazy as it sounds, many self-proclaimed foreclosure investors push for short sales when there is no hardship, and then they can't understand why a lender turns them down. As an advanced foreclosure investor, don't let that happen to you. Ascertain the hardship up front, and then work to make the foreclosing lender understand it, too.

Beyond loss of job and inability to get another one, real hardships include medical problems that preclude a homeowner from getting another job, crippling and unexpected medical expenses, terminal illnesses, and more.

The homeowner in default and facing foreclosure must explain his problem in a hardship letter, which is part of the short-sale package submitted by the investor. The hardship letter states the problem, provides proof of the problem, and then explains why the homeowner is financially insolvent as a result. The key here is to give the lender plenty of reasons to justify writing off the loan.

For example, if Eric, an unemployed contractor in Detroit, can't get work because the local market has collapsed, the letter had better explain the situation and show how Eric already has tried to get work. Simply not wanting to work doesn't cut it as an excuse for copping out on a mortgage debt.

If Jake recently fought with his boss and lost his job as a computer programmer (a job in high demand), that's too bad, but he'll have to find some way other than a short sale to resolve his mortgage default problems.

Do yourself a favor and carefully check out the hardship claimed by a homeowner in default. Don't simply take his word for it. Your integrity and reputation with the lender are on the line.

Elements of the Hardship Letter

The contents of a hardship letter that accompanies the short-sale deal proposed to the lender (see Figure 9.1) include:

- Nature of the hardship, such as a medical issue combined with unemployment, or job loss and inability to get another one.

- Proof of the hardship.

- How the hardship creates financial difficulties that preclude repayment of the loan.

- Details of the homeowner's insolvency.

RE: Loan No. 000123456789

TO: Acme Mortgage
FROM: Mr. and Mrs. John Q. Public
Date: September 2, 2007

Dear Sirs:

Regarding our loan number, 0001234546789, we would like you to strongly consider accepting a lesser payoff than the $105,000 that we show we owe you on the loan on our home at 1234 American Dream Circle, Pleasant Town, Michigan.

As you are aware, we are significantly in arrears on the above stated loan. We have no hope of catching up and fear that if you don't accept our short payoff, and if we are unable to come to a mutually acceptable agreement on this, our home will be added to your long list of foreclosures.

Please see the enclosed comparable sales data, which shows the substantial decrease in the home values and the market in our area. We attempted to sell the home at a higher price (see enclosed listing agreement). Our initial asking price was $117,000. But despite continually lowering the asking price, the home remained on the market for seven months without selling.

I am an auto welder by trade and have been out of work and unable to find another job since being laid off by General Motors in Flint, Michigan, on December 15, 2006 (see enclosed employment termination letter). My wife and I are the primary caregivers for my elderly parents who live nearby, are sickly, and are on a low fixed income, so neither of us can move from the area in search of work.

The only income we have coming in right now is from my wife, who does in-home day care for the maximum number of children allowed by law. This nominal income is barely enough to buy us food and keep our utilities turned on.

As you will see with the information we've included with this letter, I haven't worked all year, and my wife has made very little. With the region's depressed economy and high jobless rate, our prospects are bleak for any additional income going forward into next year, too.

Please consider approving our hardship in that we ask you to accept a discounted payoff of $71,000 on our loan above (Reference Loan No. 0001234456789). We have a fully qualified buyer for our home only for that amount (see the enclosed prequalification letter from ABC Bank). We will receive no money at the close of escrow.

Please do consider our offer. Thank you.

Mr. and Mrs. John Q. Public

Enc: 1099s; 2005 tax return; 2006 tax return; bank statements (January-September 2007); General Motors employment termination letter; prequalification letter from ABC Bank; real estate listing agreement.

FIGURE 9.1   Hardship Letter

"One of the reasons I don't have any problems with short sales is that I always verify what the hardship is," says Maker.

Plenty of Proof and Documentation Required

When proposing a short sale, get ready to pull together extensive proof and documentation that the seller is broke and you, as the buyer, aren't. In order to agree to forgive part of the mortgage debt, the lender must know beyond a doubt that the homeowner has no other assets to tap. *Broke* means no cash flow or assets, whether savings, investments, trusts, retirement funds, or other finances that could be potential sources of cash. Again, it's about making your deal an easy write-off for the lender.

As for your part in the deal, the lender needs to know—with supporting documentation, which typically includes three months of bank statements—that you have the cash to do the deal and won't default. The lender, understandably, doesn't want to throw away his money or his property.

Remember, you're dealing with major, impersonal corporations that must justify their gains, losses, and bottom lines to shareholders. You can't escape the numbers.

Deficiency Judgment

Complicating a short sale in some instances is the possibility of a deficiency judgment that can be levied against the homeowner for the part of the debt that's forgiven. A deficiency is the difference between the amount of the outstanding loan and the fair market value of the property as determined by the court in a judicial foreclosure (not in nonjudicial ones). If it's discovered that a borrower has liquid assets to cover the loss, some lenders will decline the short sale and require the owner to pay the loss.

However, judicial foreclosure is expensive and deficiency judgments can be tough to get and even tougher to collect, so some lenders may accept a short sale anyway.

The Lien Issue

Unlike an REO purchase or foreclosure sale, short sales are pre-foreclosure deals, hence they don't automatically wipe out all junior liens against a property. If you opt for a short sale, remember that you're taking the property subject to those liens. All liens and loans become your responsibility.

Last-Minute Deals

Because a short sale means a lender will take a loss on a property, many lenders refuse to discuss the possibility until the last minute before a foreclosure auction. They'll stall or reject your short-sale advances until it becomes clear the property is unlikely to sell at the auction. As a result, if a short sale is your goal, you must be prepared to move at the right time—at the end of the reinstatement period—and do so quickly. Have your documentation in place, your financing lined up, and your homeowner on board.

Finding the Deals

First, I don't search for short sales. There are just too many, and I'd rather work pre-foreclosure ones with equity instead. I only get involved in short sales when I have a pre-foreclosure deal that makes my first cut when I cull my lists for minimum equity—30 to 40 percent, depending on current market conditions. Then after talking to the owner, I may find out that he has another loan that makes my deal too thin. At that point if I want to pursue the deal, I can either take the backdoor, note-buying approach or do a short sale.

If in these situations you decide to go for the deal, check to make sure Canceled Notices of Default haven't been filed, and then get out there and talk to the homeowners, their neighbors, and relatives. Unless you talk to those people, you won't know what the hardship is or whether it's bona fide.

Your short-sale presentation to the lender is black and white—the numbers and the hardship letter tell the story. Dealing with the homeowner to discover the hardship and the details surrounding it, however, is an exercise in the art of communication. It draws on the people skills learned in pre-foreclosure investing: being compassionate yet firm, asking open-ended questions, and then truly listening to the person's answers. Keep the conversation moving with the homeowner by feeding back to him what you just heard him say, and then ask for elaboration. That way you'll get the full picture of what's happening in his life.

Whoever asks the questions is in control of the conversation.
If a homeowner asks you a question, answer it briefly, and
then end your response with another question for the
homeowner. That keeps them talking and you listening.

—Alexis McGee

In culling your lists, especially these days, pay particular attention to pre-foreclosures involving loans from troubled lenders. The abundance of such loans—we talked about some in Chapter 7—could mean deal potential. As mentioned earlier, many of these lenders have big incentive to take you up on your short-sale offer.

Working the Numbers

Short sale or not, your bottom line remains the fact that your offering price should not exceed 60 to 70 percent (the exact percentage depends on the current state of the local housing market) of a fixed-up property's market value minus the cost of its repairs and rehab.

Your Risks

Again, don't overlook or be reluctant to include your 15 percent profit—or a minimum $30,000 if the house is worth less than $200,000—in the equation. Although you have the opportunity to ascertain the condition of a property before a short sale—unlike with foreclosure auctions and deeds of trust purchases—you still incur plenty of risk. You earn your profit with that risk and all your efforts. As we've said, short sales are neither a quick nor easy approach to foreclosure investing.

Your risks are similar to any other pre-foreclosure investment. What happens if you can't get the former owners out? What happens if they trash the place? What happens if the rehabbed property doesn't sell quickly or for the price you anticipated? When vacant, how likely is the property to be vandalized? What about cost overruns on the repairs and rehab? All these unknowns and more could end up taking cash out of your pocket!

Items to Include in Your Deal Packet

- A cover letter that spells out the advantages to the lender in accepting your short-sale offer.

- The hardship letter.

- Your proposed deal—typewritten and on letterhead.

- Market statistics, including comps, average time on market, and current economic conditions.

- Documentation showing homeowner's insolvency, including tax returns, unemployment verification, liens, and more.

- Cost to foreclose and sell the property as REO, including all liens, penalties, taxes, foreclosure and selling expenses, and more, as well as repair and rehab costs.

The Equation

To determine if the numbers work, figure all the hard and soft costs we've discussed, including your profit.

If the numbers add up, go for the deal. If the numbers fall short, walk away.

Tips and Tricks

Short sale and REO agent expert Maker offers a few more tips to help ensure that a lender says yes to your short-sale offer:

- Be sure your numbers are in line and that you have all the figures to support the homeowner's claim of insolvency—tax returns, pink slips (job termination), and more.

- Know the exact dollars and cents of delinquencies, fines, taxes, and more levied against the property so you can present a complete and realistic package to the lender. You want the lender to see exactly what it will cost to take back the property through foreclosure.

- Include a complete broker price opinion (BPO) of the market value of the property. That's a broker's estimated selling price for a property.

- Include overall and local market statistics, too. If a potential short-sale property is located in a declining market, you want the lender to see easily that its best interests lie in accepting your proposed contract.

- Verify that a homeowner in default truly meets the criteria for what a lender/bank will accept as a legitimate hardship.

- Be realistic in your offer price. Don't just automatically slash the asking price to come up with your offer. After all, any deal needs to be a win-win for all parties—the lender, the REO agent, and you.

- Take an actual, physical look at the property so your offer makes sense. For example, your offer price for a property could be well below the asking price because the property needs a new roof or significant repairs.

- Look at the numbers. Know your property values.

Getting the Former Owners Out

Your hassles aren't necessarily over once you've done the short-sale pre-foreclosure deal. A big variable can be how and when to get the property's former owners out. They do have to leave—and the quicker, the better. Homeowners in this situation often think you've bailed them out, and therefore they needn't be in any hurry to vacate.

Wrong! You're an investor, and this is advanced foreclosure investing. Your responsibility is not their welfare at the expense of yours. This is, after all, about buying a property and flipping it for your own profits.

Always set a deadline in your short-sale offer contract for the former owner to move out—at most, two weeks after the closing. If you run into resistance, consider the cash-for-keys option. Offer them cash in their pocket as an incentive to leave sooner rather than later. If that doesn't work, immediately begin formal eviction as discussed in Chapter 2. Keep in mind, too, that the lender will not like (and often includes a disclosure in any short-sale contract that disallows) any money going to the former homeowner. Remember, the bank or lender agreed to settle for less than the amount due on the loan because the property's owner was destitute, so allowing that former owner any profits just doesn't fly.

The eviction process varies by state and can be quite lengthy—and costly—for you. But the former owners must vacate or else you've simply funded their living expenses with money coming out of your pocket. You would do better to donate the money to your favorite nonprofit for homeless people. That way, your dollars

Tales from Foreclosure Investors

Lou and Louise were always looking for real estate investments. They already owned several houses around town as well as a couple of condos and vacation homes. They considered all their properties solid investments. When they heard about their next-door neighbor Marie's mortgage default plight, they were sympathetic and interested in how they might help. Marie was seriously delinquent on her mortgage (more than 90 days past due), out of work, and had sold off virtually everything to pay her bills. A notice of foreclosure sale had been filed against her home.

After consulting with their real estate attorney, Lou and Louise decided to offer to buy Marie's home through a short sale. They liked the idea of owning the property next door and figured it was perfect for their son, who had recently graduated from high school and as yet had no plans for college. They thought the lender might agree to take a short payoff given that Marie really had no assets for the lender to tap. Lou and Louise could even use their own cash on hand to do the deal.

The lender was thrilled to unload the property quickly and without the expense of the foreclosure process. Lou and Louise bought the house, assuming Marie would move out or, as she promised, pay rent "for a couple of months" if necessary until she got things squared away.

A year later, without having received a single rent payment, Lou and Louise were forced to threaten eviction to get Marie to move. If only they had followed a major rule in short sales: *Set the move-out date in the contract and stick with it.*

would go a lot further toward helping others. Don't view yourself as the evil investor, either. Eviction is the very real consequence of foreclosure, which is a consequence of living beyond one's means.

Honesty versus Deception

Beyond the cash-for-keys scenario mentioned earlier, other integrity issues can arise with short sales. For example, some people suggest that the short-sale investor in some way compensate a homeowner in default so that the investor can then purchase the property via short sale. A common practice is for the buyer to write a bill of sale for furniture or something else in the home to legitimize the cash changing hands. Again, it's not something the lender would approve of, so disguising that personal property sale is really walking along the gray line of fraud, says Daryl White.

Likewise, avoid inflated comps and appraisals, phantom contracts, or under-the-table payments. They're outright fraud.

On the homeowner's side of the equation, be careful, too. Find out up front if a homeowner wasn't honest on the original loan application. His insolvency today could be rooted in financial trouble that began before he purchased the home. If he didn't reveal the issues in the beginning, that could spell trouble for your deal and fraud from the past for the homeowner.

Another bit of dishonesty that has surfaced with short sales in the past is the buyer/investor failing to tell the homeowner in default that by agreeing to a short sale, he may incur a tax liability. Traditionally, in the eyes of the IRS, the difference between the loan's full value and the amount of the sale (the amount of the loan that is forgiven in a short sale) is miscellaneous income. The lender then would issue an IRS Form 1099 to the home's seller even though he received no cash from the sale and the property is lost through foreclosure or a deed in lieu of foreclosure. Capital gains taxes are due on the *income* just as if a third-party sale occurred. The reasoning: A borrower cannot be allowed to pull his equity out (i.e., capital gain) through a loan and then dispose of the property by deed in lieu of foreclosure or foreclosure without paying taxes on the capital gain already realized from the property. However, in December 2007, as part of its Mortgage Forgiveness Debt Relief Act of 2007, Congress approved a three-year window that allows homeowners to avoid this tax catch-22 from a short sale (http://www.whitehouse.gov/news/releases/2007/12/20071220-3.html).

TAKEaway

- A short sale is a compromise in which the lender agrees to take less than the amount due on the loan in exchange for getting a nonperforming loan off its books and saving the costs of foreclosure.

- For a short sale to work, the seller must prove financial hardship, and a qualified buyer must be on hand and ready, willing, and able to purchase the property at the fair market value.

- Make sure to ascertain that a hardship truly exists. Otherwise it's a waste of your time and the lender's time.

- Make sure your deal packet that you submit to the lender is complete and includes that letter of hardship with proof.

- Know the exact dollars and cents of delinquencies, fines, taxes, and more levied against the property so that the lender knows exactly what it will cost it to foreclose.

- If you do a short sale, set a date for the former owner to move out, and stick to it. This is not about charity. It's a business deal.

- Avoid doing anything in connection with a potential short sale that could be construed as illegal or unethical from the point of view of any of the parties involved, including the lender, the homeowner, the IRS, and you as an investor.

PART V

REO AUCTIONS

The hype is part fact and part fiction. The real result is you must work hard to find the bargains.

—Alexis McGee

CHAPTER 10

The Phenomenon Is on a Roll

*Auction companies are masters at marketing and selling,
and creating a crowd of frenzied bidders. Be prepared
before you bid, and hang on tight to your wallets!*

—Alexis McGee

"**T**housands of homes for sale below market value!"

"Find your property and make your bid online from the comforts of home, then walk away a big winner!"

"No money down. Get a home for pennies on the dollar."

Welcome to today's highly publicized, heavily promoted world of REO auctions—a phenomenon that is rapidly gaining steam as bank- and lender-owned real estate gluts the market. The savvy foreclosure investor realizes, however, that the hype surrounding REO auctions is part fact and part fiction.

An REO auction occurs when a lender or bank (or group of lenders or banks) ends up with too many REO properties and, in turn, bundles those properties and contracts with a private auction house to sell them. The trend these days is to turn the auctions into big events splashed across the media and trumpeted locally, statewide, and even nationally. Although the media stories—and the auctions themselves—draw big audiences and big headlines, the fine print that can easily trip up bidders and investors is sometimes overlooked, lost in the hype and hoopla.

The purpose of the massive publicity, of course, is to drum up business, attract hordes of bidders, and drive up the prices paid for the properties. It's the law of supply and demand in action: The more bidders on a property, the more—and higher—bids there are likely to be. Thus far, the approach seems to be working well. (See Figures 10.1 and 10.2 for samples of actual auction announcements from Hudson & Marshall.)

FIGURE 10.1   Sample Auction Cover

FIGURE 10.2   Sample Auction Listings

Fact versus Fiction

Buyer beware! REO auctions are a bonanza for banks, not buyers. Don't fall for the myth that you can snatch up fistfuls of deals on foreclosed homes at the REO mega auctions popping up across the country. It's just not true.

- In April 2007, Texas-based auctioneers Hudson and Marshall (www.hudson andmarshall.com) auctioned 450 REO properties in Detroit. Initial bids were set low, but the auction drew a huge audience of bidders from across the country, with subsequent competitive bidding pushing many property prices to or above their market value.

- In May 2007, the Real Estate Disposition Corporation (REDC; www.ushome auction.com), an affiliate of LandAuction.com Inc. (www.landauction.com), auctioned off several hundred Southern California properties. Afterward, the company boasted in its ads to other REO lenders that it had sold "Over $100 Million at 95% of Sellers' BPOs!" at the auction. (BPO stands for *broker price opinion*, or the broker's estimated selling price for a property.) To put the touted 95 percent in perspective, properties that are sold conventionally on the MLS average about 90 percent of their BPO price.

Tales from Foreclosure Investors

Sharon quickly discovered that, at a foreclosure auction, not all is as some people would like you to believe!

Ready and eager for her first REO auction, Sharon had researched and visited nearly half the properties due to be auctioned, a tall order given that 178 properties were up for auction. To her surprise, instead of run-down, as-is properties, most of the homes were in decent condition. The sellers had cleaned them up in anticipation of getting top dollar for their REOs. The few properties that were terribly run-down and in bad neighborhoods showed no sign of repair or rehab—as if the sellers didn't expect them to sell anyway, so why bother to fix them up?

Then came the auction. Adding to Sharon's surprise, the audience was filled with real estate agents and homebuyers rather than investors like herself hoping to pick up good buys. As the bidding began, prices on the best properties skyrocketed quickly, thanks to what seemed to be "plants" in the audience.

No deals here for Sharon. Most properties sold with price tags close to or above their original MLS price.

The moral of the story: Do your research early, and learn to see the warning signs that spell "no deals" up front. Then forget going to the auction and enjoy life instead!

- REDC held another auction of about 200 homes in Denver, Colorado, in August 2007. The event took place in that city's convention center and almost 1,000 people turned out. The bidding was hot and heavy. Needless to say, bargains were few and far between.

The Real Competition

You get the idea. REO auctions rarely mean instant bargains. In fact, the banks holding REOs often are your competition, only with deeper pockets and sophisticated property-management departments, to boot. Contrary to what others may say, the lenders don't *have* to sell their properties. They can and will wait to maximize their profits or minimize their losses. So don't head to an REO auction expecting to get a great bargain on a wonderful house in a choice neighborhood. You should not go as a bidder at all until you know the drill and the players. Instead, attend some auctions first as an observer only.

"It's a little bit overwhelming the first time around, especially with the speed of it, understanding the auctioneer, and the fact you're already nervous from the prospect of making a big property purchase," says California foreclosure investor Doug Pereyda. "The good deals are very few and far between, depending on which auction you go to and the area. You must know what you're doing. I've seen most properties bid up to near retail prices just because of the well-oiled auction atmosphere."

Do your research on a property ahead of time. It's well worth the effort and will save you costly mistakes.

—Daryl White, ForeclosureS.com coach
and successful foreclosure investor

The Bargain Hunt

Of the REO auction craze, ForeclosureS.com coach Tim Rhode says: "With a glut of REOs, banks today are looking to REO auctions as a more efficient way of selling their properties than individual MLS sales. It's working, too, with banks getting 85 to 90 cents on the dollar. If you're a homeowner looking for a place to buy at a discount without a lot of time and effort, REO auction is a good way to go. But if you're an investor looking to buy and flip properties, I just don't think there's enough profit yet to make sense. But I am seeing a few clients get REO deals at discounts of up to 30 percent from the more aggressive banks," adds Rhode.

"The subprime mess has begun to affect the nation's economy, especially the real estate industry. I know of a title company in central California, for example, that's down to just three employees from 13 a year ago. It's beginning to spread throughout the community, too—to roofers, tradesmen, retail employees, and more. These people all have mortgages, so the banks end up deluged with people who can't pay their loans. They will either have to let these people put off their payments or sell the homes at a *deep discount*. It *is* coming!

"Whether there ever will be *enough* profit in the deal for us, though, depends on how bad things get," Rhode adds.

That's not to say bargains can't be found today. At some auctions, like a recent one in Detroit, you could pick up properties—albeit not the choice ones—for $30,000 or less.

If you want to score these gems, though, get ready to work for them! That's what Doug Pereyda did in California. Longtime foreclosure investor Mary Kay did too. The ForeclosureS.com coach recently added REO auctions to her long list of foreclosure-investing skills. You can do it, too, with the right approach and understanding. Let's look more closely.

The Real Numbers

Next time you hear the auction come-on for plenty of properties at cut rates, rather than swoon you might instead wonder how the auctioneers determine what a bargain is. Their numbers usually fail to compare the actual selling prices of these homes with their original MLS-listed prices.

To be successful at REO auction buying, you need to fully understand the different numbers used and how they relate to your bottom line. Must-know numbers include a property's MLS list price, its current market value, its auction price, and the percent discount off its current market value.

Keep in mind, too, what ForeclosureS.com coach Daryl White learned while dealing in REOs: A lender may artificially jack up its listed *market value* of a house in anticipation of you, the investor, looking for a *discount* purchase. So don't rely on what a bank, agent, or auctioneer says is the market price of a property. Determine it for yourself.

A buyer must also beware of *previously valued prices* that turn up in auction catalogs and listings, says Pereyda. Such numbers could be the absolute highest price a property sold for in the past (as in perhaps two years ago) and have little bearing on its market value today.

What the Numbers Signify

A property's key numbers that you hear tossed around in REO auctions by participants, auctioneers, and others include:

- *List price*. The asking price for a property as listed in the local MLS.
- *Assessed valuation*. The value of a property for tax purposes; in some cases it can be higher or lower than market value, depending where in the country the property is located. You can get that information from ForeclosureS.com's premium foreclosure-listing service or find it in the county's property tax rolls. (See Figure 10.3 for a sample property listing.)
- *Previous value*. The price paid for the home by the owner who lost it to foreclosure—often years out of date and much higher than the property's current market value. (See Figure 10.4 for a sample property deed/transfer history.)

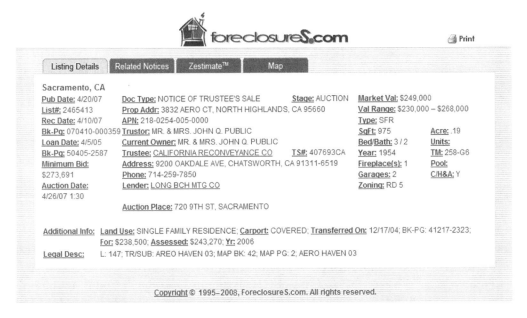

FIGURE 10.3   Sample Notice of Trustee's Sale, from ForeclosureS.com

---

Subject Property Deed/Transfer History:

Prior Transfer

Recording Date:	08/20/2007	Sales Price:	$152,500
Document #:	BK-PG 20070820-0361	Type of Sale:	Full-Computed from Transfer Tax
Document Type:	Grant Deed		
Multi APN Flag:			
Buyer Names:	MR. AND MRS. JOHN Q. PUBLIC	Buyer Vesting	Joint Tenancy
Care of Name:			

Mailing Address: 1234 ANY STREET, PLEASANT TOWN, USA
Seller Name: DEUTSCHE BANK NATIONAL TRUST, ; LONG BEACH MORTGAGE LOAN TRUST,

Mortgage Doc #:		Loan Amount:	N/A
Lender Name:		Interest Rate:	
Loan Type:		2nd Loan Amt:	N/A
Type Financing:			

Legal Description:
Lot: 147 Subdivision: AERO HAVEN UNIT 3 Map Ref: MAP2 MB42
City/Muni/Twp: NORTH HIGHLANDS

FIGURE 10.4   Sample Property Deed/Transfer History
© 2008, SiteXdata™, Fidelity National Information Services, Inc., all rights reserved.

- *Auction price*. The dollar amount a property sells for at auction; generally slightly lower than market value but, in the case of many current auctions, comparable to list price.

- *Percent discount off assessed value*. A common number used at auctions, it usually involves a discount from the *tax-assessed* value, which can be higher than actual *market* value.

- *Market value*. The dollar amount a property is likely to sell for, given the current market, after it's fixed up and rehabbed.

To figure the market value, once again you'll need the prices of comps—properties similar in size, age, construction, and style—that have sold in the past three months (up to six months if necessary) near your potential property. Use only those comps that are in top-notch condition. Then, using the same criteria, look for active and pending properties on your local MLS, Realtor.com, Metrolist.com, and other listings of properties for sale. Drive by those properties to make sure you can match them. Toss out those that obviously require too much updating/repairs to allow for a realistic purchase price/discount given current market conditions. Be conservative—use the lower end of the pricing numbers. What's left is your appraisal of the property after it's fixed up.

Understanding the Numbers

Here's a breakdown on some of the numbers for a typical property:

Original purchase price	$389,900
Original loan amount (10 percent down)	$350,000
Trustee sale minimum bid	$368,987
Trustees deed amount (REO)	$368,987
Current tax assessor's value	$399,000
Market value (current as-is)	$340,000
MLS-listed as-is price	$350,000
Opening bid at REO auction	$290,000
Sold price at REO auction	$310,000
Discount from tax assessed value	22%
Discount from current market value	9%

Source: ForeclosureS.com.

"Those comps are everything," says Pereyda. "Depending on the property's location and market conditions, before you set the market value you may also want to consider what those comparable properties will be selling for three months down the road, especially in today's market," he adds.

Why Deal with the Confusion?

Why bother with all the jargon, hoopla, and hassles in search of a foreclosure deal? Is this circus worth the price of admission?

Yes. If you do your background work on the properties, REO auctions definitely can be worth your while. At the Detroit auction mentioned earlier, the minimum bid on a property was only $1, with a $3,000 deposit required to bid. (The deposit is refundable if you're not the winning bidder). That kind of low-cost entrée into bidding on a property can translate into bargains. Some run-down properties in less desirable Detroit neighborhoods sold for less than the price of a car—and not a luxury model, either!

This is not as easy as people might think.
It takes an incredible amount of work.
Is the effort worth it? Stay tuned.

—Doug Pereyda, REO auction investor
and ForeclosureS.com student

How Skeptical Should You Be?

Before you get too enthusiastic about REO auctions, consider that at the Detroit auction, the desirable properties—great homes in great locations—brought in big money, while several other properties drew no bidders and remained REO. The moral of the story is that no matter what you hear, not every property sold at an REO auction is a bargain or even a sensible buy. It's up to you as an advanced foreclosure investor to recognize the difference between a deal and a dog, and to know when to walk away.

Don't, however, automatically reject REO auctions because of all the hassles, hype, and work involved. Like the other types of foreclosure investing described in this book, REO auctions should be considered one more valuable tool for a well-prepared advanced foreclosure investor.

Great bargains on properties to flip may not yet be widespread, but, as Rhode said earlier, be prepared and stay tuned. Those widespread discounts on prime properties at REO auctions may be closer than you think. As fallout from the sub-prime lending epidemic spreads across the housing industry, and as liquidity (the availability of credit) for everyone tightens, more homeowners will be left with fewer options. In that scenario, foreclosure numbers will continue to climb, and lenders' REO portfolios will keep growing.

Maximize Your Opportunities

If you want to maximize your chances to pick up a deal as a foreclosure investor, you must be patient and prepared to bid on all the properties in your selected geographic area of concentration. You'll need to review the properties, their titles, and their numbers. Auctions provide for several days or hours of open houses for potential buyers to see inside the homes. Absolutely and unequivocally, take the opportunity to physically visit the properties and their environs if you intend to bid on them.

> *I've watched people bid on some properties that I know*
> *they've never seen and don't really have a clue about,*
> *whether it's the condition of the property, the*
> *location, or some title complication.*

—Mary Kay, ForeclosureS.com coach, investor

Consider how Mary Kay prepared for one recent REO auction:

I preregistered online for the auction of approximately 200 properties. Of course you can't see all 200 properties in the time allotted for open houses, so after thoroughly reviewing the online auction catalog, I culled the list to 40 that matched my preset criteria. They were in my chosen geographic area, the right price range, right size to flip, and sounded like they had good potential.

Next I did my due diligence—still on the Web—with the help of DataQuick (www.dataquick.com; SiteXdata is another good source). The data service provides mortgage and lien histories of the properties, which includes the final dollar amount of the loan in default that resulted in the foreclosure and the lender subsequently taking back the property (the amount of the trustee's deed), and many more details.

Then I headed out to see all 40 properties in the three days of open houses. Some properties I immediately rejected due to either their poor location, floor plan, condition, or something else. Other properties I looked at, reviewed the title and pest reports provided on each property, assessed the condition of the properties and the cost of repairs and rehab. I was all business and not what I call a *lookie-lou*—peering into cupboards or opening closets—otherwise, I couldn't have seen all the properties in that short a time.

Instead I look at the big-ticket items—windows, roof, heating/cooling system, structural issues. The other things, like paint, replacing counters, cupboards, carpet, and whatever, are merely cosmetic and minor. But if a roof must be replaced, that can be $10,000; an air conditioner $5,000 to $10,000; and windows can run $6,000 to $10,000. If all three need replacing, that's a lot off the deal, so you must learn how to look quickly for signs and analyze potential repair issues. Stains on walls, for example, could mean water leaks, or dirt caked on the foundation might indicate termites.

Then I headed back to the office to do my comps. For each property, I looked at sales of similar properties over the past three months, considered the prices of current properties on the market, tossed out those that couldn't be replicated, and then averaged the rest to determine the market value for each property. I settled on eight properties that interested me. On each of those, I factored in the repair costs for each, subtracted out the buyer's premium—that's an extra cost tacked onto the winning bid that's a set percentage of the bid—then arrived at my maximum bid for each property. Whew!

The day of the auction, more than 3,000 people showed up to bid on just 200 properties! The auction was well coordinated from beginning to end, with various tables set up and staffed to provide every service you need to buy a property, from financing to escrow, immediate and on-site. Bidders beware here. Auction companies like novices, because with all the hype and auction fervor they're easy to bid up—to cajole into higher bids for properties. The auction company can also make money off any financing you do through their companies.

Admission to the auction was free, but bidding required a $5,000 cashier's check made out to me to be endorsed over to the auction company should I be a winning bidder. (The money goes toward the percentage of the down payment required if you're a winning bidder. Payment in full would then be due 21 days later *if* the REO property owner accepts the bid.) I showed the check and the letter from my lender stipulating preapproved financing, and picked up my 8-by-11 paper bidding card with my number on it. If you don't have financing, you're referred to one of the tables where ever-so-helpful people immediately run your credit and, of course, provide on-site financing.

If you're a winning bidder on a property, the auctioneer's helpers imme-diately escort you into a room to open escrow and make sure your financing is approved. If it's not, the property goes back out to auction, real time. If your deal is approved, you're in and out with escrow opened and the deal signed in two hours. (Not every auction or auction company is quite as efficient or thor-ough.) Of course, the REO property-owning bank/lender reserves the right to reject the bid within a certain length of time, as stipulated in the auction catalog.

A total of 147 properties sold at Mary Kay's auction. Based on a very conserva-tive estimate, the average selling price for a property was $250,000. That's a total of

Tales from Foreclosure Investors

Foreclosure investor Doug Pereyda talks about the carnival-like atmosphere at a California auction held by major national auctioneer, the Real Estate Disposition Corporation (REDC):

This particular auction drew at least 1,500 people to bid on only 65 properties. It was like a cattle auction and carnival combined. The right to bid cost $5,000 in the form of a cashier's check made out to oneself. You'd think that would limit attendance, but it didn't. (Winning bidders endorse the check over to the auctioneer and then make up the difference in the required down payment with a personal check.)

The fast-paced auctioneer would bring up a property, then begin his selling rant/chant. Meanwhile, auction assistants—I call them *yellers*—scurried around in the audience, and whenever someone raised a bidding card they'd run up to them, get in their face, and coach them to crank up their bid. It was comical and crazy, and—predictably—the audience would laugh, even as the bids went higher and higher.

I did make some bids, but it was a little overwhelming the first time around. Adding to the confusion was the fact that REDC completes the deals in real time during the auction so that if a property sells during the auction, the winning bidder is immediately taken into the backroom to finalize the deal. If the financing doesn't go through, the property is brought back into the auction and bidding on it resumes.

You have to know what you're doing, and you can't be intimidated by the process. Hudson and Marshall auctions that I've attended are a bit less performance, but just as fast-paced.

about $36.75 million taken in at that one auction alone. Each and every winning bidder paid a 5 percent buyer's premium. That's 5 percent of their winning bid that goes to the auctioneer to put on the auction, for a total of more than $1.837 million. Of course, the auctioneer must pay the cost of marketing the event and putting on the auction, as well as pay for escrow and other services, but however you add it up, the REO auction phenomenon sweeping this country involves big bucks for auctioneers, banks, and lenders.

You, too, *can* come away a winner, though. Mary Kay succeeded at this auction (more on that in Chapter 11), but it's not easy. "You must know your numbers. It's the only way to make it work. If you don't, you will get swallowed," she says.

Tom H. thought an upcoming REO auction in his hometown sounded like the perfect venue to pick up a property or two that he could then fix up and flip for a tidy profit. He dutifully checked out the properties and numbers that he thought would prepare him for the auction. Nearly 200 properties were on the auction block, but Tom was interested in only four, which he researched thoroughly. The day of the auction, Tom arrived early to get a good seat. Armed with his data on each of the four properties, he was sure he'd walk away a winner on at least one of the houses.

You can probably guess the rest of the story. Tom had run the numbers on those four homes only. All four were in demand and drew many bidders, who jacked up the prices well beyond Tom's maximum bids. A couple of great bargain homes came up later, but Tom missed out because he hadn't done all the work necessary on those deals. You don't know ahead of time which properties will end up being bargains at auction, so in this business you must be prepared to jump at whatever, whenever necessary.

Now for the Good News

If, as a foreclosure investor, you like the impersonal nature of the auction process, consider the distinct advantages of an REO auction over a courthouse or sheriff's sale, which is the individual property sale on the courthouse steps or lawn of the property in foreclosure. Although profits on REOs may not be as consistent or dramatic as profits from a courthouse sale, the upside is that you know what you're getting when you buy an REO property. As an investor, you have the opportunity to see inside an REO auction property before you buy. Take advantage of that opportunity! Walk the property with your contractor and see firsthand exactly what it is you'll be getting in exchange for your money.

No small advantage, either, is that REO auction properties come with clear title and title insurance. Aunt Bessie can't come knocking to collect the $20,000 she loaned so-and-so for a down payment, and Acme Plumbing can't try to collect that unpaid $18,000 mechanic's lien. If you have the winning bid at an REO auction, the property is yours, period. Of course, if a property has any outstanding IRS liens against it, that will be disclosed in your title report. If you opt to go through with the purchase, you're responsible for dealing with the liens. (Of note: Most lenders with a foreclosed property that has an IRS lien against it wait until after the 120-days redemption period is over before selling the property.)

"A healthy dose of skepticism is good," says Pereyda. "Be skeptical of some of the numbers the auction companies provide on properties, and be aware that just because you win a bid doesn't necessarily mean you'll get the house. The bank/lender owner generally has a specified window of time in which to accept or reject your bid.

"But if," Pereyda adds, "based on my research, a property is valued at $500,000 and my winning bid is $340,000 and the deal goes through, it's free and clear—no pre-foreclosure emotions, no fuzzy liens. It's an unemotional way to buy property. It's ironic that the setting you buy it in is so emotional."

A Word about Auctioneers

As we've mentioned, auctioneers can be a big variable. At Mary Kay's auction described earlier, REDC was the perfect picture of efficiency. Mary Kay, like Doug Pereyda, has been to other auctions that aren't as efficient. It depends on the auctioneer, the auction, and the location.

The National Auctioneers Association lists more than 6,000 auctioneers that sell real estate across the country. Not all states require them to be licensed, either, so pay attention to who is promoting and conducting an REO auction.

To help verify the legitimacy of an auction or auctioneer, check out its track record. Google the name and check for complaints through your local Better Business Bureau (or online at www.bbbonline.org). Don't forget to read real estate blogs, either. If many different people have complained about an auctioneer or have unresolved issues with it, you may want to avoid that auctioneer or, at the very least, pay close attention to what goes on at its auction.

Many of the most reputable auctioneers have national or state certification and belong to the National Auctioneers Association (www.auctioneers.org).

How to Decipher Auction Catalogs

Once again, ignore the hype. Hype equals higher prices, lower discounts, and more competitive bidding. You're far better off to pay close attention to the fine print. You may be surprised at what you find.

The Fine Print

The auction catalog takes various forms. If you are preregistered and request a catalog, some auctioneers will send you a full-color brochure via regular mail; others simply post it online and expect you to print it out. In whatever form it takes, the catalog includes the terms of the auction; the method of payment, including the amount down and when the full bid amount is due; the amount of the buyer's premium, which is that extra cost tacked onto winning bids to pay for the auction and auctioneer; and a brief description of each property.

Watch for the small print that says the auctioneer has the right to bid against bidders so the selling price meets the minimum reserve for that property. Minimum reserve is the lowest amount the bank/lender will accept for a property. Some auctions do not have minimum reserves. Others do.

Some fine print in the catalog may state that the auctioneer or bank/lender reserves the right to pull a property from the auction if that minimum reserve is not met. The bank or lender, too, can reject what you thought was a winning bid.

Mary Kay was ecstatic. She won the bidding with her $120,000 bid on a property ($126,000 total including the buyer's premium) that had a conservative market value of $199,000. The house needed $10,000 to $15,000 in repairs, but that still left a comfortable $58,000 to take care of buying, holding, and selling costs, as well as profit. All in all, it seemed a comfortable deal. Not so fast, however. Several days later the REO lender came back and wanted $145,000. Mary Kay's $120,000 bid did not make their unpublished minimum reserve, so she countered with $128,500. The seller rejected that, and Mary Kay walked away. Several months later the property remained unsold.

Pereyda won the bidding on a $160,000 property. He paid the $8,400 required down payment at the auction, and had 21 to 30 days to come up with the rest. Meanwhile, the REO owner had a certain number of days to reject his winning bid. Two hours before that time window closed, the owner called Doug and told him no deal, no explanation. He never saw mention of the property again, anywhere. "They sent the money back a month later," Pereyda adds.

Looking for Auctions or Auctioneers?

Some sources of information on REO auctions include:

- AuctionGuide.com (www.auctionguide.com).
- Hudson and Marshall Inc. (www.hudsonandmarshall.com).
- National Auctioneers Association (www.auctioneer.org).
- Real Estate Disposition Corporation (www.ushomeauction.com).
- Williams & Williams (www.williamsauctions.com).

Meanwhile, however, Pereyda found auction success elsewhere, buying a $272,000 property ($385,000 market value) at a Hudson and Marshall event in Modesto, California. "I've inspected many properties and attended numerous auctions," adds Pereyda. "You'll find a few diamonds in the rough, but don't underestimate the amount of work it takes to find the right deal."

Ask Questions

If you're not sure about something or if you have any questions, contact the auctioneer. They are well paid and have customer service departments that can help you. Many of the major auctioneers' sites as well as the National Auctioneers Association have very good FAQs and tutorials on auctions, too. Another source of information is The Gwent Group, a Bloomington, Indiana-based financial services consulting group that has analyzed trends in the auction industry (www.gwent group.com).

If you feel that something isn't right at the auction, challenge it. Don't let the auctioneers or their helpers—what Pereyda calls the *yellers*—intimidate you into bidding higher than you intend, either.

TAKEaway

- Ignore the hype, hunker down, and research the properties.
- For the maximum opportunity to pick up a good deal, you'll have to review all the properties up for auction.

- Always see any property you plan to bid on before the auction. If you can't physically see them all, limit your bidding to a predetermined group of properties and see all those.

- Be accurate in your assessments of the cost of rehab and repairs, as well as the comps for a property. As with other forms of foreclosure investing, you need to know these things so that you can figure your numbers accurately.

- Tune out the hoopla, and don't allow anyone to force you into raising your bid beyond your predetermined maximum.

- Make sure to include the cost of the buyer's premium in figuring your maximum bid.

- Watch for the small print in the auction catalog, contracts, and more. Sellers' contracts aren't generally buyer-friendly.

- Don't hesitate to ask questions.

CHAPTER 11

Time to Deal

Auctioneers work very hard at making an event fun. And it is, especially when no one is bidding on your deal!

—Alexis McGee

When someone suggests that REO auctions are a quick and easy avenue to investment riches, turn around and walk, no, run, to the nearest exit. No need to panic, though. As with every aspect of foreclosure investing, you get out of your investment what you put into it—whether time, commitment, money, or all three. Keep in mind Tim Rhode's advice in Chapter 2 on the importance of establishing personal key performance indicators (KPIs). If you use your KPIs as a map and truly follow it, you can realize tremendous financial gains from foreclosure investing.

But you can't rush the learning curve. Take your time to learn and understand the processes, legalities, and procedures—as well as the catch-22s—and when you know how to apply your knowledge to the opportunities at hand, you'll come out a winner.

Unique Requirements

Every REO auction is different. The terms of each vary depending on participating lenders, auctioneers, and even the locale. Following are some of the general terms and conditions from only two different auctioneers.

Auction Terminology

Absolute sale: Sold to the highest bidder (no minimum reserve).

As-is: No warranties expressed or implied.

Buyer's premium: An amount tacked onto the winning bid that's either a set fee or a percentage of the winning bid, which must be figured into the cost of a property; premiums based on a percentage should be clearly stated in an auction brochure.

Earnest money: Generally a set amount or a percentage of a sale price required to be paid by personal check, certified funds, or a cashier's check in order to bid on a property at auction.

Minimum reserve/seller's reserve: A minimum acceptable price set by the seller, who also has the last word on whether to accept the final bid.

Open bidding: Anyone who has registered to bid (and generally paid a preset deposit in the required form) may do so.

Opening bid: The minimum amount set by the auctioneer to open bidding—not the minimum price set by the seller.

Requirements of the Real Estate Disposition Corporation (REDC), which held the large auction in Northern California that we mentioned in Chapter 10, include:

- Each bidder must have a $5,000 cashier's check made payable to himself (or cash equivalent) in order to bid at any of the auctions.

- Winning bidders must have a personal or business check to cover the balance of the 5 percent total deposit required for any property purchased at the sale.

- Bidders must have a valid driver's license.

- Open houses must be held for bidders to inspect the properties prior to auction.

- Sellers guarantee clear title and buyer receives title insurance with purchase.

- Winning bidders have 21 days to close on the property.

- REO lender/bank maintains the right to reject the winning bid.

Compare and contrast those requirements with the some of the terms for the Hudson and Marshall Detroit-area auction that we also mentioned in the previous chapter:

- Bidders must have a valid driver's license and a $3,000 cashier's check deposit per property bid on.
- Generally, if you're the winning bidder, you must put down a total 10 percent (including your initial deposit) of the purchase price the day of the auction. You can pay the additional via personal or company check.
- Closing occurs 30 to 40 days after the auction date.
- If you're the winning bidder and don't close, your initial deposit ($3,000) may be forfeited.
- Open houses are held for bidders to inspect the properties before the auction.
- Full title insurance is provided and properties are free of all liens and encumbrances.
- Commissions are paid to buyer's agents who attend the auction with their buyer.

Terms and conditions at a particular auction can change at the last minute, too. Although you may be well informed about the specifics listed in a particular auction's catalog, listen to what's being said at the auction—it's the equivalent of reading the fine print in the catalog—and double-check to make sure you thoroughly understand the requirements.

Their Financing or Yours?

Pay attention to your financing, too. Although an auctioneer may tout the ease of its financing option—REDC folks are at the front door of some auctions, ready and waiting for you—choose your own instead. Stick to your own investor (hard-money) loans, lines of credit, your own mortgage brokers, or your investment cash supplier. You're likely to get a better deal in the long run, especially because you're interested only in an interim, short-term loan until you flip the property or, as may be the case in today's cooler market, refinance for more favorable terms. If you take another route, you could get slapped with fees and penalties for early payoff and more.

If you don't have either the ready cash or access to it (including the ability to qualify for a new loan), or a Rolodex of cash suppliers for your investments, or some other means of coming up with the money you need, you're probably not yet ready to buy investment properties at REO auctions. After all, a cornerstone of pre-foreclosure and foreclosure investing is knowing how and being able to quickly access ready cash for your deals. We talked a bit about where you can find the money in Chapter 8. Some sources include:

- "Money Available," "Cash for Real Estate," or "Investments Wanted" classified ads in your local or regional newspaper or online at sites such as Craigslist (www.craigslist.com), Creative Real Estate Online (www.creonline.com), and ForeclosureS.com (www.foreclosures.com).

- Google "hard money" and your city name to find local hard-money lenders, brokers, and their web sites.

- Real estate message boards such as Real Estate Forum (www.realestate forum.com), Real Estate Discuss (www.realestatediscuss.com), and Bigger-Pockets Forums (http://forums.biggerpockets.com) also can yield cash.

- Equity lines of credit on your house or margin accounts on your stock portfolios are a possibility, too, but do read the fine print first.

Your To-Do List

Once you have the financing covered, get ready to hunker down and perform the due diligence that's essential to these auction deals. Get connected to the Internet and grab a calculator, plenty of scratch paper, and a pencil, and get busy.

Preview the Properties

As an investor at an auction, you don't know in advance which property will end up being the best deal. That depends on the bidders and the bidding—or lack thereof. To maximize your investment opportunities, you must first review *all* the properties being auctioned. In an ideal world, you would visit every property, determine the necessary repairs for each, run the numbers on them, and then have a bid prepared for every one.

But, as Mary Kay pointed out in Chapter 10, it's almost impossible to visit each and every property for sale at a mega REO auction in the one to three days allotted for open houses. (With smaller auctions with fewer properties, it may be possible to preview every property, or you may have other opportunities to see them. With the latter, for example, if you're a Realtor and the homes are on the MLS, they may have key lockboxes so you can visit the homes over a longer period of time.) Take advantage of every opportunity to visit as many properties as possible. The more properties you see, the greater your chances of coming out a winner.

Mary Kay suggests starting your research by reviewing—at least on paper or computer—*all* the properties. Then, for practical purposes, cull the properties to those that conform to your investment criteria—the right price range, location, size, resale possibility, and more. What's left then becomes a much more manageable and realistic number of properties for your thorough review and inspection.

As you become more discerning and gain more auction experience, you, like Mary Kay, can be more selective in those auction properties that catch your eye.

Title Issues

The good news is that, no matter how many properties you review, you won't have to run title on each. Each property is REO, owned free and clear by the bank or lender, and comes with title insurance. Nonetheless, you still must perform the due diligence of discovering whether any federal tax liens are outstanding against a property. Remember, IRS liens have a 120-day redemption right to buy the house back from the REO lender. Hopefully the lender waited until after the 120-day period expired before selling the property. But there's no guarantee of that, so it's up to you to make sure. It's also to your bidding advantage to learn the amount of the foreclosed loan on each property, because that number represents the property's basic cost/loss to the bank—plus, of course, its internal management costs.

Historical information on an individual property's loans is available by subscription online through companies such as DataQuick (www.dataquick.com), SiteXdata (www.sitexdata.com), or other real estate information sources. Alternatively—and sometimes in addition to these—if you have a good relationship with a title company, you can work with them to get the information you need, or you can review the county's grantor/grantee directory online or off.

Drive by the Properties

Once you've done the preliminary paperwork, get in your car and start driving. "I spent three solid days looking at properties," says Mary Kay, and that was to review only 40 of the 200 properties scheduled for a particular auction. But, to emphasize: If you are considering bidding on a property, you must see it first. One look may dissuade you.

"I went to one property that sounded great on paper, but when I drove by, I discovered it was in the middle of an industrial area," says Mary Kay. "I immediately crossed it off my list without even going inside. With that location, there's no way it would be a good candidate for resale.

"At another potential property, the minute I walked in I turned around and walked out," she adds. "The floor plan was just too odd."

Remember, when selecting properties you plan to bid on, look for those with solid potential to flip quickly for a profit. Stick with middle-of-the-road, ordinary, starter-type homes with broad appeal. They are always in demand. By appealing to the broadest spectrum of potential buyers, you'll go a long way toward insulating yourself and your investments from the ups and downs of the market. Plus, if you decide to keep a house as a rental, small houses are a much safer investment because the cash flow is much better on a small, entry-level home rather than a larger, move-up size home. You also don't want a one-of-a-kind property that requires just the right buyer. That's not good business sense in foreclosure investing.

Estimate the Repairs

As you visit each property, assess the needed repairs. You likely won't have time to take your contractor with you, which means you must hone your observation skills so your cost estimates are accurate. Jot down the needed repairs and their costs for each house. A handy way to do that is to attach a bid repair sheet to a printout of each property listing. If you're not sure about the dollar amount for a particular repair, check with your contractor. In fact, you may want to show your contractor those bid repair sheets anyway just to double-check some of your numbers. After all, the more accurate the assessment, the more accurate your bid.

Keep in mind, too, the rule of thumb that ForeclosureS.com coach White has learned over the years: The cost of repairing normal wear and tear on a typical house averages about $15 a square foot.

Determine Property Market Values

After seeing the properties on your list and figuring repair costs for each, you must determine the market value for each house if it were fixed up to cherry condition. Given your time constraints, it makes no sense to order formal appraisals, so check those comps and the MLS to put together your own appraisals for *all* the properties.

Are you beginning to get the time-consuming picture? This form of foreclosure investing has nothing to do with your emotional involvement with a property or a homeowner. It is purely a question of dollars and cents and whether you are flexible enough to bid wisely on any property if, during the actual bidding, it turns out to represent a good deal.

Set Maximum Bids

Add to your lists a maximum bid for each property, and don't forget to factor in the buyer's premium. If you've been lucky enough to visit every property, make sure you set maximums even for those properties in terrible shape and the ones you can't stand. With the worst properties, figure in a profit greater than 15 percent as a cushion for the unknowns. It would be a shame to pick up a property for a good price only to have your gains eaten up by costs you didn't consider. As with other forms of foreclosure investing, I make sure to have at least 15 percent off the top, or $30,000 profit from the resale, no matter what.

Bottom line: Never, ever go over your maximum bid. It's easy to get caught up in the auction bidding frenzy, but don't. The auctioneer's job is to fuel that frenzy, and he is good at it. Bidding frenzy equates to higher prices for his clients' properties. When the bidding goes past your maximum, mentally let go of that property and wait for the next one.

Don't let an auctioneer or his assistants bully you into a higher bid, either. Auctioneers typically will try to bump up each bid in $5,000 increments. For example, if you bid $150,000, the auctioneer then would ask for $155,000. But anyone can bump up the bid by any amount unless the auction terms stipulate otherwise.

Mary Kay recalls an experience in which an auction assistant tried to raise her bid without her consent. To his chagrin, she objected and prevented him from doing so. Here's what happened.

A bidding auditorium or area typically is divided into sections with an easily identifiable auction assistant working each area. (These are the people referred to as *yellers* by investor Pereyda because they relay the bids to the auctioneer on the stage.) At this particular auction, Mary Kay raised her bidder's card to indicate she bid $150,000 for a property. Someone countered with $155,000, and the auctioneer looked to Mary Kay for $160,000.

"I countered with $155,500. But the assistant turned away from me and yelled to the auctioneer, '*$160,000*.' I was furious. I hadn't bid that, and I objected to his attempt to raise my bid. He was simply trying to bully me into a higher bid. But I stood my ground and told the assistant my bid was $155,500, period. He looked at me with disgust but changed the bid to $155,500. I ended up not getting that property," Mary Kay recalls.

"But no matter what, you can't allow them to bump your bids," she adds. "It's your money, and unless stipulated otherwise, you technically can raise a bid by $1 and they can't refuse it."

Winning Numbers

Let's see how the numbers add up for a condo Mary Kay recently purchased at an REO auction in Northern California.

Fixed-up market value	$230,000
Winning bid at auction	$165,000
Buyer's premium (5 percent)	$8,250
Total purchase price	$173,250
Minimal repairs/rehab	$8,000
Soft costs (quick deal with minimal buy, hold, and selling expenses)	$14,500
Total cost	$195,750
Profit of 15 percent	$34,250

Just as Mary Kay's bid was bumped without her authorization, yours could be, too. You may say, "No way," but believe me, it happens. Everything in an auction moves so quickly and so chaotically, anything can happen. And the auctioneers and their assistants do all they can to whip up the chaos because it helps them extract higher bids.

So stand your ground. It's easy to cave in, but that's not how you succeed in this business.

"I once allowed someone to outbid me by $5,000 on a property valued at $250,000 because I stuck to my guns on my maximum bid," says Pereyda. "Many people at auctions are buying for homeownership and are looking to get a good price on a property. So for those folks, going over a maximum bid might work out. But investors need bigger margins."

A Word on Buyer's Premiums

We've already said this, but it bears repeating as an absolute must: When figuring your maximum bid on a property, don't forget to factor in the buyer's premium. That's the amount that generally goes to the auctioneer for the cost of running the auction, and it can be either a set fee or a percentage of the winning bid. Whether set fee or percentage, it should be clearly stated in the auction catalog. Either way, it's added to the winning bid to arrive at the final selling price.

If, for example, your winning bid for a property is $200,000 and the buyer's premium is 5 percent, you're actually paying $210,000 for the property. If the buyer's premium is 10 percent, that cost rises to $220,000.

"One of the biggest mistakes people make in setting their maximum bids on a property is that they forget to include the buyer's premium," says Mary Kay.

> *Don't forget to subtract the cost of the buyer's premium from the amount you've figured as your maximum bid on a property. That premium varies and is part of the amount you ultimately must pay for a property at REO auction.*
>
> —Alexis McGee

Auctioneers don't hide it, but the buyer's premium can and does sneak up on buyers. It represents thousands of extra dollars tacked onto each and every winning bid. If you forget the buyer's premium, you can easily exceed your maximum bid amount.

Open Your Ears and Be Patient

Pay attention to what's going on around you at an auction. That doesn't mean you must listen in on everyone's conversations—we've already discussed the value of not believing everything you hear. But pay attention to the formal announcements at an auction. They supersede the written information and could correct, delete, or update information on a property.

Another reason to pay attention is that, at some auctions, *already sold* properties can resurface for sale again. That happens at REDC auctions, for example, when the initial winning bidder's financing falls through. It can happen in real time at an auction because, as we indicated, once you win a bid, you're immediately escorted to the area where financing is finalized and escrow is opened to ensure the sale is complete then and there, unless the seller rejects the bid. If a deal isn't completed, the property then can go back up for sale later at that same auction without delays. Or the property may come up again at a later auction.

So if you miss out on a property its first time around, don't give up hope. You could get another shot at it if you're patient and observant. At the very end of a recent auction, a pair of older investors picked up four properties that had come back up for bid after their initial deals fell though. In fact, one of Doug Pereyda's very first REO auction deals was a holdover from a Sacramento auction.

Pay close attention to the bidding, too, because it's fast and furious, especially the early bidding on a property. The auctioneer may open bids on a property at $50,000, but a couple minutes later that same property may end up sold for $350,000.

Online Options

Online REO auctions are yet another phenomenon following in the footsteps of eBay, the online marketplace that sells everything under the sun. In fact, some real estate auctions are "online only" or offer certain properties only online.

No matter how they're sold, property auctions require the same due diligence before you make a bid. See the property, estimate repairs, check the title, review the liens, look at the comps, determine the market value, subtract the cost of repairs, subtract the buyer's premium, and then arrive at your maximum bid. As usual, stick to your guns and don't overbid.

If REO banks and lenders have the option to reject a *winning bid* anyway after an on-site auction, why not make the auctions online, says Mary Kay, who is registered with the online auctioneer Bid4Assets Inc. (www.bid4assets.com). "Those properties usually go for more than 70 cents on the dollar (not a big enough discount), so I don't bid on many. But it's the same approach—research the properties, visit the open houses, and get your numbers lined up," she adds.

Bargains and Today's Market

As we've mentioned, REO auctions haven't yet hit their peak, at least from an investor's point of view.

The national foreclosure epidemic is far from over, and banks' and lenders' REO portfolios are growing. Nonetheless, lenders across the board haven't yet given in to big, widespread discounting on property sales. In part, that's due to the phenomenally successful REO auction. As long as buyers by the thousands fill auditoriums for these auctions and willingly pay premium prices, discounts will remain elusive to all but the best-prepared and most effective foreclosure investors.

As an advanced foreclosure expert, you can discover and snap up those bargains if you understand the process, are aware of the nuances and legalities involved, pay attention to the details, and take advantage of your opportunities.

TAKEaway

- Terms for each auction can vary, so pay attention to the details. They can change at the last minute, too.

- Opt for your own financing versus that provided by an auctioneer. That way you'll avoid unnecessary fees, and won't have to worry about any prepayment penalties.

- Though REO properties are 100 percent owned by the bank or lender and come with title insurance, do your due diligence to determine if there are any outstanding federal tax liens against a property.

- Be patient. If you don't pick up a property the first time it's up for bid, at many auctions it may come back up for sale.

- Take advantage of online opportunities to streamline the REO auction process, even if it's just checking out the auction catalogs online.

- The more properties (and their titles and numbers) you can check out thoroughly, the greater your opportunities for bargains at REO auctions.

PART VI

SELLING IN A SOFT MARKET

Get ready to be more aggressive in your marketing and spend more to sell your property. That means you can earn solid profits when you buy—and sell—right in any market.

—Alexis McGee

CHAPTER 12

Winning in Today's Market

It's never easy to buy and sell at the same time. But you better know how to do both perfectly!

—Alexis McGee

To succeed in the business of foreclosure investing, you must know how to buy right—at that minimum 30 to 40 percent discount depending on current market conditions—and how to sell right, too. Selling right doesn't necessarily mean at a discount, but it does mean at a profit. (Remember, your minimum profit should be 15 percent of the market value of the fixed-up property minus repair and rehab costs, or $30,000.)

As we've discussed, to ensure that you do buy—and sell—right, you need to know your options, your market, and how to capitalize on both. We hope that, so far, this book has helped you understand how to make savvy purchases. Now let's consider how to sell for serious profits, too. That's especially important in today's rocky—and in some cases cold—market.

The Housing Picture

The housing chill is on across much of the country. Many areas are flooded with properties—foreclosure and otherwise—that are languishing on the market; home prices are stagnant or dropping, and buyers are scarce. No one welcomes such a chill, but in large part it's simply the market—which had been spiraling upward out of control—correcting itself back to reality.

That adjustment, however, could take up to two years to complete as the market works off its excess inventories of homes, said Alphonso Jackson, HUD secretary, in prepared remarks at the FHA Regional Homeownership Summit in Los Angeles on June 25, 2007 (see http://www.hud.gov/news/speeches/2007-06-25b.cfm). "At the same time, it could be up to five years before we see the housing market return to where it would have been without the dramatic up/down cycle during this decade," Jackson added.

Boom or Bust for Investors?

Sounds like a pretty dismal picture for foreclosure-property investors, doesn't it? Nope—at least not for wise investors. Keep in mind that despite all the negatives swirling around the glut of foreclosures—including the subprime market debacle and subsequent liquidity crisis, broader economic fallout, and more—the nation's economy remains sound!

- Nationally, unemployment is low—about 5 percent.
- Interest rates remain low.
- FHA reform, versions of which have been passed by both the Senate and the House, will make it easier for our homebuyers to qualify for new loans when we sell our houses for profit.
- And, in certain geographic areas, real estate remains a hot commodity.

Those investors who jump in now with both feet will likely reap the rewards later, many times over. In hindsight, you will look back at this period as the best buying opportunity in seven years or more. If, after the last market bottom in the late 1990s, you wished you had bought more property, now is your second chance to come out a big winner. Think of it as the sale of the decade on real estate.

Right Positioning

Positioning yourself and your deals properly is essential to your investing success now. Instead of figuring your numbers and your deals for fast property flips, consider the current and future national and local markets, then base your numbers on what's right for the state of your market, your financing, your goals, and your risk-tolerance levels. Despite drops in home sales and rising foreclosure rates, for example, 93 of 150 metropolitan statistical areas registered third-quarter 2007 increases in median existing home prices from a year earlier, according to the National Association of Realtors quarterly survey.

On the other hand, let's assume that your market is Sacramento County, California, where property speculation ran rampant and where, as a result, a glut of properties are in foreclosure, with many more to follow. Basing your deal on buying a property at a big discount and then flipping it for a fast buck may not be a realistic investment approach in this market.

> *What makes this market so unique for investors is that prices are massively correcting with some great buys available, and interest rates are extremely attractive, which makes the environment very favorable for a long-term hold.*
>
> —Tom Daves, successful REO investor,
> and 30-year real estate industry veteran

REO and real estate veteran Tom Daves certainly doesn't think now is the time for a fast flip. A year ago, Daves had 36 homes in his inventory that were being fixed up with the intent to flip. But when he saw the subprime mess unfold and numbers of REOs start to mount up, he quickly switched gears.

"I knew the bottom was falling out [of the market] and I had to dump those homes," Daves says. "Since I worked with REOs in the 1990s, I knew that REOs would be a good thing to do again. But I had no idea it was going to explode the way it did.

"What makes our market so unique for investors this time around," he adds, "is that prices are massively correcting with some great buys available. Interest rates are extremely attractive, which makes the environment very favorable for a long-term hold. The last time we had all these REOs (on the market or nearing market) the interest rates were 9 to 10 percent. Now they're just 5 to 6 percent."

Where's the Money?

With the glut of inventory on the market, it's much easier to buy at 30 to 40 percent off now than it has been for a long time. But is there still money to be made?

"Right now the money is in buying and holding. It's not in flipping," Daves says. "Why? First, you always have to make your money when you buy, and now it's very, very difficult to get a huge buy from these banks. They're more interested in selling to an end user, an owner-occupier [instead of an investor]. Only about 1 to 2 percent of properties are now sold at a deep discount.

"Second, it's not easy to sell that flipped property right now. It's a buyers' market. One strategy would be to wait and perhaps rent out the property for a few years. That's where you'll get much greater return on your investment," Daves adds.

What about Your Cash Needs?

Daves has it right. After all, if you don't need the money anytime soon, the best time to build up your rental properties portfolio is in a down market. All those folks who can't afford to buy or keep their home need a place to rent! Plenty of great buys are available, too, if your pockets (read "cash supplier") are deep enough and you are patient.

However, if you need to raise cash yourself, your best bet in a down market is to get in, get out, and bank the money for the next deal.

To Sell or Not

Suppose, however, that you're not interested in becoming a landlord, even if only a temporary one, and instead still like the idea of flipping properties. After all, there is *always* a ready market for the right homes in any market, hot or cold. How then do you move a property in today's market? Let's look more closely for answers.

Price It Right

A big element in moving a house in today's market is price. Price a property right—for you and the seller—and you'll move it, period. "Today you must have the property priced $10,000 to $15,000 below the next comparable active home currently on the market in order to procure a sale," says Daves.

We talked in Chapter 2 about how to figure a home's market value for resale with the help of comparable property sales, pending sales, and active listings in the same neighborhood—factoring in market conditions, subtracting the cost of repairs and rehab, and more. We also briefly mentioned the cost differences associated with moving a house in a colder market. But how else is pricing different in today's market?

> *Another reason to buy entry-level houses as foreclosure investments: Their prices don't drop very fast in a down market. In a worst-case investment scenario of a four- to six-month property hold time, an entry-level home may have only a 3 to 5 percent price correction. On a move-up or nicer home, the downside risk can be two to three times that!*
>
> —Alexis McGee

In a buyers' market, you must be more aggressive in your marketing and probably will need to spend more to sell your property. That means you will have to drop your maximum purchase offer price for a property from 70 percent of the fixed-up market value of the property (minus repair and rehab costs) to perhaps 60 to 65 percent to still make your profits.

How Much Is Too Much?

Because all transactions are unique, your property pricing must be flexible, too.

For example, suppose three comparable properties have sold recently, and the sale prices in the down market have ranged from $400,000 to $425,000. If the market has slowed even further, $399,000 and even $395,000 may be the right price point to attract buyers and move your property.

Even if you've priced your property right *by the numbers*, drive past your house and others in the neighborhood with an objective eye. What do you see? How do you feel about how your house compares with the others? Does your home seem inviting? Does it look well maintained? Do you see more value in your home than in the others? Would you want to buy this home over the rest? Your answers to those questions should all be yes if you want to move the property. If you say "no" to one or more of those questions, head back to the drawing board!

Repair It Right

Driving by those other properties will also help you determine what repair and rehab needs to be done to your property to move it. Pay attention to comparable homes in the neighborhood when determining just how much you need to do to a property in order to move it quickly. Cleanup and cosmetic work, of course, as we discussed in Chapter 2, are a given. Don't go overboard beyond the lipstick, but do aim for the top-level condition of comparable homes in your neighborhood.

Putting together a winning combination for your property—a short-term or realistic market-wise flip for solid profits—is part science, partly subjective, and a great deal dependent on your understanding of all the variables. Each transaction is different. No conclusion is foregone. If it all works out as planned—you made the proper repairs, you figured your numbers based on what you paid for the property combined with its repair costs, and you pegged the current and future market correctly—you should make a 15 percent net profit on the resale of your foreclosure investment. That is, that should be the case *if* you pay attention to yet one more thing: marketing your property.

The Marketing Link

To sell a property in any market—hot, cold or degrees of lukewarm—you need to make the right marketing moves that draw buyers in and persuade them to buy. You may know you've put together a solid deal, but if you don't get the word out, no one else will. As your property languishes on the market, your holding costs eat up any profits—your cash cushion.

In normal markets, I advocate four steps to selling success: mailers to neighbors; MLS listing and for sale by owner (FSBO) services; advertising the property; and holding an open house. In colder markets, though, it's generally a good idea to add market incentives such as picking up the buyer's title costs. Consider bringing in a professional Realtor or listing agent as opposed to FSBO, too. Even if you pay them 6 percent or more, it is worth it to get the exposure for your property and, in turn, a quicker sale.

Mailer to Neighbors

Before you bring in a professional to do your selling, try mailers to neighbors. Use tax assessor's data (available at SiteXdata.com) for current neighbors, ownership, and property information, and print postcard mailer labels to properties within a one-mile radius of your property. The postcard should say something as simple as this:

> Hi, I just bought your neighbor's house at (property's address). I'm fixing it up and plan to sell it. This is your chance to choose your neighbors. Have your friend or family member call me at (your contact number) ASAP. If they call quickly, they can even pick their colors!

> P.S. I am very interested in investing in your community. If you're thinking about selling, call me (your number here). Thank you!

MLS Listing and FSBO Services

You can opt to list a property with a full-service Realtor or the for sale by owner flat-rate, do-it-yourself program. Whichever option you choose, it's essential to get the word out about your house. If you go the FSBO route, you can pay a flat-rate broker to list the property on the MLS and then offer the buyer's agent 3 to 4 percent commission for producing a bona fide buyer. Flat-rate broker web sites include Homeseller's Assistance (www.whypay6.com) and FlatFeeMLSListing.com (www.flatfeemlslisting.com). For as low as $399 to $799, depending on your area and the services provided, you'll get the opportunity to list a property on the local MLS as well as listings on FSBO sites, yard signs, disclosure and purchase agreements, online photos, lockbox, and more.

With this approach, you'll have to show the house, qualify the buyer, write the contract, and close the deal. For only a 3 to 4 percent commission, though, a buyer's agent will handle those responsibilities for the buyer. If you want help negotiating the deal, you should expect to pay the full 6 percent and hire a listing agent to handle all the details for you.

Advertising Your Property

Try placing a classified ad in the local major Sunday newspaper (print and online) as well as on Craigslist (www.craigslist.com) and other real estate advertising web sites. Make your ad brief, and make sure it announces your open house with the address and hours.

Hold an Open House

Open houses are a good tool to bring in the neighbors and get new people in to check out an area. (Provide a guest register as a way to collect names and contact information. Whatever their reasons for visiting, they could be your future clients.)

During the open house, make sure your property is inviting. Perhaps bring a few barstools into the kitchen. Open the curtains, turn on the lights, and think airy as a way to enhance a property's attractiveness. Have cookies available—home-baked in the house, if possible, adds a homey smell—and perhaps milk or bottles of water to drink. Beside your cookie plate, have a list of "what's on the market." Ask your buyers if they have seen those houses. How does your house look compared with the others? Do they see more value in your home than in the others? Listen carefully and note all feedback. This will help you find out quickly if you have properly priced your property.

The Role of Incentives

In normal markets, if you've done everything right, including pricing the property correctly, you're likely to quickly sell any property with little more than an MLS listing, postcards to neighbors, and a well-executed open house. But with today's uncertainties, it's often not quite that easy. You'll need to plan for additional expenses related to the cold market. Those costs can include paying full sales commissions, buyer's closing costs, and increased mailing/advertising to attract buyers.

As a result, when you initially buy the foreclosure property, your maximum purchase offer price will have to compensate for those costs so that you still realize your minimum 15 percent net profit from the resale of every house you buy.

If It Still Doesn't Sell

If, despite all your efforts, a property doesn't sell in today's market, it's probably because you haven't been aggressive enough in one of the following ways:

- You didn't complete the proper repairs to maximize your property's value.
- The price you're asking isn't consistent with the quality of your product and the condition of your local market.
- You haven't properly marketed your product.

Every investor wants the best price and terms when selling a property. Remember, though, the definition of *best* is fluid depending on the condition of markets, properties, individuals, and corporations involved. If, for example, you want to buy an REO, you may have better luck getting a discount from a smaller lender whose pockets are not quite as deep as those of a huge money-center bank with a well-oiled REO department and a sizable portfolio. However, if it's the financial reporting period for that big lender and the corporation wants a better balance sheet to show its shareholders, you could hit deal pay dirt.

In the same vein, if the property is in an area with a seriously depressed economy, you'll likely have to buy at a much bigger discount, plan on a longer hold time, and seriously discount your selling price to move the property. Alternatively, as Daves suggests, you may want to buy and rent out the property temporarily until the local market shifts.

The keys are to be prepared, pay attention, be persistent, and don't forget to factor in your full profit before you buy. If property hold times are running six to nine months in your locale, figure those holding costs into your deal numbers. Consider discounting your offer price to 65 or even 60 percent of the fixed-up market value of a property minus the rehab and repair costs, too. Otherwise, your numbers and your needed profit simply won't add up.

Selling your investment property is an important event. Big profits are involved and complex issues negotiated, so it's critical, especially in a cold market, that you position yourself to do it properly. If you've done everything right thus far, you likely will bring in buyers. In today's market, though, you'll probably get fewer offers than in a market primed for sellers. Don't fret. Instead, evaluate each offer realistically.

- Is it at or near your asking price?
- How much down payment and deposit will the buyer put down?
- Is the potential buyer preapproved or prequalified, and is the approval in writing?
- How far along is the potential buyer in the application process?
- If a contract were signed today, how soon could the buyer's lender fund the loan and close?

If a potential buyer meets your needs, go for it. If not, move on to the next one. Remember, your investment is about meeting your numbers and then closing as quickly as possible with the fewest contingencies. As I mentioned earlier, get in, get out, and bank the cash for your next deal.

No matter the market conditions, the sky is your limit *if* you're knowledgeable, prepared, and persistent. Now is *your* time to come out a winner. You've earned it!

TAKEaway

- To come away a foreclosure investment winner, you must know how to adjust your approach to selling your property in alignment with the existing market in your geographic area.
- Despite today's generally colder markets, the nation's overall economy remains relatively sound.
- Think of today's market as the sale of the decade on real estate. Find the right deal, buy now, and reap instant rewards.
- Slower markets mean you must adjust your maximum purchase offer down from the normal 70 percent of a fixed-up property's market value minus the

cost of repairs and rehab to 65 percent and even 60 percent to compensate for the cost of longer hold times and lower resale prices.

- You may want to consider buying and holding a property as a rental until markets pick up.

- Buyer's markets require more aggressive marketing of a property, too, often including adding buyer incentives.

A dvanced foreclosure investing isn't easy. In these pages we've shown you that. But I hope in reading this book you've also learned that the various types of foreclosure investing are doable, profitable, and rewarding with the right approach, knowledge, and understanding of the processes, the legalities, and the details. Yes, there's much to consider.

I hope, however, you now recognize that investing in deeds of trust, buying properties at courthouse auctions, short sales, REOs, and REO auctions are essential tools in the savvy foreclosure investor's toolbox. They give you, as an advanced foreclosure investor, the ability to capitalize on whatever situation comes your way. You now know what to do and how to do it, no matter the foreclosure scenario, and no matter current market conditions. Where other investors see no deal, shrug, and walk away, you can seize the opportunity to achieve the successes you so deserve.

Throughout this book we've discussed the basic tenets that apply to foreclosure investing across the board:

- Knowing and understanding your state's laws on foreclosure.
- Identifying potential investment properties with the help of reliable and accurate foreclosure lists.
- Culling those lists based on key criteria ranging from geographic location to size, age, price, and more.
- Knowing the importance and essentials of running title on a property, including how to identify red flags such as liens, multiple mortgages, and more.
- Knowing when to turn to and how to use a county's grantor/grantee index.
- Understanding how to determine the real market value of a property and how to assess repairs and rehab on that property.
- Considering your various financing options and what works best in a particular situation.
- Realizing what details make the difference in a deal.

- Figuring the numbers in a prospective deal so they add up to a win-win situation for both parties involved.
- Don't forget to factor in your 15 percent profit.
- And don't forget to consider current market conditions that affect the potential hold time—and your costs—on a property.

You can do it all. It's that simple. Don't be discouraged if, despite the glut of foreclosures today, banks and lenders aren't yet ready for big discount sales. (Remember, those discounts translate to your bottom line.) Instead, dig deeper. Look for another approach to obtaining your target property. Or stay tuned and get prepared. The discounts *will* materialize as lender and bank portfolios of REOs grow thicker and thicker.

Foreclosure investing, after all, is a business that booms no matter the state of the nation's economy. With your newfound foreclosure investing skills, you can capitalize on that!

Good luck and happy deal making. If you need more assistance, feel free to e-mail me (alexis@foreclosures.com) or contact one of my consultants at ForeclosureS.com, 800-310-7730.

Sample Documents

Deed of Trust 206

    Available at http://www.chicagotitle.com/pdfs/LegalForm/CA/DEED%
        20OF%20TRUST.pdf

Assignment of Deed of Trust 213

    Available at http://www.chicagotitle.com/pdfs/LegalForm/CA/ASSDT.pdf

Promissory Note 214

    Available at http://www.chicagotitle.com/pdfs/LegalForm/CA/
        PROMISSORY%20NOTE.pdf

Trustee's Deed 215

    Available at http://www.chicagotitle.com/pdfs/LegalForm/CA/T-DEED.pdf

Notice of Default 217

    Available at http://www.chicagotitle.com/pdfs/LegalForm/CA/N-D.pdf

Notice of Trustee Sale 219

    Available at http://www.chicagotitle.com/pdfs/LegalForm/CA/N-S.pdf

Judgment Lien 220

    Available at http://www.sos.ca.gov/business/ucc/ra_9_jl1_barcode.pdf

Preliminary Title Report 224

    Available at http://www.dearborn.com/download/CAREEscrow/
        SamplePreliminaryReport.pdf; Also available from http://www
        .chicagotitle.com/pdfs/prelim.pdf

RECORDING REQUESTED BY

AND WHEN RECORDED MAIL TO

DEED OF TRUST
WITH ASSIGNMENT OF RENTS AS ADDITIONAL SECURITY

This DEED OF TRUST, made   , between

herein called TRUSTOR,
whose address is

CHICAGO TITLE COMPANY, a California Corporation, herein called TRUSTEE, and

                                        , herein called BENEFICIARY,

Trustor irrevocably grants, transfers and assigns to Trustee in Trust, with Power of Sale that property in
            County   California, described as:

Together with the rents, issues and profits thereof, subject, however, to the right, power and authority hereinafter given to and conferred upon Beneficiary to collect and apply such rents, issues and profits.

For the Purpose of Securing (1) payment of the sum of $ _____ with interest thereon according to the terms of a promissory note or notes of even date herewith made by Trustor, payable to order of Beneficiary, and extensions or renewals thereof; (2) the performance of each agreement of Trustor incorporated by reference or contained herein or reciting it is so secured; (3) payment of additional sums and interest thereon which may hereafter be loaned to Trustor, or his successors or assigns, when evidenced by a promissory note or notes reciting that they are secured by this Deed of Trust.

To protect the security of this Deed of Trust, and with respect to the property above described, Trustor expressly makes each and all of the agreements, and adopts and agrees to perform and be bound by each and all of the terms and provisions set forth in subdivision A of that certain Fictitious Deed of Trust referenced herein, and it is mutually agreed that all of the provisions set forth in subdivision B of that certain Fictitious Deed of Trust

FIGURE A.1   Deed of Trust

Courtesy of Fidelity National Title Group.

recorded in the book and page of Official Records in the office of the county recorder of the county where said property is located, noted below opposite the name of such county, namely:

COUNTY	BOOK	PAGE	COUNTY	BOOK	PAGE	COUNTY	BOOK	PAGE	COUNTY	BOOK	PAGE
Alameda	1288	556	Kings	858	713	Placer	1028	379	Sierra	38	187
Alpine	3	130-31	Lake	437	110	Plumes	166	1307	Siskiyou	506	762
Amador	133	438	Lassen	192	367	Riverside	3778	347	Solano	1287	621
Butte	1330	513	Los Angeles	T-3878	874	Sacramento	71-10-26	615	Sonoma	2067	427
Calveras	185	338	Madera	911	136	San Benito	300	405	Stanislaus	1970	56
Colusa	323	391	Marin	1849	122	San Bernardino	6213	768	Sutter	655	585
Contra Costa	4684	1	Mariposa	90	453	San Francisco	A-804	596	Tehama	457	183
Del Norte	101	549	Mendocino	667	99	San Joaquin	2855	283	Trinity	108	595
El Dorado	704	635	Merced	1660	753	San Luis Obispo	1311	137	Tulare	2530	108
Fresno	5052	623	Modoc	191	93	San Mateo	4778	175	Tuolumne	177	160
Glenn	469	76	Mono	69	302	Santa Barbara	2065	881	Ventura	2607	237
Humboldt	801	83	Monterey	357	239	Santa Clara	6626	664	Yolo	769	16
Imperial	1189	701	Napa	704	742	Santa Cruz	1638	607	Yuba	398	693
Inyo	165	672	Nevada	363	94	Shasta	800	633			
Kern	3756	690	Orange	7182	18	San Diego Series 5 Book 1964, Page 149774					

shall inure to and bind the parties hereto, with respect to the property above described. Said agreements, terms and provisions contained in said subdivisions A and B (identical in all counties) are preprinted on the following pages hereof and are by the within reference thereto, incorporated herein and made a part of this Deed of Trust for all purposes as fully as if set forth at length herein, and Beneficiary may charge for a statement regarding the obligation secured hereby, provided the charge thereof does not exceed the maximum allowed by laws.

The undersigned Trustor requests that a copy of any notice of default and any notice of sale hereunder be mailed to him at his address hereinbefore set forth.

_____

_____

FIGURE A.1 *(Continued)*
Courtesy of Fidelity National Title Group.

CERTIFICATE OF ACKNOWLEDGEMENT OF NOTARY PUBLIC

STATE OF CALIFORNIA,)

)

COUNTY OF   )

       On _____ before me, _____ , personally appeared _____ personally known to me (or proved to me on the basis of satisfactory evidence) to be the person(s) whose name(s) is/are subscribed to the within instrument and acknowledged to me that he/she/they executed the same in his/her/their authorized capacity(ies), and that by his/her/their signature(s) on the instrument the person(s), or the entity upon behalf of which the person(s), acted, executed the instrument.
       WHEREAS my hand and official seal.

                                                   _____

                                               (Signature of Notary Public)

FIGURE A.1 *(Continued)*

Courtesy of Fidelity National Title Group.

DO NOT RECORD

The following is a copy of Subdivisions A and B of the fictitious Deed of Trust recorded in each County in California as stated in the foregoing Deed of Trust and incorporated by reference in said Deed of Trust as being a part thereof as if set forth at length therein.

A. To protect the security of this Deed of Trust, Trustor agrees:
(1) To keep said property in good condition and repair; not to remove or demolish any building thereon; to complete or restore promptly and in good and workmanlike manner any building which may be constructed, damaged or destroyed thereon and to pay when due all claims for labor performed and materials furnished therefor; to comply with all laws affecting said property or requiring any alterations or improvements to be made thereon; not to commit or permit waste thereof; not to commit, suffer, or permit any act upon said property in violation of law; to cultivate, irrigate, fertilize, fumigate, prune and do all other acts which from the character or use of said property may be reasonably necessary, the specific enumerations herein not excluding the general.

(2) To provide, maintain and deliver to Beneficiary fire insurance satisfactory to and with loss payable to Beneficiary. The amount collected under any fire or other insurance policy may be applied by Beneficiary upon any indebtedness secured hereby and in such order as Beneficiary may determine, or at option of Beneficiary the entire amount so collected or any part thereof may be released to Trustor. Such application or release shall not cure or waive any default or notice of default hereunder or invalidate any act done pursuant to such notice.

(3) To appear in and defend any action or proceeding purporting to affect the security hereof or the rights or powers of Beneficiary or Trustee; and to pay all costs and expenses, including cost of evidence of title and attorney's fees in a reasonable sum, in any action or proceeding in which Beneficiary or Trustee may appear, and in any suit brought by Beneficiary to foreclose this Deed.

(4) To pay: at least ten days before delinquency all taxes and assessments affecting said property, including assessments on appurtenant water stock; when due, all encumbrances, charges and liens, with interest, on said property or any part thereof, which appear to be prior or superior hereto; all costs, fees and expenses of this Trust.

Should Trustor fail to make any payment or to do any act as herein provided, then Beneficiary or Trustee, but without obligation so to do and without notice to or demand upon Trustor and without releasing Trustor from any obligation hereof, may make or do the same in such manner and to such extent as either may deem necessary to protect the security hereof, Beneficiary or Trustee being authorized to enter upon said property for such purposes; appear in and defend any action or proceeding purporting to affect the security hereof or the rights or powers of Beneficiary or Trustee; pay, purchase, contest or compromise any encumbrance, charge, or lien which in the judgment of either appears to be prior or superior

FIGURE A.1   *(Continued)*

Courtesy of Fidelity National Title Group.

hereto; and, in exercising any such powers, pay necessary expenses, employ counsel and pay his or her reasonable fees.

(5) To pay immediately and without demand all sums so expanded by Beneficiary or Trustee, with interest from date of expenditure at the amount allowed by law in effect at the date hereof, and to pay for any statement provided for by law in effect at the date hereof regarding the obligation secured hereby, any amount demanded by the Beneficiary not to exceed the maximum allowed by law at the time when said statement is demanded.

B. It is mutually agreed:

(1) That any award of damages in connection with any condemnation for public use of or injury to said property or any part thereof is hereby assigned and shall be paid to Beneficiary who may apply or release such moneys received by him or her in the same manner and with the same effect as above provided for regarding disposition of proceeds of fire or other insurance.

(2) That by accepting payment of any sum secured hereby after its due date, Beneficiary does not waive his or her right either to require prompt payment when due of all other sums so secured or to declare default for failure so to pay.

(3) That at any time or from time to time, without liability therefor and without notice, upon written request of Beneficiary and presentation of this Deed and said note for endorsement, and without affecting the personal liability of any person for payment of the indebtedness secured hereby, Trustee may: reconvey any part of said property; consent to the making of any map or plat thereof; join in granting any easement thereon; or join in any extension agreement or any agreement subordinating the lien or charge hereof.

(4) That upon written request of Beneficiary stating that all sums secured hereby have been paid, and upon surrender of this Deed and said note to Trustee for cancellation and retention or other disposition as Trustee in its sole discretion may choose and upon payment of its fees, Trustee shall reconvey, without warranty, the property then held hereunder. The recitals in such reconveyance of any matters or facts shall be conclusive proof of the truthfulness thereof. The Grantee in such reconveyance may be described as "the person or persons legally entitled thereto."

(5) That as additional security, Trustor hereby gives to and confers upon Beneficiary the right, power and authority, during the continuance of these Trusts, to collect the rents, issues and profits of said property, reserving unto Trustor the right, prior to any default by Trustor in payment of any indebtedness secured hereby or in performance of any agreement hereunder, to collect and retain such rents, issues and profits as they become due and payable. Upon any such default, Beneficiary may at any time without notice, either in person, by agent, or by a receiver to be appointed by a court, and without regard to the adequacy of any security for the indebtedness hereby secured, enter upon and take possession of said property or any part thereof, in his or her own name sue for or otherwise

FIGURE A.1 *(Continued)*

Courtesy of Fidelity National Title Group.

collect such rents, issues, and profits, including those past due and unpaid, and apply the same, less costs and expenses of operation and collection, including reasonable attorney's fees, upon any indebtedness secured hereby, and in such order as Beneficiary may determine. The entering upon and taking possession of said property, the collection of such rents, issues and profits and the application thereof as aforesaid, shall not cure or waive any default or notice of default hereunder or invalidate any act done pursuant to such notice.

(6) That upon default by Trustor in payment of any indebtedness secured hereby or in performance of any agreement hereunder, Beneficiary may declare all sums secured hereby immediately due and payable by delivery to Trustee of written declaration of default and demand for sale and of written notice of default and of election to cause to be sold said property, which notice Trustee shall cause to be filed for record. Beneficiary also shall deposit with Trustee this Deed, said note and all documents evidencing expenditures secured hereby.

After the lapse of such time as may then be required by law following the recordation of said notice of default, and notice of sale having been given as then required by law, Trustee, without demand on Trustor, shall sell said property at the time and place fixed by it in said notice of sale, either as a whole or in separate parcels, and in such order as it may determine, at public auction to the highest bidder for cash in lawful money of the United States, payable at time of sale. Trustee may postpone sale of all or any portion of said property by public announcement at such time and place of sale, and from time to time thereafter may postpone such sale by public announcement at the time fixed by the preceding postponement. Trustee shall deliver to such purchaser its deed conveying the property so sold, but without any covenant or warranty, express or implied. The recitals in such deed of any matters or facts shall be conclusive proof of the truthfulness thereof. Any person, including Trustor, Trustee, or Beneficiary as hereinafter defined, may purchase at such sale.

After deducting all costs, fees and expenses of Trustee and of this Trust, including cost of evidence of title in connection with sale, Trustee shall apply the proceeds of sale to payment of: all sums expended under the terms hereof, not then repaid, with accrued interest at the amount allowed by law in effect at the date hereof; all other sums then secured hereby; and the remainder, if any, to the person or persons legally entitled thereto.

(7) Beneficiary, or any successor in ownership of any indebtedness secured hereby, may from time to time, by instrument in writing, substitute a successor or successors to any Trustee named herein or acting hereunder, which instrument, executed by the Beneficiary and duly acknowledged and recorded in the office of the recorder of the county or counties where said property is situated, shall be conclusive proof of proper substitution of such successor Trustee or Trustees, who shall, without conveyance from the Trustee predecessor, succeed to all its title, estate, rights, powers and duties. Said instrument must contain the name of the original Trustor, Trustee and Beneficiary hereunder, the book and page where this Deed is recorded and the name and address of the new Trustee.

FIGURE A.1 *(Continued)*

Courtesy of Fidelity National Title Group.

(8)   That this Deed applies to, inures to the benefit of, and binds all parties hereto, their heirs, legatees, devisees, administrators, executors, successors, and assigns. The term Beneficiary shall mean the owner and holder, including pledgees of the note secured hereby, whether or not named as Beneficiary herein. In this Deed, whenever the context so requires, the masculine gender includes the feminine and/or the neuter, and the singular number includes the plural.

(9)   The Trustee accepts this Trust when this Deed, duly executed and acknowledged, is made a public record as provided by law. Trustee is not obligated to notify any party hereto of pending sale under any other Deed of Trust or of any action or proceeding in which Trustor, Beneficiary or Trustee shall be a party unless brought by Trustee.

DO NOT RECORD   REQUEST FOR FULL RECONVEYANCE

TO CHICAGO TITLE COMPANY

The undersigned is the legal owner and holder of the note or notes and of all other indebtedness secured by the foregoing Deed of Trust. Said note or notes, together with all other indebtedness secured by said Deed of Trust, have been fully paid and satisfied; and you are hereby requested and directed, on payment to you of any sums owing to you under the terms of said Deed of Trust, to cancel said note or notes above mentioned, and all other evidence of indebtedness secured by said Deed of Trust delivered to you herewith, together with the said Deed of Trust, and to reconvey, without warranty, to the parties designated by the terms of said Deed of Trust, all the estate now held by you under the same.

Dated

Please mail Deed of Trust,
Note and Reconveyance to _____

Do not lose or destroy this Deed of Trust OR THE NOTE which it secures. Both must be delivered to the Trustee for cancellation before reconveyance will be made.

FIGURE A.1   *(Continued)*
Courtesy of Fidelity National Title Group.

RECORDING REQUESTED BY

AND WHEN RECORDED MAIL TO:

Name

Street
Address

City &
State
Zip

Title Order No.   Escrow No.

SPACE ABOVE THIS LINE FOR RECORDER'S USE

Assignment of Deed of Trust

Assessors Parcel Number:

FOR VALUE RECEIVED, the undersigned hereby grants, assigns and transfers to

all beneficial interest under that certain Deed of Trust dated

executed by

, Trustor,

to   , Trustee,

and recorded as Instrument No.   on   in book   , page   , of

Official Records in the County Recorder's office of   County, California, describing land therein as:

TOGETHER with the note or notes therein described or referred to. the money due and to become due thereon with interest,
and all rights accrued or to accrue under said Deed of Trust.

Dated _____

STATE OF CALIFORNIA
COUNTY OF _____ } S.S.

On _____ before me,

a Notary Public in and for said County and State, personally appeared

_____

personally known to me (or proved to me on the basis of satisfactory
evidence) to be the person(s) whose name(s) is/are subscribed to the
within instrument and acknowledged to me that he/she/they executed
the same in his/her/their authorized capacity(ies), and that by
his/her/their signature(s) on the instrument the person(s), or the entity
upon behalf of which the person(s) acted, executed the instrument.

WITNESS my hand and official seal

Signature _____

(This area for official notarial seal)

FIGURE A.2   Assignment of Deed of Trust

Courtesy of Fidelity National Title Group.

PROMISSORY NOTE

For value received , I, the undersigned, promise to pay to the order of
_____ the principal sum of
$ _____ on _____, 20___ (maturity date) with interest at
the rate of _____ percent per year, interest payable
_____, beginning _____, 20___, and continuing until
maturity date at which time all unpaid sums of principal and interest shall be due and
payable.

Should default be made in payment of the principal or interest, the whole sum of principal
and interest shall, at the option of the holder of this note, become immediately due.

This Note is subject to Section 2966 of the California Civil Code, which provides that the
holder of this Note shall give written notice to the trustor, or his successor in interest, of
prescribed information at least 90 and not more than 150 days before any balloon payment
is due.

_____

(Delete acceleration and balloon notice provisions if not applicable.)

FIGURE A.3   Promissory Note

Courtesy of Fidelity National Title Group.

RECORDING REQUESTED BY

AND WHEN RECORDED MAIL TO:

Name

Street
Address

City &
State

SPACE ABOVE THIS LINE FOR RECORDER'S USE

Trustee's Deed Upon Sale   T.S. NO

The undersigned grantor declares:
(1) The grantee herein was/was not the foreclosing beneficiary.
(2) The amount of the unpaid debt together with costs was . . . . $
(3) The amount paid by the grantee at the trustee's sale was . . . . $
(4) The documentary transfer tax is . . . . $
(5) Said property is in (   ) unincorporated area; (   ) City of _____ , and
CHICAGO TITLE COMPANY, a corporation (herein call Trustee), as the duly appointed Trustee under the Deed of Trust hereinafter
described, does hereby grant and convey, but without covenant or warranty, express or implied, to

(herein called Grantee), all of its right, title and interest in and to that certain property situated in the City
of _____ , County of _____ , State of California, described as
follows:

TRUSTEE STATES THAT:
This conveyance is made pursuant to the powers conferred upon Trustee by that certain Deed of Trust dated
and executed by

as trustor, and recorded   in Book/Reel/Instrument No.
Page/Image   of Official Records of   County, California, and after fulfillment of the conditions
specified in said Deed of Trust authorizing this conveyance.
Default occurred as set forth in a Notice of Default and Election to Sell which was recorded in the office of the Recorder of said County.
All requirements of law regarding the mailing of copies of notices and the posting and publication of copies of the Notice of Sale which was
recorded have been complied with.
Said property was sold by said Trustee at public auction on   at the place
named in the Notice of Sale, in the County of   , California, in which the property is situated.
Grantee being the highest bidder at such sale, became the purchaser of said property and paid therefor to said Trustee the amount
Bid $, in lawful money of the United States, or by the satisfaction, pro tanto, of the obligations then secured by said
Deed of Trust.
In Witness Whereof, said CHICAGO TITLE COMPANY, a corporation, as Trustee, has this day caused its corporate name to be hereunto
affixed by its Vice President and Assistant Secretary, thereunto duly authorized by resolution of its Board of Directors.

Dated _____   Chicago Title Company,
                               as Trustee aforesaid

CERTIFICATE OF ACKNOWLEDGMENT OF NOTARY PUBLIC

STATE OF CALIFORNIA,   )
COUNTY OF _____)

On _____ before me, _____ , a notary public in and for said County and State, personally appeared _____
personally known to me (or proved to me on the basis of satisfactory evidence) to be the person(s) whose name(s) is/are subscribed to the within instrument
and acknowledged to me that he/she/they executed the same in his/her/their authorized capacity(ies) and that by his/her/their signature(s) on the instrument
the person(s), or the entity upon behalf of which the person(s) acted, executed the instrument.
WITNESS my hand and official seal.

FIGURE A.4   Trustee's Deed
Courtesy of Fidelity National Title Group.

_____ (Signature of Notary Public)

FIGURE A.4 *(Continued)*
Courtesy of Fidelity National Title Group.

RECORDING REQUESTED BY

WHEN RECORDED MAIL TO

Name

Street
Address

City &
State

TITLE ORDER NO.	T.S. NO.	SPACE ABOVE THIS LINE FOR RECORDER'S USE
		COMPUTER NO.
LOAN NO.	OTHER REF.	T.S. NO.

NOTICE OF DEFAULT AND ELECTION TO SELL UNDER DEED OF TRUST
IMPORTANT NOTICE
IF YOUR PROPERTY IS IN FORECLOSURE BECAUSE YOU ARE BEHIND
IN YOUR PAYMENTS, IT MAY BE SOLD WITHOUT ANY COURT ACTION,

and you may have the legal right to bring your account in good standing by paying all of your past due payments plus permitted costs and expenses within the time permitted by law for reinstatement of your account which is normally five business days prior to the date set for the sale of your property. No sale date may be set until three months from the date this notice of default may be recorded (which date of recordation appears on this notice).

This amount is   as of   and will increase until your account becomes current.

While your property is in foreclosure, you still must pay other obligations (such as insurance and taxes) required by your note and deed of trust or mortgage. If you fail to make future payments on the loan, pay taxes on the property, provide insurance on the property, or pay other obligations as required in the note and deed of trust or mortgage, the beneficiary or mortgagee may insist that you do so in order to reinstate your account in good standing. In addition, the beneficiary or mortgagee may require as a condition to reinstatement that you provide reliable written evidence that you paid all senior liens, property taxes, and hazard insurance premiums.

Upon your written request, the beneficiary or mortgagee will give you a written itemization of the entire amount you must pay. You may not have to pay the entire unpaid portion of your account, even though full payment was demanded, but you must pay all amounts in default at the time payment is made. However, you and your beneficiary or mortgagee may mutually agree in writing prior to the time the notice of sale is posted (which may not be earlier than the end of the three-month period stated above) to, among other things, (1) provide additional time in which to cure the default by transfer of the property or otherwise; or (2) establish a schedule of payments in order to cure your default; or both (1) and (2).

Following the expiration of the time period referred to in the first paragraph of this notice, unless the obligation being foreclosed upon or a separate written agreement between you and your creditor permits a longer period, you have only the legal right to stop the sale of your property by paying the entire amount demanded by your creditor.

FIGURE A.5   Notice of Default

Courtesy of Fidelity National Title Group.

To find out the amount you must pay, or to arrange for payment to stop the foreclosure, or if your property is in foreclosure for any other reason, contact:

Name of Beneficiary or Mortgagee:

Phone:

If you have any questions, you should contact a lawyer or the Governmental agency which may have insured your loan.

Notwithstanding the fact that your property is in foreclosure, you may offer your property for sale, provided the sale is concluded prior to the conclusion of the foreclosure.

Remember, YOU MAY LOSE LEGAL RIGHTS IF YOU DO NOT TAKE PROMPT ACTION.

NOTICE IS HEREBY GIVEN: CHICAGO TITLE COMPANY, a California Corporation, is duly appointed Trustee under a Deed of Trust dated   executed by

                                                                                                as Trustor, to secure certain obligations
in favor of
                                                                                                        , as beneficiary,

recorded   as instrument no.   in book   page

of Official Records in the Office of the Recorder of   County, California, describing the land therein as:

said obligations including   note(s) for the   sum of $

that a breach of, and default in, the obligations for which such Deed of Trust is security has occurred in that payment has not been made of:

that by reason thereof, the undersigned, present beneficiary under such Deed of Trust, has executed and delivered to said duly appointed Trustee, a written Declaration of Default and Demand for Sale, and has deposited with said duly appointed Trustee, such Deed of Trust and all documents evidencing obligations secured thereby, and has declared and does hereby declare all sums secured thereby immediately due and payable and has elected and does hereby elect to cause the trust property to be sold to satisfy the obligations secured thereby.

> THIS NOTICE MUST BE RECORDED BY
> CHICAGO TITLE COMPANY, a
> California Corporation

Dated _____   _____

FIGURE A.5   *(Continued)*
Courtesy of Fidelity National Title Group.

RECORDING REQUESTED BY

WHEN RECORDED MAIL TO
Name

Street
Address

City &
State

NOTICE OF TRUSTEE'S SALE
T.S. No. _____
YOU ARE IN DEFAULT UNDER A

_____

(Deed of Trust or mortgage)
DATED _____ **UNLESS YOU TAKE ACTION TO PROTECT YOUR PROPERTY, IT MAY BE SOLD AT A PUBLIC SALE. IF YOU NEED AN EXPLANATION OF THE NATURE OF THE PROCEEDING AGAINST YOU, YOU SHOULD CONTACT A LAWYER.**

On _____, at 9:00 A.M., **Chicago Title Company**, a corporation, as duly appointed Trustee under and pursuant to Deed of Trust recorded _____, as Inst. No _____, in book _____, page _____, of Official Records in the office of the County Recorder of _____ County, California, WILL SELL AT PUBLIC AUCTION TO HIGHEST BIDDER FOR CASH OR CASHIER'S CHECK OR OTHER INSTITUTIONAL CHECK ACCEPTABLE TO THE TRUSTEE (payable at time of sale in lawful money of the United States) at

all right, title and interest conveyed to and now held by it under said Deed of Trust in the property situated in said County and Slate described as:

A. P. N.

Trustor:

The street address or other common designation, if any, of the real property described above is purported to be:

The undersigned Trustee disclaims any liability for any incorrectness of the street address or other common designation, if any, shown herein.

Said sale will be made, but without covenant or warranty, express or implied, regarding title, possession, or encumbrances, to pay the unpaid balance of the note(s) secured by said Deed of Trust, to-wit: $ _____, including as provided in said note(s), advances, if any, under the terms of said Deed of Trust, fees, charges and expenses of the Trustee and of the trusts created by said Deed of Trust. Accrued interest and additional advances, if any, will increase this figure prior to sale.

The beneficiary under said Deed of Trust heretofore executed and delivered to the undersigned a written Declaration of Default and Demand for Sale, and a written Notice of Default and Election to Sell. The undersigned caused said Notice of Default and Election to Sell to be recorded in the county where the real property is located on _____ as Inst. No. _____.

Trustee or party conducting sale   Chicago Title Company, a corporation
CHICAGO TITLE COMPANY

Date: _____   _____

FIGURE A.6   Notice of Trustee Sale
Courtesy of Fidelity National Title Group.

JUDGMENT LIEN FILING INSTRUCTIONS

Please type or laser-print information on this form. Be sure information provided is legible. Read all instructions and follow them completely. Complete the form very carefully as mistakes may have important legal consequences. Do not insert anything in the open space in the upper right portion of this form as it is reserved for filing office use. Do not staple or otherwise mutilate the barcode in the upper left corner of the document, this will render the barcode ineffective.

To provide the requester with an acknowledgment of filing, the original and a duplicate copy of the notice must be presented for filing. This Notice of Judgment Lien must be filed according to provisions of Section 697.510 of the Code of Civil Procedure.

Section A:	To assist filing office communication with the filer, information in this section should be provided.
Section B:	Enter name and mailing address of requester in this section. This is required information.
ITEM 1a or 1b:	Enter the exact legal name of the organization or the name of the individual that is the debtor appearing on the court judgment. Use the judgment lien addendum to add additional judgment debtor names.
ITEM 1c:	Enter the last known mailing address of the judgment debtor.
ITEM 2a or 2b:	Enter the exact legal name of the organization or the name of the individual that is the creditor appearing on the court judgment. Use the judgment lien addendum for additional judgment creditor names.
ITEM 2c:	Enter the last known mailing address of the judgment creditor.
ITEMS 3A–E:	Enter information from the court judgment.
ITEM 3F:	Enter the amount of the court judgment adjusted for interest and payments to the date of the notice.
ITEM 3G:	The date of the statement will normally be the date the notice is executed.
ITEM 4:	The signature of either the judgment creditor or the judgment creditor's attorney is required. (Section 697.550, Code of Civil Procedure)
	If the individual signing the statement signs on behalf of a law firm, which is the attorney of record, the name of the law firm should be entered BENEATH, not above, the signature. If the signature is for a judgment creditor, which is an entity, the name of the entity should be entered BENEATH, not above, the signature of the person signing for the judgment creditor.

The Judgment Lien must be submitted with a filing fee of ten dollars ($10.00) if the original document is two pages or less and twenty dollars ($20.00) if the original document is three pages or more. Please send a check made payable to the **Secretary of State**. DOCUMENTS NOT ACCOMPANIED BY THE FILING FEE WILL NOT BE PROCESSED.

When properly completed, send **payment**, and the **original** and a **duplicate copy** of the notice to:

Secretary of State
P.O. Box 942835
Sacramento, CA 94235-0001

FIGURE A.7   Judgment Lien (California)

JUDGMENT LIEN ADDENDUM INSTRUCTIONS

This form is to be used for listing additional judgment debtors and/or creditors to the NOTICE OF JUDGMENT LIEN.

Please type or laser-print information on this form. Be sure information provided is legible. Read all instructions and follow them completely. Complete the form very carefully as mistakes may have important legal consequences. **Attach this ADDENDUM to the completed NOTICE OF JUDGMENT LIEN.**

ITEM 5:   Provide the name of the judgment debtor shown in Item 1 of the original NOTICE OF JUDGMENT LIEN. Provide only one name by completing either 5a or 5b, as applicable.

ITEMS 6, 7, 8: To add additional debtor names to the judgment lien record, enter the appropriate information in Item 6, 7 or 8, as needed. For each of these items, enter either an organization name or an individual name, not both.

Provide the complete mailing address for each judgment debtor.

ITEMS 9, 10: To add additional creditor names to the judgment lien record, enter the appropriate information in Item 9 or 10, as needed. For each of these items, enter either an organization name or an individual name, not both.

Provide the complete mailing address for each judgment creditor.

FIGURE A.7   *(Continued)*

NOTICE OF JUDGMENT LIEN
FOLLOW INSTRUCTIONS CAREFULLY (front and back of form)

A. NAME & PHONE OF FILER'S CONTACT (optional)

B. SEND ACKNOWLEDGMENT TO: (NAME AND ADDRESS)

THIS SPACE FOR FILING OFFICE USE ONLY

1. JUDGMENT DEBTOR'S EXACT LEGAL NAME –Insert only one name, either 1a or 1b. Do not abbreviate or combine names.

1a. ORGANIZATION'S NAME

1b. INDIVIDUAL'S LAST NAME	FIRST NAME	MIDDLE NAME	SUFFIX
1c. MAILING ADDRESS	CITY	STATE	POSTAL CODE	COUNTRY

2. JUDGMENT CREDITOR'S NAME– Do not abbreviate or combine names.

2a. ORGANIZATION'S NAME

2b. INDIVIDUAL'S LAST NAME	FIRST NAME	MIDDLE	SUFFIX
2c. MAILING ADDRESS	CITY	STATE	POSTAL CODE	COUNTRY

3. ALL PROPERTY SUBJECT TO ENFORCEMENT OF A MONEY JUDGMENT AGAINST THE JUDGMENT DEBTOR TO WHICH A JUDGMENT LIEN ON PERSONAL PROPERTY MAY ATTACH UNDER SECTION 697.530 OF THE CODE OF CIVIL PROCEDURE IS SUBJECT TO THIS JUDGMENT LIEN.

A.   Title of court where judgment was entered: _____

B.   Title of the action: _____

C.   Number of this action: _____

D.   Date judgment was entered: _____

E.   Date of subsequent renewals of judgment (if any): _____

F.   Amount required to satisfy judgment at date of this notice: $ _____

G.   Date of this notice: _____

4. *I declare under penalty of perjury under the laws of the State of California that the foregoing is true and correct:*

_____
SIGNATURE – SEE INSTRUCTION NO. 4

Dated: _____
(If not indicated, use same as date in item 3G.)

FOR: _____

FILING OFFICE COPY

NOTICE OF JUDGMENT LIEN (FORM JL1) (Rev. 6/01)
Approved by the Secretary of State

FIGURE A.7   *(Continued)*

JUDGMENT LIEN ADDENDUM
FOLLOW INSTRUCTIONS CAREFULLY (FRONT AND BACK OF FORM)

5. NAME OF JUDGMENT DEBTOR: (NAME OF FIRST DEBTOR ON RELATED JUDGMENT LIEN)

5a. ORGANIZATION'S NAME			
5b. INDIVIDUAL'S LAST NAME	FIRST NAME	MIDDLE NAME	SUFFIX

6. ADDITIONAL JUDGMENT DEBTOR – insert only one name (6a or 6b):

6a. ORGANIZATION'S NAME				
6b. INDIVIDUAL'S LAST NAME	FIRST NAME	MIDDLE NAME		SUFFIX
6c. MAILING ADDRESS	CITY	STATE	POSTAL CODE	COUNTRY

7. ADDITIONAL JUDGMENT DEBTOR – insert only one name (7a or 7b):

7a. ORGANIZATION'S NAME				
7b. INDIVIDUAL'S LAST NAME	FIRST NAME	MIDDLE NAME		SUFFIX
7c. MAILING ADDRESS	CITY	STATE	POSTAL CODE	COUNTRY

8. ADDITIONAL JUDGMENT DEBTOR – insert only one name (8a or 8b):

8a. ORGANIZATION'S NAME				
8b. INDIVIDUAL'S LAST NAME	FIRST NAME	MIDDLE NAME		SUFFIX
8c. MAILING ADDRESS	CITY	STATE	POSTAL CODE	COUNTRY

9. ADDITIONAL JUDGMENT CREDITOR – insert only one name (9a or 9b):

9a. ORGANIZATION'S NAME				
9b. INDIVIDUAL'S LAST NAME	FIRST NAME	MIDDLE NAME		SUFFIX
9c. MAILING ADDRESS	CITY	STATE	POSTAL CODE	COUNTRY

10. ADDITIONAL JUDGMENT CREDITOR – insert only one name (10a or 10b):

10a. ORGANIZATION'S NAME				
10b. INDIVIDUAL'S LAST NAME	FIRST NAME	MIDDLE NAME		SUFFIX
10c. MAILING ADDRESS	CITY	STATE	POSTAL CODE	COUNTRY

(1) FILING OFFICE COPY – JUDGMENT LIEN ADDENDUM FORM (REV. 6/01)

CA Secretary of State

FIGURE A.7 *(Continued)*

Sample
Preliminary
Title
Report

FIGURE A.8   Preliminary Title Report

Courtesy of Fidelity National Title Group.

Review of Sample Preliminary Title Report

1. Under Schedule A Item C. The Tract No. is incorrect. It should be Tract 56, not 53.

2. Under Notes and Requirements Item 4. Homeowners Exemption: Shows NONE. This may not be an error. If the transaction is for an owner-occupied refinance, with cash out, why has the owner not taken the exemption to reduce the property taxes? Refer this to the agents and lender for their review

3. Under Schedule B Item 5. Under Trustor: Charles C. & Elizabeth D. Byer. This should be Charles D. & Elizabeth C. Byer, husband and wife.

4. This is the wrong plat map.

FIGURE A.8 *(Continued)*
Courtesy of Fidelity National Title Group.

SAMPLE PRELIMINARY TITLE REPORT
Title/Escrow Company, Inc.
1111 Main Street
Coastal Inlet, CA 99999

Client's Name:
Client's Address: 1111 Main Street Ste. 201
City & State with Zip Code: Coastal Inlet, CA 99999
Attention: Contact person at the escrow: Becky Repp
Your No.: Escrow number 99-8888BR
Our No.: Preliminary Title Report Number 77777

Dated as of: April 15, 20___ 7:30 a.m.

IN RESPONSE TO THE ABOVE REFERENCED APPLICATION FOR A POLICY OF TITLE
INSURANCE, (TITLE INSURANCE COMPANY'S NAME), a California Corporation, hereby reports that it is
prepared to issue, or cause to be issued, as of the date hereof, a (Title Insurance Company's Name) Policy or
Policies of Title Insurance describing the land and the estate or interest therein hereinafter set forth, insuring
against loss which may be sustained by reason of any defect, lien, or encumbrance not shown or referred to as
an Exception in Schedule B or not excluded from coverage pursuant to the printed Schedules, Conditions and
Stipulations of said forms.

The printed exceptions and exclusions from the coverage of said Policy or Policies are set forth in the attached
cover sheet. Copies of the Policy forms should be read. They are available from the office which issued this
report.

Please read the exceptions shown or referred to in Schedule B of this report and the exceptions and exclusions
set forth in the cover sheet attached to this report carefully. The exceptions and exclusions are meant to provide
you with notice of matters which are not covered under the terms of the title insurance policy and should be
carefully considered.
It is important to note that this preliminary report is not a written representation as to the conditions of title and
may not list all liens, defects, and encumbrances affecting title to the land.

THIS REPORT (AND ANY SUPPLEMENTS OR AMENDMENTS HERETO) IS ISSUED SOLELY FOR
THE PURPOSE OF FACILITATING THE ISSUANCE OF A POLICY OF TITLE INSURANCE AND NO
LIABILITY IS ASSUMED HEREBY. IF IT IS DESIRED THAT LIABILITY BE ASSUMED PRIOR TO
THE ISSUANCE OF A POLICY OF TITLE INSURANCE, A BINDER OR COMMITMENT SHOULD BE
REQUESTED.
The form of Policy of Title Insurance contemplated by this report is:
    1. Land Title Association Standard Coverage Policy   ( )
    2. American Land Title Association Owner's Policy   ( )
    3. American Land Title Association Residential Title Insurance Policy   ( )
    4. American Land Title Association Loan Policy   ( )

Title Officer: Mark Taber
Direct Telephone Line: (415) I-M-Title
FAX Line: (415) fax-mark

FIGURE A.8 *(Continued)*
Courtesy of Fidelity National Title Group.

SCHEDULE A

The estate or interest in the land hereinafter described or referred to covered by this report is:

A.   A FEE

Title to said estate or interest at the date hereof is vested in:

B.   Charles D. Byer and Elizabeth C. Byer, Husband and Wife, as Joint Tenants.

The land referred to in this report is situated in the State of California, County of Anywhere, and is described as follows:

C.   Lot 17, Tract 53, in the City of Anytown, County of Anywhere, State of _____, as per map recorded in Book 789, Page 12 and 13, inclusive of Miscellaneous Maps, in the office of the County Recorder of said County.

D.   EXCEPT all oil, gas and hydrocarbon substances and other mineral rights, without however, the right to enter the surface of said land down to a distance of 500 feet from the surface thereof, as reserved in the Deed recorded October 11, 1955, in Book 5654, page 140 of Official Records.

FIGURE A.8 *(Continued)*
Courtesy of Fidelity National Title Group.

ORDER NO.: 77777

SCHEDULE A-1

NOTES AND REQUIREMENTS

NOTE NO. 1:

California Insurance Code Section 12413.1 which was enacted by Chapter 598 of the Laws of 1989 (AB 512) effective January 1, 1990, regulates the disbursement of escrow funds by Title Companies. Funds received by (Title Insurance Company's Name) via wire transfer may be disbursed upon receipt. Funds received by this Company via cashier's check or teller's check may be disbursed on the next business day after the day of deposit. IF ESCROW FUNDS (INCLUDING SHORTAGE CHECKS) ARE DISBURSED TO THIS COMPANY OTHER THAN BY WIRE TRANSFER OR CASHIER'S CHECK OR TELLER'S CHECK, DISBURSEMENT AND/OR CLOSING WILL BE DELAYED 3 TO 7 BUSINESS DAYS. Questions concerning deposit and/or disbursement of escrow and sub-escrow funds and recording should be directed to your title officer, escrow officer or loan payoff officer.

     1. Outgoing wire transfers will not be authorized until we have confirmation of our recording and one (1) of the following:

     A. We have received confirmation of the respective incoming wire.

     B. Collection of a deposited check.

Wires directed to this office of (Title Insurance Company's Name) must be directed to:

     Title Wire Bank
     123 ABC Street
     Anytown, CA 90505
     Acct. # 55555
     ABA# 2222
     FOR: 4321-5

NOTE NO. 2:

     2. Please be advised that this Company will require that the beneficiary or beneficiaries sign an estimated settlement statement any time we are presented for payoff:

     A. a NET PROCEEDS demand; or
     B. a SHORT PAYOFF demand in which the beneficiary or beneficiaries are accepting for payoff an amount that is less than the total amount owed.

NOTE NO. 3:

     We will require a statement of information from the parties named below in order to complete this report, based on the effect of documents, proceedings, liens, decrees, or other matters which do not specifically describe said land, but which, if any do exist, may affect the title or impose liens or encumbrances thereon.

Parties: All Parties

FIGURE A.8 *(Continued)*

Courtesy of Fidelity National Title Group.

ORDER NO.: 77777

NOTES AND REQUIREMENTS
(Continued)

3. (NOTE: The statement of information is necessary to complete the search and examination of title under this order. Any title search includes matters that are indexed by name only, and having a completed statement of information assists the Company in the elimination of certain matters which appear to involve the parties but in fact affect another party with the same or similar name. Be assured that the statement of information is essential and will be kept strictly confidential to this file.)

NOTE NO. 4:

Property taxes, including general and special taxes, personal property taxes, if any, and any assessments collected with taxes, for the fiscal year shown below are paid. For proration purposes the amounts are:

Fiscal year 2000–2001

4.	1st Installment:	$982.57
	2nd Installment:	$982.56
	Homeowners Exemption:	NONE
	Code Area:	01-003
	Assessment No.:	123-456-78

NOTE NO. 5:

5. There are no conveyances affecting said land, recorded with six (6) months of the date of this report.

NOTE NO. 6:

6. None of the items shown in this report will cause the Company to decline to attach CLTA Endorsement Form 100 to an ALTA loan policy, when issued.

NOTE NO. 7:

7. There is located on said land a single family residence known as 123 Elm Street, in the City of Coastal Inlet, County of Anywhere, State of California, 99999.

NOTE NO. 8:

8. The charge for a policy of title insurance, when issued through this title order, will be based on the short-term rate. (If this applies. Usually requires less than two years of ownership.)

FIGURE A.8 *(Continued)*

Courtesy of Fidelity National Title Group.

ORDER NO.: 77777

SCHEDULE B

AT THE DATE HEREOF EXCEPTIONS TO COVERAGE IN ADDITION TO THE PRINTED EXCEPTIONS AND EXCLUSIONS IN THE POLICY FORM DESIGNATED ON THE FACE PAGE OF THIS REPORT WOULD BE AS FOLLOWS:

A.   Property taxes, including general and special taxes, personal property taxes, if any, and any assessments collected with taxes, to be levied for the fiscal year 1996–1997 which are a lien not yet payable.

B. Supplemental or escaped assessments of property taxes, if any, assessed pursuant to the Revenue and Taxation Code, of the State of _____.

1. An easement for the purposes shown below and rights incidental thereto as shown or as offered for dedication on the recorded map shown below.

Map of:	Tract 56
Purpose:	Pipeline
Affects:	The Southerly 10 feet of said land

2. An easement for the purpose shown below and rights incidental thereto as set forth in a document.

Granted to:	Southern California Edison Company
Purpose:	Public utilities
Recorded:	March 6, 1969
	in Book 4798, Page 368 of Official Records
Affects:	The Northerly 6 feet of said land

3. An easement for the purpose shown below and rights incidental thereto as set forth in a document.

Granted to:	General Telephone Company
Purpose:	Pole lines
Recorded:	June 15, 1970
	in Book 4850, Page 114 of Official Records
Affects:	The exact location and extent of said easement is not disclosed of record.

Note: If a CLTA Form 103.3 Endorsement with respect to said easement is desired, please advise so that a determination can be made whether such endorsement can be issued.

4. Covenants, conditions and restrictions (deleting therefrom any restrictions based on race, color or creed) as set forth in the document.

Recorded:	July 15, 1970
	in Book 4855, Page 112 of Official Records

Said covenants, conditions and restrictions provide that a violation thereof shall not defeat the lien of any mortgage or deed of trust made in good faith and for value.

Modification(s) of said covenants, conditions and restrictions	
Recorded:	October 10, 1971
	in Book 4901, Page 110 of Official Records

FIGURE A.8   *(Continued)*

Courtesy of Fidelity National Title Group.

SCHEDULE B (continued)

5. A Deed of Trust to secure an indebtedness in the amount shown below, and any other obligations secured thereby.

Amount:	$200,000.00
Dated:	October 10, 1991
Trustor:	Charles C. Byer and Elizabeth D. Byer, husband and wife
Trustee	Title Insurance Company, a California Corporation
Beneficiary:	Fly-By-Night Savings and Loan Association, a California corporation
Recorded:	October 20, 1991 as Instrument No. 91-611311 of Official Records

An assignment of the beneficial interest under said Deed of Trust which names

As Assignee:	Gooddeed Savings and Loan Association, a corporation
Recorded:	January 5, 1992 as Instrument No. 92-0003546 of Official Records

6. A Deed of Trust to secure an indebtedness in the amount shown below, and any other obligations secured thereby.

Amount:	$40,000.00
Dated:	October 10, 1991
Trustor:	Charles C. Byer and Elizabeth D. Byer, husband and wife
Trustee:	Title Insurance Company, a California corporation
Beneficiary:	Your Friendly Credit Union
Recorded:	October 20, 1991 as Instrument No. 91-611312 of Official Records

A Notice of Default under the terms of said deed of trust

Executed by:	Your Friendly Credit Union
Recorded:	April 15, 1993 as Instrument No. 93-0112456 of Official Records

A Substitution of Trustee under said Deed of Trust which names as the substituted trustee, the following.

Trustee:	Title Insurance Company, a California corporation
Recorded:	April 15, 1993 as Instrument No. 93-0112457 of Official Records

7. An abstract of judgment for the amount shown below and any other amounts due.

Debtor:	Charles C. Byer and Elizabeth D. Byer
Creditor:	Cool Pool Inc., a state corporation
Date entered:	May 5, 1992
County:	Bay Area
Court:	Central court of Anytown
Case No.:	AO3914
Amount:	$2,365.30, plus interest and costs
Recorded:	June 17, 1992 as Instrument No. 92-214567 of Official Records

FIGURE A.8   *(Continued)*

Courtesy of Fidelity National Title Group.

SCHEDULE B (continued)

8. A tax lien for the amount shown and any other amounts due, in favor of the United States of America, assessed by the District Director of Internal Revenue.

Federal Serial No.:	93641
Taxpayer:	Charles C. Byer and Elizabeth D. Byer
Amount:	$936.40
Recorded	July 15, 1993
	as Instrument No. 93-21568

9. A tax lien for the amount shown and any other amounts due, in favor of the State of California.

Amount:	$320.45
Filed by:	State Board of Equalization
Taxpayer:	Charles C. Byer and Elizabeth D. Byer
Certification No.:	73492
Recorded:	August 1, 1993
	as Instrument No. 93-216789

10. A lien for unsecured property taxes filed by the tax collector of the county shown, for the amount set forth, and any other amounts due.

County:	Bay Area County
Fiscal Year:	1992–1993
Taxpayer:	Charles C. Byer and Elizabeth D. Byer
County Identification No.:	513456
Amount:	$193.60
Recorded:	August 15, 1993
	as Instrument No. 93-217890 of Official Records

11. A judgment lien for child support.

Debtor:	John G. Martinez
Recorded:	June 1, 1986
	as Instrument No. 86-771320
Case No.:	86-220-971
Filed by:	County of Greenville
Amount:	None given

END OF SCHEDULE B

IMPORTANT INFORMATION: PLEASE REFER TO THE "NOTES AND REQUIREMENTS SECTION" FOR ANY INFORMATION NECESSARY TO COMPLETE THIS TRANSACTION.

FIGURE A.8 *(Continued)*

Courtesy of Fidelity National Title Group.

Plat Map

Borrower: <u>MARTINEZ</u>
Property Address <u>7711 PLEASANT DRIVE</u>
City <u>HOMETOWN</u>   County <u>ORANGE</u>   State <u>CA</u>   Zip Code <u>00000</u>
Lender/Client <u>NATIONAL MUTUAL SAVINGS</u>   Address <u>19623 Bone Road   Anytown, CA 12345</u>

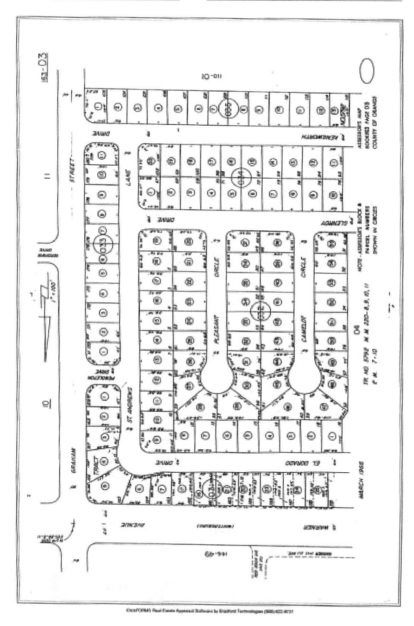

FIGURE A.8 *(Continued)*

Courtesy of Fidelity National Title Group.

State Foreclosure Laws in Brief

Following is a brief look at basic provisions of some foreclosure rules and regulations in various states. Keep in mind that the rules vary widely. For more details by state, visit ForeclosureS.com, click on "Learn" and then "Foreclosure Laws" in the drop-down box. You'll also find direct links to the individual state statutes that regulate a particular aspect of foreclosure law.

Alabama
Judicial foreclosure: Yes.
Nonjudicial foreclosure: Yes.
Security instruments: Deed of trust, mortgage.
Right of redemption: Yes.
Deficiency judgments: Yes.
Time frame: 30 to 60 days.

Alaska
Judicial foreclosure: Yes.
Nonjudicial foreclosure: Yes.
Security instruments: Deed of trust, mortgage.
Right of redemption: Nonjudicial foreclosure only.
Deficiency judgments: Judicial foreclosure only.
Time frame: Usually 90 days.

Arizona
Judicial foreclosure: Sometimes.
Nonjudicial foreclosure: Yes, most common.
Security instruments: Deed of trust, mortgage.
Right of redemption: No.
Deficiency judgments: Varies.
Time frame: Usually 90 days.

Arkansas
Judicial foreclosure: Yes.
Nonjudicial foreclosure: Yes.
Primary security instruments: Deed of trust, mortgage.
Right of redemption: Judicial foreclosure only.
Deficiency judgments: Nonjudicial foreclosure only.
Time frame: Usually 120 days.

California
Judicial foreclosure: Sometimes.
Nonjudicial foreclosure: Yes, most common.
Security instruments: Deed of trust, mortgage.
Right of redemption: Judicial foreclosure only.
Deficiency judgments: Judicial foreclosure only.
Time frame: 111 days or more.

Colorado
Judicial foreclosure: Yes.
Nonjudicial foreclosure: Yes.
Primary security instruments: Deed of trust, mortgage.
Right of redemption: Yes.
Deficiency judgments allowed: Yes.
Time frame: Usually 60 days.

Connecticut
Judicial foreclosure: Yes.
Nonjudicial foreclosure: No.
Security instrument: Mortgage.
Right of redemption: Court's discretion.
Deficiency judgments: Yes.
Time frame: Varies from 60 to 150 days.

Delaware
Judicial foreclosure: Yes.
Nonjudicial foreclosure: No.
Security instrument: Mortgage.
Right of redemption: No.
Deficiency judgments: No.
Time frame: Usually 90 days.

District of Columbia
Judicial foreclosure: No.
Nonjudicial foreclosure: Yes.
Security instrument: Deed of trust.
Right of redemption: No.
Deficiency judgments: Yes.
Time frame: Usually 60 days.

Florida
Judicial foreclosure: Yes.
Nonjudicial foreclosure: No.
Security instrument: Mortgage.
Right of redemption: Yes, brief and subject to court procedure.
Deficiency judgments: Yes.
Time frame: Usually 180 days.

Georgia
Judicial foreclosure: Yes.
Nonjudicial foreclosure: Yes.
Security instruments: Deed of trust, mortgage.
Right of redemption: Yes.
Deficiency judgments: Yes.
Time frame: Usually 90 days.

Hawaii
Judicial foreclosure: Yes.
Nonjudicial foreclosure: Yes.
Security instruments: Deed of trust, mortgage.
Right of redemption: No.
Deficiency judgments: Yes.
Time frame: Usually 60 days.

Idaho
Judicial foreclosure: No.
Nonjudicial foreclosure: Yes.
Security instrument: Deed of trust.
Right of redemption: Yes.
Deficiency judgments: Yes.
Time frame: Approximately 150 days.

Illinois
Judicial foreclosure: Yes.
Nonjudicial foreclosure: No.
Security instrument: Mortgage.
Right of redemption: Yes, limited.
Deficiency judgments: Varies.
Time frame: Usually 210 days.

Indiana
Judicial foreclosure: Yes.
Nonjudicial foreclosure: No.
Security instrument: Mortgage.
Right of redemption: Yes.
Deficiency judgments: Yes.
Time frame: Usually 150 days.

Iowa
Judicial foreclosure: Yes.
Nonjudicial foreclosure: No, but deed in lieu permitted.
Primary security instrument: Mortgage.
Right of redemption: No.
Deficiency judgments: No.
Time frame: Usually 150 days.

Kansas
Judicial foreclosure: Yes.
Nonjudicial foreclosure: No.
Primary security instrument: Mortgage.
Right of redemption: Yes.
Deficiency judgments: Yes.
Time frame: Usually 120 days.

Kentucky
Judicial foreclosure: Yes.
Nonjudicial foreclosure: No.
Security instrument: Mortgage.
Right of redemption: Yes.
Deficiency judgments: Yes, with restrictions.
Time frame: Varies.

Louisiana
Judicial foreclosure: Yes.
Nonjudicial foreclosure: No.
Primary security instrument: Mortgage.
Right of redemption: No.
Deficiency judgments: Yes.
Time frame: Usually 60 days.

Maine
Judicial foreclosure: Yes.
Nonjudicial foreclosure: No.
Security instrument: Mortgage.
Right of redemption: Yes.
Deficiency judgments: Yes.
Time frame: Usually 90 days.

Maryland
Judicial foreclosure: Yes.
Nonjudicial foreclosure: Yes.
Security instrument: Deed of trust, mortgage.
Right of redemption: No.
Deficiency judgments: Yes.
Time frame: Usually 90 days.

Massachusetts
Judicial foreclosure: Yes.
Nonjudicial foreclosure: Yes.
Security instruments: Deed of trust, mortgage.
Right of redemption: Yes, in foreclosure by possession.
Deficiency judgments: No.
Time frame: Usually 90 days.

Michigan
Judicial foreclosure: Yes.
Nonjudicial foreclosure: Yes.
Security instruments: Deed of trust, mortgage.
Right of redemption: Yes.
Deficiency judgments: Varies, case by case.
Time frame: Usually 60 days.

Minnesota
Judicial foreclosure: Yes.
Nonjudicial foreclosure: Yes.
Primary security instruments: Deed of trust, mortgage.
Right of redemption: Yes.
Deficiency judgments: Yes.
Time frame: Usually 60 days.

Mississippi
Judicial foreclosure: Yes.
Nonjudicial foreclosure: Yes.
Security instruments: Deed of trust, mortgage.
Right of redemption: No.
Deficiency judgments: No.
Time frame: Usually 60 days.

Missouri
Judicial foreclosure: Yes.
Nonjudicial foreclosure: Yes.
Security instruments: Deed of trust, mortgage.
Right of redemption: Yes.
Deficiency judgments: No.
Time frame: Usually 60 days.

Montana
Judicial foreclosure: Yes.
Nonjudicial foreclosure: Yes.
Security instruments: Deed of trust, mortgage.
Right of redemption: No.
Deficiency judgments: Judicial foreclosure only.
Time frame: Usually about 150 days.

Nebraska
Judicial foreclosure: Yes.
Nonjudicial foreclosure: No.
Security instrument: Mortgage.
Right of redemption: None, after confirmation of sale.
Deficiency judgments: No.
Time frame: Usually 180 days.

Nevada
Judicial foreclosure: Sometimes.
Nonjudicial foreclosure: Yes, most common.
Security instruments: Deed of trust, mortgage.
Right of redemption: Judicial foreclosure only.
Deficiency judgments: Yes.
Time frame: Usually 120 days.

New Hampshire
Judicial foreclosure: Yes.
Nonjudicial foreclosure: Yes.
Security instruments: Deed of trust, mortgage.
Right of redemption: No.
Deficiency judgments: Yes.
Time frame: Usually 60 days.

New Jersey
Judicial foreclosure: Yes.
Nonjudicial foreclosure: No.
Security instrument: Mortgage.
Right of redemption: Yes, limited.
Deficiency judgments: Yes, restricted.
Time frame: Usually 90 to 120 days unless contested.

New Mexico
Judicial foreclosure: Yes
Nonjudicial foreclosure: No, except commercial properties.*
Security instrument: Mortgage.
Right of redemption: Yes.
Deficiency judgments: Yes.
Time frame: Usually 120 days.

New York
Judicial foreclosure: Yes.
Nonjudicial foreclosure: Yes, but rarely used.
Security instruments: Deed of trust, mortgage.
Right of redemption: No.
Deficiency judgments: Yes.
Time frame: Usually 12 to 19 months.

---

*Nonjudicial foreclosure is available only for commercial or business properties valued at $500,000 or more.

North Carolina
Judicial foreclosure: Yes.
Nonjudicial foreclosure: Yes.
Security instruments: Deed of trust, mortgage.
Right of redemption: Yes.
Deficiency judgments: Varies case by case.
Time frame: Usually 60 days.

North Dakota
Judicial foreclosure: Yes.
Nonjudicial foreclosure: No.
Security instrument: Mortgage.
Right of redemption: Yes.
Deficiency judgments: Yes.
Time frame: Usually 90 days.

Ohio
Judicial foreclosure: Yes.
Nonjudicial foreclosure: No.
Security instrument: Mortgage.
Right of redemption: Yes.
Deficiency judgments: Yes.
Time frame: Usually 150 days.

Oklahoma
Judicial foreclosure: Yes.
Nonjudicial foreclosure: Yes.
Security instruments: Deed of trust, mortgage.
Right of redemption: None, upon confirmation of sale.
Deficiency judgments: Yes, with time limitation of filing.
Time frame: Usually 90 days.

Oregon
Judicial foreclosure: Yes.
Nonjudicial foreclosure: Yes.
Security instruments: Deed of trust, mortgage.
Right of redemption: Judicial foreclosure only.
Deficiency judgments: Judicial foreclosure only.
Time frame: Typically 120 to 180 days.

Pennsylvania
Judicial foreclosure: Yes.
Nonjudicial foreclosure: No.
Security instrument: Mortgage.
Right of redemption: No.
Deficiency judgments: Yes.
Time frame: Usually 90 days.

Rhode Island
Judicial foreclosure: Yes.
Nonjudicial foreclosure: Yes.
Security instruments: Deed of trust, mortgage.
Right of redemption: Varies by process.
Deficiency judgments: Yes.
Time frame: Usually 60 days.

South Carolina
Judicial foreclosure: Yes.
Nonjudicial foreclosure: No.
Security instrument: Mortgage.
Right of redemption: No.
Deficiency judgments: Yes.
Time frame: Varies.

South Dakota
Judicial foreclosure: Yes.
Nonjudicial foreclosure: Yes.
Security instruments: Deed of trust, mortgage.
Right of redemption: Yes, but various time periods.
Deficiency judgments: Varies on case-by-case basis.
Time frame: Usually 90 days.

Tennessee
Judicial foreclosure: Yes.
Nonjudicial foreclosure: Yes.
Security instruments: Deed of trust, mortgage.
Right of redemption: Nonjudicial foreclosure only.
Deficiency judgments: Yes.
Time frame: Usually 60 days.

Texas
Judicial foreclosure: Yes.
Nonjudicial foreclosure: Yes.
Security instruments: Deed of trust, mortgage.
Right of redemption: No.
Deficiency judgments: Yes.
Time frame: Usually 60 days.

Utah
Judicial foreclosure: Yes.
Nonjudicial foreclosure: Yes.
Security instruments: Deed of trust, mortgage.
Right of redemption: Yes.
Deficiency judgments: Yes.
Time frame: Varies.

Vermont
Judicial foreclosure: Yes, in strict foreclosure process.
Nonjudicial foreclosure: Yes.
Security instruments: Deed of trust, mortgage.
Right of redemption: Yes.
Deficiency judgments: Yes.
Time frame: Usually 210 days.

Virginia
Judicial foreclosure: Yes.
Nonjudicial foreclosure: Yes.
Security instruments: Deed of trust, mortgage.
Right of redemption: Varies.
Deficiency judgments: Yes.
Time frame: Usually 60 days.

Washington
Judicial foreclosure: Yes, but not commonly used in Washington.
Nonjudicial foreclosure: Yes.
Security instruments: Deed of trust, mortgage.
Right of redemption: Judicial foreclosure only; very rare.
Deficiency judgments: Judicial foreclosure only.
Time frame: 190 days.

West Virginia
Judicial foreclosure: Yes.
Nonjudicial foreclosure: Yes.
Security instruments: Deed of trust, mortgage.
Right of redemption: No.
Deficiency judgments: No.
Time frame: Usually 60 days.

Wisconsin
Judicial foreclosure: Yes.
Nonjudicial foreclosure: Yes.
Security instruments: Deed of trust, mortgage.
Right of redemption: Yes, if no court confirmation of sale.
Deficiency judgments: Yes, unless waived.
Time frame: Usually 90 days, but may be one year.

Wyoming
Judicial foreclosure: Yes.
Nonjudicial foreclosure: Yes.
Security instruments: Deed of trust, mortgage.
Right of redemption: Yes.
Deficiency judgments: Yes.
Time frame: Usually 90 days.

abandonment Situation in which homeowner leaves house with no intention to return.

abstract of judgment Summary of a judgment in a lawsuit; includes who won, who lost, amount owed, the court making the decisions, date of judgment, and winning attorney. Once recorded (filed with county clerk or recorder), it creates a general lien on judgment debtor's property that's usually discovered by title company in conjunction with property sale. Most title companies require lien be paid as a condition of insuring resale.

acceleration clause Part of trust deed or mortgage that gives lender right to call/demand all money owed as due and payable immediately in the event a specific event (such as a sale) occurs.

acceptance When seller's or agent's principal agrees to terms of the agreement of sale, approves negotiation on the part of agent, and acknowledges receipt of deposit.

accrued items of expense Incurred expenses not yet payable; seller's accrued expenses credited to purchaser in closing statement.

adjustable rate mortgage (ARM) Loan with an interest rate that can vary up or down at certain intervals (periods) and within certain limits (caps); loan is secured by house on which lender will foreclose if loan is not paid.

alienation Transferring property from one person to another.

alienation/acceleration/due on sale clause States that on sale or transfer of certain property, a loan is immediately due and payable.

all-inclusive deed or trust Also known as a *wraparound contract*, a mortgage document that includes amount actually financed as part of a property purchase as well as amounts of any prior deeds of trust.

amortization Repayment of a debt in installments.

amortization mortgage A debt in which periodic repayments reduce the outstanding principal and pay off current interest charges.

apportionment Adjustment of income, expenses, or carrying charges on real estate, usually computed to the date of closing of title so seller pays all expenses to that date and buyer assumes all expenses after that.

appraisal   Estimate of property's value as made by a trained, licensed professional.

appraisal by comparison   Estimate of property value made by comparing sale prices of similar properties in the same area.

appurtenance   Something outside of a property but belonging to the land and adding to its greater enjoyment, such as a right-of-way, barn, or dwelling.

as-is   When a property is sold as-is, its seller does not warrant or guarantee the property is free of defects; buyer accepts property in present condition without modification.

assessed valuation   Value placed on property by public officer or board as basis for taxation.

assessment   Charge against real estate made by a unit of government to cover a proportionate cost of an improvement such as a street or sewer.

assessor   Official who has responsibility for determining assessed valuation.

assessor's parcel number   Numeral assigned by county tax assessor to identify parcel of real property.

assignment   Method or manner by which a right or contract is transferred from one person (the assignor) to another (the assignee).

assignment of rents   Procedure in which borrower gives lender the right to receive rents collected from a tenant in a house owned by borrower.

assumes and agrees to pay   Clause in deed or related document in which a buyer who takes over payments on a seller's old loan also agrees to pay the old loan; buyer normally receives title and makes payments. Clause is often found in section of document that transfers title from the seller to the buyer; seller may or may not be released from liability.

assumption of mortgage   Occurs when person takes title to property and assumes liability for payment of existing note or bond secured by mortgage against the property.

auction   Process of selling property at public sale to highest bidder.

automatic stay   Court order when bankruptcy is filed that prevents any creditor from attempting to collect any debt from the person who declared bankruptcy; creditors may not undertake foreclosure, repossession, eviction, or seizure, or even call or write the debtor demanding payment, and instead must join all other creditors and go through bankruptcy court to seek any money owed them.

balance owed on loan   The part of the original loan that remains unpaid by the borrower at a given point in time.

balloon payment   Final installment on a loan that pays off debt; larger than previous installments.

bankruptcy   Action filed in federal bankruptcy court that allows creditor to reorganize or discharge credit obligations due to insolvency; property owner may restrain foreclosure action by filing bankruptcy.

bearer   Lender in whose hands the promissory note remains until it is paid in full.

beneficiary   (1) One entitled to the benefit of a trust; (2) one who receives profit from an estate, the title of which is vested in a trustee; (3) lender on a security of a note and deed of trust.

beneficiary's statement   Also known as a *benny statement*, a written statement of conditions and remaining balance on loan secured by a deed of trust.

bill of complaint   Initial paperwork filed in many states to begin foreclosure; part of the process of filing a lawsuit.

bill of sale   Document that passes title to personal property from seller to buyer.

bond   Set sum of money or assets available if needed to pay to court or other named person upon a certain event.

broker price opinion   Real estate broker's estimate of property's reasonable selling price; often less than professional appraisal but often more useful because it's a realistic marketing price.

buydown   Arrangement in which seller pays some or all of buyer's loan costs, usually measured by increments (points) of 1 percent of loan. Seller pays enough points so that lender can offer loan at reduced interest rate (and lower monthly payment). Cost to seller is small, but the reduction in payments to buyer can be substantial; often structured to reduce interest rates (and payments) in early years of loan. In a 3-2-1 buydown, the seller pays enough points to reduce the buyer's interest rate 3 percent the first year, 2 percent the second year, and 1 percent the third year; in the fourth year, the loan interest rate and the monthly payments would return to the normal market rate of interest as set initially.

buyer's premium   An amount tacked onto the winning bid at an REO auction that's either a set fee or a percentage of the winning bid, and that must be figured into the cost of a property; premiums based on a percentage should be clearly stated in an auction brochure.

capital improvement   Permanent structure change that extends useful life and value of a property, such as a new roof.

certificate of sale   Document indicating a property has been sold to a buyer at foreclosure sale subject to right of redemption for a set period after the sale; redemption periods vary, but with IRS, it's 180 days. Foreclosures often take place without a certificate of sale indicating sale is final or near final, and buyer gets deed instead.

chain of title   History of conveyances and encumbrances affecting a title from the time the original patent or right to the land was granted, or as far back as records are available.

Chapter 7   Chapter in the federal Bankruptcy Code that calls for liquidation. A debtor's nonexempt assets are gathered together and given up or sold for benefit of creditors in order of their priority; debts are not discharged; secured creditors receive continued payments or the asset as collateral for the loan; unsecured creditors usually get little or nothing.

Chapter 13   Chapter in the federal Bankruptcy Code that gives wage earner the right to reduce debt payments through a bankruptcy court order according to the terms of a plan that will allow the debtor to pay much or even all of the original amounts owed.

chattel   Personal property such as household goods or fixtures.

chattel mortgage   Mortgage on personal property.

clear title   Ownership rights to piece of real estate that are not diminished by liens, leases, or other encumbrances.

client   Principal who employs and compensates a broker.

closing costs   Title, escrow, and other costs associated with the closing of the purchase or resale of a property.

closing date   Date on which buyer takes over the property.

cloud on the title   Outstanding claim or encumbrance that, if valid, affects or impairs owner's title.

collateral   Property pledged as security for payment of debt.

collections   Activity in which lenders or their agents employ various techniques to pressure borrowers to pay what's owed.

color of title   Apparent invalid title.

condemnation   Acquisition of private property for public use with what's considered fair compensation to the owner.

conditional sales contract   Contract for sale of property that calls for seller to deliver property, but title remains vested in the seller until conditions of contract are fulfilled.

condominium   Land ownership arrangement in which one owns an individual unit and a percentage of common area.

conforming loans   Loans that meet Federal National Mortgage Association (Fannie Mae) standards.

conservatorship   When the Federal Deposit Insurance Corporation takes over and runs a bank or savings and loan (S&L) until it can be sold either complete or broken down into its major components. (During the S&L crisis of the 1980s, the Resolution Trust Corporation was also involved in conservatorship.)

consideration   When parties in a contract exchange something of value such as goods, services, or promises.

constructive notice   Information someone is assumed by law to have because it could be ascertained by proper diligence and inquiry in public records.

contingency fee   Employment arrangement commonly used by attorneys in which payment is a percentage of whatever monetary damages are awarded in a lawsuit's final judgment.

contract for deed   Sales arrangement in which seller holds title until buyer completes payment for property and then receives title/deed; terms of sale and payments are set in written contract signed by buyer and seller.

conventional lender Group or individual that makes conventional loans.

conventional loan Private loan not insured or guaranteed by any agency of the federal government.

conversion Exchange of personal real property of one character or use for another.

conveyance Process of transferring title or some interest in real estate to a new owner.

correlation Final state of the appraisal process in which appraiser reviews data and estimates property's value.

covenants Agreements written into deeds and other instruments promising performance or nonperformance of certain acts or stipulating certain uses or restrictions on a property.

coverage Amount of money insurance company will pay in response to a claim.

cram-down Chapter 13 bankruptcy arrangement in which plan to repay lenders and creditors developed by debtor's attorney is ordered into effect by the court; it is *crammed down* on sometimes unwilling creditors.

credit Willingness of borrower to repay loaned money; usually measured by borrower's past record of payments on loans and debts as maintained in a *credit report*.

cured default When borrower's failure to make payments or meet the terms of a loan is corrected to the lender's satisfaction.

current value Value of a property at time of appraisal.

damages Monetary compensation set by court for loss suffered by party to a lawsuit.

debt service Annual amount to be paid by debtor for money borrowed.

decree Final order of a court in many states.

deed Legal document commonly used to transfer ownership of real estate from one owner to the next.

deed in lieu of foreclosure Borrower deeds property, usually to lender, instead of waiting for lender to force sale of house in foreclosure.

deed of reconveyance Instrument that releases and discharges deed of trust.

deed of restriction Limits use of land; might include clauses preventing sale of liquor on property or defining size, type, value, or placement of improvements.

deed of trust (trust deed) Type of mortgage given by property owner to secure performance of an act (such as making payments on a loan).

default Failure to fulfill duty or promise, or to discharge an obligation; omission or failure to perform an act. In property foreclosure, usually the failure to pay loan installment repayments when they become due.

defeasance clause Part of a mortgage that permits borrower to redeem his property on payment of mortgage obligations.

defeased To lose ownership; in medieval times ownership rights constituted a fee and to be defeased meant to lose the fee.

defendant's original answer   First responsive pleading of a defendant in a lawsuit.

deficiency   Money that a borrower who has lost real estate in foreclosure still owes to the lender because the foreclosure sale failed to generate enough money to pay off the loan. Frequently lenders acquire title to real estate at foreclosures and often only credit fair market value of property against balance due on the loan; any unpaid balance on loan after all just credits are applied generally is amount of deficiency. Many states limit or restrict deficiencies.

deficiency judgment   A court judgment that the defaulting borrower owes a deficiency.

delinquency   The state of affairs when payments on a note or other loan obligation are past due.

demand note   A note payable on demand of the holder.

Department of Veterans Affairs   Federal government department that guarantees loans and performs other services for veterans; formerly known as Veterans Administration (VA).

discharge of indebtedness or debt   Lender informs borrower a loan does not have to be repaid.

discovery   Phase of lawsuit when parties may ask each other formal written and oral questions, obtain copies of documents, and in general find out facts related to the lawsuit.

documentary transfer tax   Applicable to transfers of real property, notice of payment entered on face of the deed or on a separate paper filed with the deed.

double whammy   When lenders refuse to permit loan assumptions while, at the same time, insisting on hefty prepayment penalty when a nonassumable loan is paid off early.

down payment   Initial cash a borrower pays to seller to purchase a property; does not include closing costs.

due on encumbrance   Clause in mortgage preventing a borrower from encumbering title to the property with liens, leases, or other encumbrances without the lender's consent.

due on sale   Mortgage clause demanding that borrower pay off the loan in full if the house is ever sold; lender can't prevent sale but can demand payment in full on the loan balance. Without a due on sale clause, loan is assumable without lender's consent; older FHA and DVA loans are assumable without lender's consent.

earnest money   Down payment made by purchaser of real estate as evidence of good faith.

earnest money contract   Agreement in which seller agrees to sell and the buyer agrees to buy.

easement   Right that may be exercised by the public or individuals on, over, or through the property of others.

encroachment Building, part of building, or obstruction that intrudes on the property of another.

encumbrance Any right to or interest in property interfering with its use or transfer, or subjecting it to an obligation; with foreclosures, encumbrance likely includes mortgages and unpaid tax claims.

entry and possession Method of foreclosure in some states in which lender, who already owns property, reenters it and takes possession away from borrower, either peacefully or by court order.

equity Excess of fair market value over the outstanding loan balance.

equity cushion Amount of equity required before lender will make a loan.

equity loan Junior (subordinate) loan based on a percentage of the equity.

equity right of redemption Right of property owner to avert foreclosure by paying the debt, interest, and costs.

equity skimmer Scam artist who assumes loan, collects money up front, and possibly rents, then refuses to pay the payments on assumed loan while keeping cash paid up front.

escrow Deposit held ready for some use, such as to pay taxes and insurance on a mortgaged property.

estate Degree, quantity, nature, and extent of interest (ownership) that a person has in real property.

estoppel certificate Instrument executed by the mortgagor, setting forth status of and balance due on mortgage as of date of certificate execution.

eviction Legal procedure to forcibly remove a tenant from dwelling.

exclusive right to sell Agreement to give, for a specified period, only one broker the right to sell a property; if sale during term of agreement is made by owner or any other broker, the broker holding exclusive right is entitled to compensation.

execution sale Sale of property by a sheriff pursuant to a court order.

extending loan term Giving borrower more time to repay a loan.

extension agreement Accord that extends life of a mortgage.

Fair Credit Reporting Act Federal law regulating credit bureaus and credit reports that grants individuals certain rights regarding both.

fair market value Amount a willing and knowledgeable buyer would pay and seller would accept in a property transaction.

Fannie Mae See *Federal National Mortgage Association*.

FCL Abbreviation for *foreclosure*, used on borrower's credit record.

Federal Deposit Insurance Corporation (FDIC) Agency set up by the federal government to insure deposits at banks and S&Ls.

Federal Home Loan Mortgage Corporation (FHLMC) A government-chartered, privately owned entity that buys mortgages from S&Ls; also known as *Freddie Mac*.

Federal Housing Administration (FHA) Federal agency that regulates many aspects of the real estate industry and insures repayment of certain home loans.

Federal National Mortgage Association (FNMA)   Government-chartered, privately owned corporation that buys mortgages from mortgage companies; also known as *Fannie Mae*.

Federal Savings and Loan Insurance Corporation (FSLIC)   Corporation formerly run by the federal government that insured deposits in S&Ls; FDIC took over its function; leftover FSLIC deposit insurance funds were transferred to Savings Association Insurance Fund (SAIF).

FHA guidelines   Rules specifying income and credit requirements for borrower and condition and value of property to allow an insured loan of a specific amount.

FHA mortgage   Loan insured by Federal Housing Administration.

FHLMC   See *Federal Home Loan Mortgage Corporation*.

first lien   Debt recorded first against a property.

first mortgage   Loan with priority as a lien over all other mortgages; in cases of foreclosure, the first mortgage must be satisfied before other mortgages are paid off.

FNMA   See *Federal National Mortgage Association*.

for sale by owner (FSBO)   A property marketed by its owner without help of a real estate broker.

forbearance   Lender voluntarily accepts lower payments than originally agreed to in loan documents for a specific time period to allow borrower to recover financially; borrower eventually must repay missing or reduced payments and all other remaining payments on loan.

foreclosure   Forced sale of real estate to repay debt.

fraud   Intentionally false statements made by one individual and believed and relied on by another individual who suffers a loss as a result.

Freddie Mac   See *Federal Home Loan Mortgage Corporation*.

freeze order   Automatic stay; bankruptcy court order that prevents creditors from attempting to collect debt from individual who declared bankruptcy. Creditors may not undertake foreclosure, repossession, eviction or seizure, or even call or write the debtor demanding payment, and instead must join all other creditors and go through bankruptcy court to seek any money owed them.

FSA   Designation for Federal Savings Association.

full assumption   Arrangement in which buyer takes title to property and takes over payments on seller's old loan with the full permission of lender; new buyer also must prove to lender (qualify) adequate income and creditworthiness.

Ginnie Mae   See *Government National Mortgage Association* (*GNMA*).

good repair   Borrower's obligation to maintain condition of mortgaged property.

Government National Mortgage Association   Also known as Ginnie Mae (GNMA), arm of federal government that purchases loans.

grace period   Additional time allowed to perform an act or make payment before a default occurs.

grant   Term used in deeds of conveyance of land to indicate a transfer.

grant deed   Conveyance document that implies grantor (seller) is granting an actual interest and has not previously granted such interest to anyone else.

grantee   Party to whom the title to real property is conveyed.

grantor   Person who conveys real estate by deed; the seller.

guarantee   Federal insurance, such as from the Department of Veterans Affairs, that agrees to cover loss up to a certain dollar figure on a loan made by a private lender if it goes into default and foreclosure.

hearing   A proceeding in court.

homestead   Special legal protection that many states give to an individual's principal residence.

Housing and Urban Development (HUD)   Department of federal government that administers housing programs.

hypothecate   To use something as security without giving up possession of it.

impound account   Account held by lender, used to advance payments of certain expenses or charges incidental to property ownership and that may protect lender's security.

installment   Parts of the same debt, payable at successive periods as agreed; payments made to reduce a mortgage.

instrument   Written legal document.

Internal Revenue Service (IRS)   Arm of the U.S. government that collects taxes.

involuntary lien   Lien imposed against property without consent of owner—such as taxes, special assessments.

jeopardy   To have property or liberty subjected to a possibly adverse decree of a court or agency.

joint tenancy   Ownership of property by two or more individuals, each with an undivided interest and right of survivorship.

judgment   Final decision of court.

judicial foreclosure   Foreclosure action executed by the court.

junior lien holder   Holder of a right to force sale of property that is subordinate to another lien holder's right to do the same. A junior lien holder who forces the sale of real estate must either pay off senior lien or make arrangements to make payments on it to prevent it from being foreclosed. Foreclosure of first lien eliminates right of junior lien holder to foreclose, but foreclosure of a junior lien does not affect right of senior lien to foreclose.

junior mortgage   Mortgage second or subsequent in lien to a previous mortgage.

land sale contract   Document transferring ownership rights but not title that may be used to sell property.

late payment   Set amount that may be paid past its due date in accordance with loan documents.

lease with option to buy   Arrangement in which property owner rents to a tenant who has the right to purchase the property on agreed terms.

lender approval   Lender's agreement to allow assumption after review of borrower's creditworthiness and income; can also apply to initial loan.

lender liability   Holds lenders legally responsible to pay damages for legal misdeeds committed against borrowers in course of making loans.

liability   Obligation to pay a debt.

lien   Right to force sale of property to pay a debt.

lien holder   Person or institution that controls a lien.

life estate   Conveyance of title to property for duration of the life of grantee.

life tenant   Holder of a life estate.

liquidating plan   Arrangement in which borrower repays missed payments to lender over time.

liquidation appraisal   Estimate of property's value in a forced sale (when it's sold quickly); usually less than fair market value.

lis pendens   Recorded notice indicating a lawsuit is in progress that could affect title to a piece of land.

listing agreement   Accord in which seller hires a real estate broker to sell a property, usually for a commission.

loan balance   Amount a borrower owes on a loan.

loan modification   Procedure in which a loan's terms, such as interest rate, monthly payment, or duration, are altered.

loan officer   Person who is paid commissions to find and sign up borrowers for loans.

loan pool   Group of mortgages in which investors own shares.

loan processor   Person who gathers and prepares paperwork used by lender to determine whether to make loan.

lot book report   Document from title company that identifies encumbrances recorded against a particular property; does not identify liens recorded in the name of the owner that may affect property.

marketable title   Property title considered free from defect by court that will enforce its acceptance by purchaser.

maven (also mavin)   Regarded by cohorts as a trusted expert in a particular field, and who seeks to pass his knowledge on to others.

mechanic's lien   Claim that secures the price of labor done on and materials furnished for uncompensated improvements.

metes and bounds   Land description that sets forth all boundary lines together with their uncompensated improvement.

minimum reserve   The lowest amount the bank/lender will accept for a foreclosure property at auction.

misrepresentation   Making false statements in the course of a business transaction.

mortgage   Instrument in writing, duly executed and delivered, that creates a lien on real estate as security for payment of specified debt, usually in the form of a bond.

mortgage commitment   Formal indication made by lender that grants a mortgage loan on property for a specified amount and terms.

mortgage company   Group that makes home loans to borrowers; most then resell the loans on secondary market to loan buyers but continue to service the loans under contracts, collecting payments from borrowers and handling trouble (such as default and foreclosure) with the loan.

Mortgage Guaranty Insurance Corporation (MGIC)   Major private insurer of mortgage loans in the United States.

mortgage instrument   Legal paperwork to create mortgage.

mortgage lien   Right of lender to force sale of mortgaged property if borrower fails to repay the loan as agreed.

mortgage reduction certificate   Instrument executed by mortgagee that gives status of and balances due on loan as of the date document is executed.

mortgagee   Lender.

mortgagee's title policy   Title insurance policy that will pay off lender's loss if title to the mortgaged property fails.

mortgagor   Borrower.

motion to lift stay   Formal request to bankruptcy court to dissolve an automatic stay that prevents a lender from foreclosing; once granted, lender may proceed to foreclose unless borrower can keep up payments.

negative equity   Position in which outstanding loans on property exceed its worth.

nonjudicial foreclosure   Foreclosure on a mortgage without filing lawsuit or obtaining court order; generally occurs because borrower has signed a document such as a deed of trust that gives trustee right to sell property to pay off debt.

notary public   Person legally authorized to take sworn affidavits and certify certain classes of documents, such as deeds, contracts, and mortgages.

note   Legal document specifying terms of a loan (including rate, duration, and provisions dealing with failure to pay in timely manner).

notice of default   Letter sent to party as reminder loan has not been paid; may include a grace period and penalties for failing to cure the default.

notice of rescission   Document that cancels notice of default.

one-action rule   Rule of law, used heavily in California, forcing lender to bring only one court action or proceeding against a borrower in foreclosure; hampers lender's ability to obtain deficiency judgment.

open bidding   Anyone who has registered to bid (and generally paid a preset deposit in the required form) may do so.

open mortgage   A mortgage that has matured or is overdue and, therefore, may be foreclosed at any time.

origination   Creation of a loan.

owner-occupied   Home used by borrower as his primary residence.

partial payments   Payments that are less than the full amount borrower owes on a loan.

performance bond   Used to guarantee completion of an endeavor in accordance with a contract.

plat book   Public record containing maps of land showing division into streets, blocks, and lots and indicating the measurements of individual parcels.

PMI-assisted presale   Private mortgage insurance (PMI) company pays part of loss when house with negative equity (loans exceed property value) is sold by regular means prior to foreclosure.

points   Discount charges by lenders that raise loan yields.

positive equity   When a property's value exceeds amount due on mortgage.

posting   Placing legal notice of foreclosure sale on public display as legally specified.

power of attorney   Document signed and executed by owner of property that authorizes agent to act on his behalf.

power-of-sale clause   Portion of deed of trust or mortgage in which borrower preauthorizes sale of property to pay off loan balance in case of default.

prepaids   Costs of purchasing home that buyer pays at closing to a third party.

prepayment clause   Statement in mortgage granting mortgagor right to pay off debt early.

primary lender   Lender that deals directly with borrower.

private mortgage insurance (PMI)   Insurance that protects a lender in the event borrower defaults on loan.

property condition   Property's physical state.

prorations   Allocation of closing costs and credits to buyers and sellers.

purchase money mortgage   Mortgage given by grantee in part payment of purchase price of real estate.

qualifying   Process lender undertakes prior to agreeing to make a loan that evaluates a buyer's income and credit, the property's physical condition, and compares figures with the lender's guidelines.

quiet title suit   Lawsuit to ascertain legal rights of an owner to a certain parcel of real property.

quitclaim deed   Conveys grantor's rights or interest in real estate; generally considered inadequate except when interests are being passed from one spouse to the other.

real estate owned (REO)   Property acquired by lender through foreclosure and held in inventory.

recasting   Restructuring loan with new interest rate and term; can be same loan from same lender.

receivership   What happens when FDIC takes over bank to liquidate its assets; REO is taken over by FDIC's liquidation division; existing contracts with institution can be voided at the option of the FDIC.

recording   Act of writing or entering in public record instruments affecting the title to real property.

recourse   Right to claim against prior owner of property or note.

redemption   Right of mortgagor to property by paying debt before sale at foreclosure; right of owner to reclaim property after its foreclosure sale to settle claims for unpaid taxes.

refinance   Process of replacing old loan with new one, usually at lower interest rate.

release clause   Statement in mortgage that gives property owner right to pay off part of debt, thus freeing part of property from mortgage.

release of liability   Document relieving individual's obligation to pay loan; may be obtained when buyer takes over payments on seller's old loan if buyer meets lender's standards for income and creditworthiness.

relief   Various types of special payment plans or other assistance offered to borrowers who have missed payments; enables borrower to bring loan current.

removal   Process of transferring a case from state to federal court.

repayment plan   Plan for repaying missed payments over time.

request for notice of default   Document that under statutory provisions allows certain interested parties to request and be entitled to notification of default.

right of rescission   Authorization to back out of contract.

right of survivorship   Opportunity for surviving joint owner to take over interests of deceased joint owner; a distinguishing feature of joint tenancy or tenancy by the entirety.

sales contract   Legal document in which buyer and seller agree to terms of sale.

satisfaction piece   Receipt for paid-off mortgage.

scire facias   Court order to borrower to attend hearing and show cause why foreclosure should not be authorized.

second deed of trust   Subordinate position to another deed of trust securing same parcel.

second mortgage   Mortgage made by home buyer in addition to existing first mortgage.

secondary market   The market in which investors buy loans from primary lenders, who deal directly with borrowers to originate loans.

servicing   Process of administering mortgage loan including collecting payments, maintaining insurance, and undertaking special measures such as workouts and foreclosures as necessary.

short sale (also *short payoff*)   Workout procedure in which lender accepts less than full balance due on loan as part of deal in which borrower cooperates with lender to obtain quick sale.

simple assumption   Arrangement in which seller conveys property's title to buyer and moves out while buyer moves in and makes payments on old loan; lender does not qualify buyer's credit and income, so this may be a *no-approval loan*; seller remains liable on old loan under such circumstances. (Only loans without strong *due on sale* clauses are assumable without approval, including DVA loans made before March 1, 1988; FHA loans made before December 15, 1989; and conventional loans made before 1973.)

special assessment   Assessment made against a property to pay for a public improvement.

strict foreclosure   Legal premise in some states that gives lender ownership to property, allows borrower to be evicted for nonpayment, and then gives lender full and complete title by waiting a set time period until borrower's right to redeem ends (lender also gets any property value in excess of what's owed on loan).

subdivision   Tract of land divided into lots or plots.

subject-to clause   Statement in a deed that transfers title from seller to buyer in an assumption transaction, or in other paperwork for the assumption transaction, in which buyer refuses to accept legal liability to make payments, although buyer expects to make them; lender's remedy for nonpayment is limited to foreclosure, and lender can't sue defaulting buyer for missed payments on the loan balance.

subordinate clause   Statement in a mortgage that gives priority to mortgage taken out at later date.

subrogation for mortgage insurers   Right of mortgage insurance company to file suit to recover losses due to borrower's default from the money borrower already paid to lender.

summary judgment   Legal procedure in which one side wins lawsuit without trial by showing the case involves no material fact issues but only legal issues that can be decided by the judge; if judge agrees, then one side wins by *summary judgment*.

survey   Process by which parcel of land is measured and its area ascertained; also the blueprint showing measurements, boundaries, and area.

tax sale   When property is sold after a period of nonpayment of taxes.

temporary injunction   Court order freezing the status quo for extended time period, typically until full court trial can determine merits of case; can require posting bond, although many states' laws waive that in cases involving home foreclosure.

temporary restraining order   Court command that freezes status quo for short time until other legal relief is awarded or settlement between litigants can be reached.

tenancy at will   A license to use or occupy lands and tenements at the will of the owner.

tenancy by the entirety   An estate that exists only between husband and wife with equal right of possession and enjoyment during their joint lives and with right of survivorship.

tenancy in common   Ownership of real estate by two or more people, each of whom has an undivided interest without right of survivorship.

title   Evidence of ownership of land.

title defect   Unresolved claim against ownership of property that prevents presentation of marketable title; such claims may arise from failure of owner's spouse or former part-owner to sign deed, as well as from current liens against property or interruption in title's records of property.

title insurance   Insurance policy that protects holder from any loss caused by defects in title.

title report   Document indicating current state of title, including easements, covenants, liens, and any other defects; does not describe the chain of title.

title search   Examination of public records to determine ownership and encumbrances affecting real property.

trust deed   A type of mortgage that gives lender the power to foreclose and take title away from borrower.

trustee   Person named in deed of trust or other mortgage to conduct any foreclosure proceedings and sell property to pay off mortgage loan balance.

trustee's deed   Type of deed issued to buyer at foreclosure by trustee.

trustee's sale   Nonjudicial action in which trustee may auction and sell property secured by a deed of trust subsequent to default in terms and conditions of loan.

trustee's sale guarantee   Title insurance policy for benefit of trustee handling foreclosure action.

Truth in Lending Act   Federal law that requires lenders to make certain disclosures (such as interest, annual percentage rate, total cost of loan, total of all payments, and use of disclosure forms at the loan application and closing) to borrowers concerning loan.

turnover order   Court command to debtor to give title to certain assets to creditor.

underwriter   Person who makes final decision at most mortgage companies on whether loan should be granted.

undivided interest   Ownership of real estate by joint tenants or tenants in common under the same title.

upside-down home   A house worth less than what is owed on the mortgage it secures.

vendee's lien   A lien against property under contract of sale to secure a deposit paid by purchaser.

verification of deposit   Form sent to bank by lender to verify that borrower has certain sum on deposit.

verification of employment   Form sent to employer by lender to verify borrower is employed at certain salary.

Veterans Administration   See *Department of Veterans Affairs*.

wage earner's plan   Nickname for Chapter 13 bankruptcy.

warranty deed   Conveyance of land in which grantor guarantees title to grantee.

without recourse   Words used in endorsing note or bill to denote that future holder is not to look to endorser in case of nonpayment.

workout   Process in which borrower comes to mutually acceptable financial arrangement with lender to avoid impending foreclosure.

wraparound   Type of mortgage in which obligation to pay second or later lien includes obligation to pay earlier lien mortgage; later mortgage wraps around the earlier mortgage; default on earlier-lien mortgage is automatically a default on later-lien mortgage.

wraparound loan   New loan encompassing any existing loans.

writ of execution   Court order authorizing holder to seize and sell debtor's property to pay off judgment.

writ of garnishment   Court order commanding someone who holds assets for another (for example, a banker who holds funds on deposit, employer who holds a paycheck, or a stock broker who holds account for investor) to give those assets up to creditor.

writ of possession   Court document authorizing constable or other law officer to break down tenant's door, drag tenant from premises, and throw tenant's belongings out of house or apartment.

wrongful foreclosure   Foreclosure that was legally improper and caused borrower to suffer damages.

A

Accredited Home Lenders, 118
Advertising, of property for resale, 199
American Home Mortgage, 118
Appraisals. *See* Resale value, determining
As is, purchasing properties:
  REO auctions, 164, 180
  REOs and short sales, 122, 127–141
  trustee and courthouse auctions, 88, 97, 103
Assignment of deed of trust, 42
  sample document, 213
Auctioneers, 174
Auctions. *See* REO auctions; Trustee and courthouse auctions

B

BNC Mortgage LLC, 118
Buyer's premium, at REO auction, 185–187

C

Capital One Financial Corporation, 117
Cash, need for:
  auctions and, 87–88, 92, 109
  deeds of trust and, 72
  REO sales and, 135
Cash-for-keys approach, to owners, 29, 89, 154
Catalogs, for auctions, 175–176
Collusion. *See* Fraud
Communication skills, 49, 50
Costs. *See* Financial issues
Countrywide Financial Corporation, 117
Courthouse auctions. *See* Trustee and courthouse auctions

D

Daves, Tom:
  on pricing of properties, 196
  on REO sales, 121, 195–196
Deeds of trust, 7, 39–55
  basics of finding and evaluating, 39–44, 59–62
  cautions about, 53–54, 73–74

Deeds of trust *(Continued)*
    financing and, 27, 64–74
    finding and contacting lender, 62–64
    information sources for, 12, 58–59
    junior notes and, 40–51, 57–58, 74
    professional assistance with, 52–53
    profiting from, 44–47, 51
    sample document, 206–212
    speed and, 51–52
    state laws and, 47–48
Deed types, 42
Deficiencies, auctions and, 87
Deficiency judgment, 150
Delinquency rates, on mortgages, 3, 5–6
Disclosure laws, 21

E

Equity, need for:
    auctions and, 100
    deeds of trust and, 59
    REO sales and, 129–130
Escrow company/attorney, deeds of trust and, 52–53
Evictions:
    auctions and, 92
    short sales and, 154–155
    tips for handling, 27–30

F

Fannie Mae, 117
Federal Housing Administration (FHA), 147
FHASecure, 147
Financial issues:
    deeds of trust, 27, 64–74
    foreclosures in general, 25–27, 54

REO auctions, 27, 181–182
REO sales, 27, 132–136
short sales, 152–154
trustee and courthouse auctions, 27, 87–88, 101–102
Finder's fee, REO sales and, 135
First Magnus Financial Corporation, 118
Forbearance, 146
Foreclosure:
    cost to lenders of, 134
    current rates of, 4–5
    ways to avoid, 146–147
Foreclosure investing:
    advantages of, 7–10
    information sources for, 10–13, 17–21
    qualities needed for success in, 14–15
    white-knight approach, 39–40, 49, 83
Foreclosure-listing services, 11–12, 58–59
    qualities of good, 20–21
ForeclosureS.com, 4
    white-knight approach to foreclosure investing, 39–40, 49, 83
Fraud:
    auctions and, 82, 93
    short sales and, 155–156
Freddie Mac, 116, 117
FSBO listings, 199
Full value transfer, 107

G

Garlick, Sarah, on deeds of trust, 40–42, 51, 52, 69
Goals, setting of, 34–35
Grant deed, 42

Grantor-grantee index, 60–61
GreenPoint Mortgage, 117

H

Hard-money loans, 135, 136,
    182
Hardship, proving for short
    sale, 146–151
HUD homes, 124
Hudson and Marshall, 163

I

Incentives, for resale in soft
    market, 200
Information sources:
    deeds of trust, 12, 58–59
    escrow companies, 53
    evictions, 29
    foreclosure investing, 10–13,
        17–21
    hard-money loans, 136
    lenders, 63, 182
    properties in foreclosure, 10–13,
        17–21
    real estate attorneys, 53,
        108–109
    real estate markets, 125
    REO auctions, 12, 176
    REO sales, 130–131
    repair costs and values, 32
    resale values, 33, 59
    subprime lending, 117–118
Internet:
    property information on, 10–13,
        18–21
    REO auctions and, 188

J

Jackson, Alphonso, 194
Judgment lien, sample document,
    220–223
Judicial foreclosure, 47
Junior notes, deeds of trust and,
    40–51, 57–58, 74

K

Kay, Mary, on REO auctions, 165,
    170–173, 175, 182–184,
    185–186, 187, 188
Key performance indicators (KPIs),
    34–35, 179

L

Legal forms, 21
Lehman Brothers Holdings
    Incorporated, 118
Lenders. *See also* REO auctions;
    REO sales
    costs of foreclosure to, 134
    information sources for, 12, 63
    right to advance funds, 45
    ways to avoid foreclosure by,
        146–147
Licensing laws, 21
Liens. *See also* Tax liens
    REO sales and, 120–121
    sample judgment lien,
        220–223
    short sales and, 150–151
Link, Gary, 28–30
Lis pendens, 47
Loan modification, 146

M

Mailer, to neighbors, 198
Maker, Ian:
    on REO sales, 120, 121, 122, 128, 132
    on short sales, 145, 148, 150, 153–154
Marketing, for resale, 198–200
Mechanic's lien, 74
Military protections, foreclosures and, 54
MLS listings, 166, 199
Mortgages. *See also* Subprime lending
    delinquency rates of, 3, 5–6
    difference from deeds of trust, 42

N

National Auctioneers Association, 174
Neighbors, sending marketing mailer to, 198
New Century Financial Corporation, 118
Nonjudicial foreclosure, 47
Notes, buying of. *See* Deeds of trust
Notice of default, sample document, 217–218
Notice of trustee sale, sample document, 167, 219

O

Open house, as marketing tool, 199
Order of appraisal, 87

P

Pereyda, Doug, on REO auctions, 165, 166, 169, 172, 174, 175–176
Pocket buyers, 122–123

Power of sale clause, 47, 48
Pre-foreclosure:
    financing and, 26–27
    sample listing for, 18
Pricing, for resale, 196–197, 200
Profit goals. *See also* Financial issues
    auctions, 101–102
    deeds of trust, 67–68
    in general, 25–27
    REO sales, 122–123
    in soft market, 193
Promissory note, sample document, 214
Property deed, transfer history sample, 167
Property information packets (PIPs), for REO sales, 120
Property inspections, 21–23. *See also* Resale value, determining

R

Race notice states, 107, 108
Real estate agents, REO properties and, 122–123, 138–141
Real estate attorneys:
    auctions and, 108–109
    finding qualified, 53
Real Estate Disposition Corporation (REDC), 163–164, 172
Real estate markets, information sources on, 125. *See also* Soft markets
Recording rules, 21
Refinancing, 146
REO auctions, 7, 161–177, 179–189
    advantages of, 173–174
    bidding on, 185–188
    competition for deals, 163–165
    financing and, 27, 181–182
    information sources for, 12, 176

online, 188
preparing for, 169–173, 182–187
prices and, 166–169
requirements of, 179–181
titles and, 24
REO sales, 7, 115–141
basics of finding and evaluating,
127–131
concerns about, 123–125, 136
financing and, 27, 132–136
information sources for, 130–131
lender contacts, 131–132, 137–138
pros and cons of purchasing, 119–123
real estate agents and, 122–123,
138–141
sample listing, 19
soft markets and, 195
subprime lending and supply of,
115–119
titles and, 24
Repair and rehab costs, 30–32
auction properties, 98–99, 102
deeds of trust, 66–67
REO auctions, 184
REO sales, 133
resale in soft market and, 197–198,
200
Repo properties, 124
Resale techniques, for soft market,
196–201
marketing and, 198–200
pricing and, 196–197, 200
repair and, 197–198, 200
Resale value, determining, 32–34
deeds of trust, 67–68
REO auctions, 184–185
REO sales, 121, 133
trustee auctions, 109–110
Rhode, Tim:
on auctions, 80, 98, 99, 104–105, 106
on formula for success, 34
on REO auctions, 165

Right of redemption, auctions and,
84–85
by state, 86–87
Risks and rewards. *See* Financial
issues
Rooney, Christian:
on auctions, 84, 88
on property research, 23

S

Sale notice sample listing, 19
Senior encumbrances, auctions and,
88–89
Sheriff sales. *See* Trustee and
courthouse auctions
Short sales, 7, 143–157
advantages and disadvantages of,
144–146
basics of finding and evaluating,
151–152
deception and, 155–156
eviction and, 154–155
financing and, 152–154
proving hardship and, 146–151
Soft markets:
investing during, 193–196
REO sales and, 129
tips for selling during, 196–201
State laws:
deeds of trust and, 47–48
disclosure and licensing, 21
foreclosure in general, 235–245
trustees auctions and, 81, 83, 86–87,
107, 108, 109
"Subject to" financing, 72
Subprime lending:
REO supply and, 115–119
short sales and, 145
Successful people, qualities of,
14–15

T

Tax liens:
    deeds of trust and, 54
    REO auctions and, 183
    REO sales and, 120
    short sales and, 156
    trustee auctions and, 88–89, 97, 106
Title insurance, 24
Titles:
    auctions and, 88, 91, 101, 103,
        104–109
    deeds of trust and, 52
    importance of researching, 23–25
    REO auctions, 183
    sample preliminary report of,
        224–233
Tracy, Brian, 13–14
Trustee and courthouse auctions, 7,
        79–111
    basics of, 79–82
    cautions about, 95–97, 103
    financing and, 27, 87–88, 101–102
    fraud and, 93
    notice of, 167, 219
    procedures for, 90–93
    property evaluation and, 97–101

    risks of, 82–89
    state laws and, 81, 83, 86–87, 107,
        108, 109
    terminology of, 85
Trustee's deed, sample document,
        215–216

U

Upset bids, 85

V

Valuations. *See* Resale value,
        determining

W

White, Daryl:
    on auctions, 25, 99
    on helping homeowner, 40
    on REO auctions, 166
    on REO sales, 132
    on short sales, 145, 156

About ForeclosureS.com

MORE THAN A DATABASE . . . A KNOWLEDGE BASE (WWW.FORECLOSURES.COM)

Foreclosure Listings, Learning, and Expert Help.
Everything You Need to Achieve Success Today.

Whether you're starting out or closing on your latest property, ForeclosureS.com has what you'll need. The Internet's original foreclosure site, ForeclosureS.com offers everything from free information to educational opportunities, expert guidance, and unsurpassed up-to-date property listings covering nearly 1,600 counties nationwide.

Serving our clients since 1995, we take the approach that true success happens when you help others first. You *can* make money honestly and ethically as a foreclosure investor! Let us show you how.

Consider the ForeclosureS.com Difference:

- **Find deals in your own backyard** in pre-foreclosure stage, scheduled for auction, or already taken back by the lender (REO). Our lists are complete, accurate, and updated daily.

- **Easy foreclosure search, display, and e-mail delivery tools** allow you to identify great deals efficiently.

- **Filter your pre-foreclosure leads based on the equity available** in a property to maximize your time and possibilities for success; a ForeclosureS.com exclusive.

- **Get current AND previous foreclosure filings attached to a property** for a quick overview of the owner's complete financial picture; another ForeclosureS.com exclusive.

- **See all properties attached to one loan in foreclosure** and find hidden profits on deals with multiple properties about to be lost to foreclosure; another ForeclosureS.com exclusive.

- **Gain direct Web links to the trustees and REO lenders** listed on your foreclosure property reports (where available); another ForeclosureS.com exclusive.

Experience the ForeclosureS.com difference
with our FREE 7-Day List Trial.

Visit www.ForeclosureS.com today!

ForeclosureS.com's teachers are nationally recognized experts and have been involved in investment property transactions since 1983.

The leader in foreclosure-investing education, ForeclosureS.com offers cutting-edge, investor-oriented learning programs for both new and seasoned professional investors. Students have access to exclusive learning programs as well as experts in foreclosure investing. Personal foreclosure-investing coaches work closely with our students, sharing up-to-date techniques and life experiences to guide each student through the investing process and ultimately to success.

Intensive Help through Our Exclusive Learning Process

Alexis McGee has developed a proven four-step system to help investors maximize their foreclosure lists and, subsequently, their foreclosure-investing success. Step 1 introduces you to what works now in the foreclosure business. Steps 2 to 4 teach you exactly what to do (and what *not* to do) so you can begin generating pre-foreclosure profits in your own backyard and without your own money!

- **Step 1: Sign up for Alexis'** *Jump-Start Your Foreclosure Profits* **Webinar and Teleconference Call:** Chat with Alexis and her guest panelists live in a 90-minute session with live chat.

- **Step 2: Order the Home-Study Course,** *Seven Steps to Mastering Foreclosures:* Step-by-step, complete systems for buying great deals and selling them in any market (home-study CD course with digital forms and bonus DVD).

- **Step 3: Enroll in Mastering Systems Lab:** Three days of hands-on tutoring from Alexis and her coaches in their new, state-of-the-art training facility.

- **Step 4: Join the Personal Foreclosure-Investor Coaching Program:** Get one-on-one training with your personal ForeclosureS.com coach (for lab graduates).

Start Learning Now!

We invite you to check us out. You'll see why so many people agree that **ForeclosureS.com** is so much more than a database. It's your knowledge base for success in foreclosure and pre-foreclosure investing.

I look forward to helping you succeed and serve others for years to come. Happy investing.

Alexis McGee and the ForeclosureS.com Team

Call us today at 800-310-7730, ext. 2

FREE TELE-CONFERENCE!

Lock In Your Foreclosure Profits NOW!

Listen to foreclosure expert <u>Alexis McGee</u> discuss her unique investing approach in a special FREE Tele-Conference for readers of <u>The ForeclosureS.com Guide to Advanced Investing Techniques You Won't Learn Anywhere Else</u>, and learn how you can Lock In Your Foreclosure Profits in today's market.

You Will Learn How to:

- Maximize your efforts when investing in today's real estate and foreclosure markets.
- Find great foreclosure deals at huge discounts in your own backyard.
- Quickly flip a house and lock in your profits in this soft market.
- Build your foreclosure business today so you won't have to work tomorrow.

As an Added Bonus:

- **Guest Panelists:** <u>Successful graduates of Alexis' learning program</u> share their inspiring foreclosure investing experiences.

FREE "Lock In Your Foreclosure Profits" Program Includes:

- **FREE audio replay** of a special Tele-Conference Call that Alexis taped just for owners of this book. *($50 Value)*
- **FREE digital outline** of the entire presentation including all of Alexis' web page links. *($40 Value)*

Here's How to Get Your FREE OFFER NOW:

- **Go to <u>www.ForeclosureS.com/book</u>.**
- **Submit your full contact information.**
- **Include your FREE OFFER CODE: <u>REOQUEEN</u>.**
- **We will e-mail you the link to download the audio file and full outline.**
- **If you need assistance, please contact 800-310-7730 x3.**

Then sit back, read, listen, and enjoy your Special Free Tele-Conference! Please e-mail us with your feedback (<u>alexis@foreclosures.com</u>). We would love to hear from you!